DROWNING
IN THE DESERT

DROWNING IN THE DESERT

A JAG's Search for Justice in Iraq

Vivian H. Gembara
with Deborah A. Gembara

ZENITH PRESS

The views presented in this book are those of the author alone and do not necessarily represent the views of the U.S. Department of Defense or any of its components, including the Department of the Army.

First published in 2008 by Zenith Press, an imprint of MBI Publishing Company, 400 First Avenue North, Suite 300, Minneapolis, MN 55401 USA

Zenith Press titles are also available at discounts in bulk quantity for industrial or sales-promotional use. For details write to Special Sales Manager at MBI Publishing Company, 400 First Avenue North, Suite 300, Minneapolis, MN 55401 USA.

To find out more about our books, join us online at www.zenithpress.com.

Designer: Helena Shimizu
Maps by: Peter J. Hutson

On the front cover: Russ Bryant

All other photographs are from author's collection except as noted.

Library of Congress Cataloging-in-Publication Data

Gembara, Vivian H., 1975–
  Drowning in the desert : a JAG's search for justice in Iraq / by Vivian H. Gembara.
    p. cm.
  ISBN 978-0-7603-3448-5 (hb w/ jkt)
  1. Gembara, Vivian H., 1975– 2. United States. Army. Judge Advocate General's Corps—Biography. 3. Judge advocates—United State—Biography. 4. Iraq War, 2003—Biography. 5. Desertion, Military—United States. 6. Trials (Military offenses)—United States.
  I. Title.
  KF373.G46A3 2008
  956.7044'3373—dc22
  [B]
                                    2008023131

Printed in United States of America

Contents

Acknowledgments	vii	
Maps	ix	
Chapter One	Rules of Engagement	1
Chapter Two	Sand Trap	15
Chapter Three	Joy Ride	29
Chapter Four	Warning Signs	43
Chapter Five	Mortarville	59
Chapter Six	The Trial	79
Chapter Seven	Blackhawk Down	97
Chapter Eight	Samarra	111
Chapter Nine	Soft Spot	123
Chapter Ten	Surfacing	133
Chapter Eleven	Odd Man Out	141
Chapter Twelve	Following Orders	151
Chapter Thirteen	Only for Flowers	157
Chapter Fourteen	Sergeant Phil	169
Chapter Fifteen	Conduct Unbecoming	177
Chapter Sixteen	Coming Unglued	189
Chapter Seventeen	The Peacemakers	197
Chapter Eighteen	Fish or Cut Bait	211
Chapter Nineteen	Standing Up	219
Chapter Twenty	A Bad Penny	229
Chapter Twenty-one	*Ovem lupo commitere*	243
Chapter Twenty-two	Bloodstains	255
Chapter Twenty-three	The Leap	267
Chapter Twenty-four	Failure to Repair	273
Chapter Twenty-five	The File	285
Epilogue	296	
Index	303	

Acknowledgments

I am grateful to my husband, Michael Williams, whose unconditional support, encouragement, and keen editing skills buoyed me along the way. I could not have done it without you. And to my parents, Andrew and Vui Gembara, whose own story is worthy of a book, you were both right: serving in the U.S. Army was a great foundation for life and an experience I'll always cherish. Thank you for your prayers and love.

I would also like to thank the following people for their assistance, or support: Timothy and Barbara Williams, Steve Williams, Albert Gembara, Thomas Roughneen, Amy Brown, Molly Cesarz, Brian Tierney, Marissa McCourry, Anh-Van Nguyen, and Anna Ghosh.

Finally, thank you to my agent, Jim Hornfischer, for believing in this project, and my editor, Richard Kane, for his experience and guidance.

—Vivian Gembara

In addition to the sentiments above, I'd like to add that Bryan Rager improves every situation he walks into and my life is no exception. Christine Coticchia picked up the phone and listened when we needed her most. For that, I will always be grateful. Leslie Donaldson said the right thing at the right time and I love her for it.

Also, thank you to our former high school journalism teacher, Meg Carnes, and her husband, Charlie Aldinger, for a lifetime of encouragement. Special thanks to my dear friends: Alex Lorman, Eliza Bussey, and Brian Eng. Victor Antonie made the resources available for us to work together on this story. Amazingly, he did this when he could least afford to. Thank you to my wonderful colleagues and everyone who shared in this adventure.

—Deborah Gembara

Maps

Peter J. Hutson

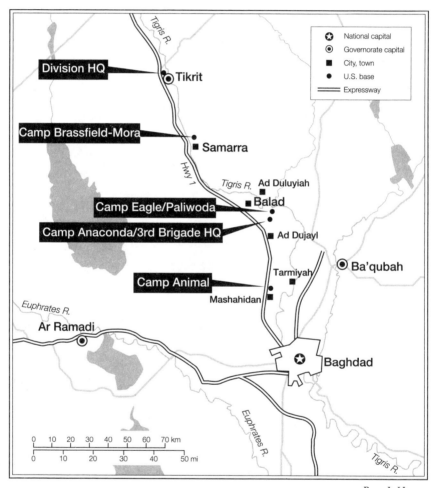

CHAPTER ONE

Rules of Engagement

THEY SAY THE ONLY GOOD morning in a war zone is the morning you leave. As a lawyer for the U.S. Army, mornings were a particularly messy affair for me. Morning was when I made legal sense of a night's worth of raids, seizures, and anything else that happened while I was asleep. It's scary how much things can change in the course of an evening, how fragile lives and reputations are. Come daybreak, it was my job to review the events of the evening and see if what had happened overnight still made sense when examined under the blazing Iraqi sun.

August 21, 2003, was not off to an auspicious start. During my several-minute walk to the brigade operations tent, I had already been told twice that Lt. Col. Paul Welsch was looking for me. Never a good sign.

I hadn't even stepped inside the tent when the battle sergeant on duty spotted me.

"Ma'am, Colonel Welsch is looking . . ."

"I know. I know. Did he say what it was about?" I asked, knowing full well it would not be that easy.

"No. He just said to find you," the sergeant said, a touch defensively.

"Oh, okay." Smiling, I added, "They always hunt you down when they've got good news to share, right sergeant?"

A throng of soldiers was already waiting in front of the "L" shape formed by the field desk and plastic table that constituted the JAG workspace. They chatted excitedly with one another, many of them still dusty from their convoy rides to our base, Camp Anaconda. Cutting a winding path through the mob, and squeezing by a soldier whose entire right side was covered in dirt, I discovered our desk was unmanned. Where the hell was Kolb? Or Carter? This desk was supposed to be manned twenty-four hours a day. Wasn't one of them supposed to be on duty?

"Excuse me, ma'am . . ."

"Captain, can you . . ."

"Ma'am, I've been waiting . . ."

Many of the waiting soldiers had made special trips in from their units specifically to obtain legal help, and they were anxious not to leave empty handed. Some way to start the day. Flipping open our laptop, I wiped a thin layer of sand from the keyboard.

Directly across the table from me, a deeply tanned soldier gestured that he was the first in line.

"Hey, ma'am, real quick," he said launching in, "I got married just before we deployed and my wife says I need to change my will so she's the beneficiary. But if I die, doesn't she get the money anyways?" Before he could finish, another soldier slid a folder across the table toward me.

Smiling, he said, "Just two seconds, captain. First sergeant sent me to get your signature."

"Okay, specialist," I said, taking the folder from him. "I'll have to read this first. And would you tell me again who your first sergeant is?" I asked, looking from him to the soldiers who seemed to occupy every inch of my peripheral vision.

Our ten-feet-by-fifteen-feet workspace inside the brigade operations tent was a one-stop shop handling everything from divorces to detainee issues; basically, any sort of "legal clutter." As the JAG (Judge Advocate General) officer for the 4th Infantry Division's 3rd Brigade Combat Team, I was legal counsel for more than three thousand soldiers. I advised commanders on almost everything, from what they could target, to how much force they could use, to the

Iraqi justice system. The fun didn't end there. My team of three paralegals and I also handled personal legal matters for the brigade's soldiers. When the soldiers were kicking down doors and clearing houses, the army couldn't afford to have them worrying about unresolved legal problems.

What specific JAG duty Lieutentant Colonel Welsch needed me for this morning was still a mystery. Was there something I had forgotten to do? There was nothing in my notebook. Maybe someone left me a note. Nothing under this stack of papers, nor on the small open surface of the desk. Increasingly, we were seeing more and more evidence left on our desk, usually items seized during raids. It wasn't unusual for me to return from a meeting and find a wad of blood-stained Iraqi dinars, a handful of bullet casings, or weapons paraphernalia. We usually stored the stuff in a large trunk at the back of our workspace that served as a catchall for office supplies, unused chemical protection gear, and now evidence. Our rolls of toilet paper and baby wipes commingled with confiscated liquor bottles and the occasional illegal weapon.

Maybe things just felt off because I was running late. The neon green numbers on my watch, however, said 0655. I wasn't late. If anything, I was early.

I stood up to get the attention of the battle sergeant. "Hey, sergeant, can you get me the INTSUM from last night?"

"One second, ma'am. Let me check," he said, rifling through the papers in front of him.

The intelligence summary, or INTSUM, was a recap of any enemy activity and intelligence gathered overnight. If soldiers conducted a raid and confiscated thirty AK-47s, it was there. If a unit detained a guy they thought was launching mortars at them, it was there. For me, it was a good heads-up about what might be coming my way. Right now, I was hoping the INTSUM contained some clue as to why Welsch was looking for me.

"No luck?" I asked, as the battle sergeant reached for a stack of binders.

Before he could answer, someone shouted from behind me, "Ma'am, I think 1-68 [1st Battalion, 68th Armor] caught two soldiers driving some Iraqi's car on Highway One last night."

"What do you mean by 'caught' two soldiers?" Surely, he wasn't talking about our own guys. "Were they special forces?" I asked.

Special forces (SF) are the army's elite operators. Trained to work with foreign armies and insurgent groups in exotic locales, they often adopt local dress and lifestyle to blend in. I knew a bit about this. My father is a retired special forces officer who, when he was on assignment in Iran, grew a beard and drove a blue van one week and a white truck the next. Highly skilled and stealthy, SF soldiers are given considerable latitude to complete their missions compared to conventional soldiers. During our five months in Iraq, it wasn't unusual for our brigade to move into an Iraqi city and discover SF guys living across the street from the mayor.

"No, ma'am," he replied, then hesitating, added, "Uh, at least I don't think so. I heard they might be 1-8 [1st Battalion, 8th Infantry] guys."

"Soldiers from *1-68* caught soldiers from *1-8* driving an Iraqi car?" I asked, looking for clarification.

"Yeah, 1-8. They stopped them at a checkpoint or something," the specialist said, eager to share what he had heard.

Soldiers from 1-8? What the hell was going on? Both 1-68 Armor Battalion and 1-8 Infantry Battalion belonged to 3rd Brigade. They handled different sections of our part of the Sunni Triangle. 1-8 handled Balad and everything between Balad and the restive city of Samarra. 1-68 was responsible for the southern part of the brigade's area of operations.

At least I had my answer as to why the Tactical Operations Center (TOC) tent felt suspiciously caffeinated this morning. Soldiers savored gossip, a welcome distraction from their anxiety. If the gossip had a whiff of scandal, it was a good bet the issue would eventually land on the JAG desk.

Finally, a soldier asked the question that seemed to be on everyone's minds, "Captain G, do you think they were trying to escape?"

Escape? Desertion. Dereliction of duty. Being absent without leave. The legal ramifications could be serious or nonexistent, depending on the circumstances.

If the rumor was true, there was no sense in broadcasting my ignorance. I busied myself with the supply of water bottles behind our desk to buy some time. *Careful here, Viv, don't get ahead of yourself. You don't know the details. Keep it light.* It was risky to show too much interest or excitement about a potential criminal case in front of soldiers. It could, and often did, fuel more rumors.

"Hey, guys," I said, turning away from the water bottles, "let's not jump to any conclusions, okay? It's still early." Clapping my hands together and assessing the crowd, I asked, "So, who needs some legal help?"

The irony was rich. These soldiers thought I was feigning ignorance. I had spent the past five months in Iraq inserting myself into every huddle and attending every brigade-level briefing, all with the goal of keeping myself "in the loop." I could never learn about a major operation or an important command decision too early. Even if it was a bad decision, I wanted to be in the huddle when the play was called. Commanders needed to be comfortable with me, and confident that I understood the mission. It wasn't enough to just understand the peripheral legal issues. I had to understand why a raid was planned, how soldiers cleared a house, that the enemy's AK-47s made a distinctive sound when fired. How else could I expect the commanders to listen to my guidance on no-fire zones and use-of-force issues?

In times of peace, a little breathing room from the brigade's leadership isn't such a bad thing for a JAG. When you are heading into a combat zone, however, it's wise to stick close to the folks making the decisions about operations and supplies. Even before we deployed, there had been warning signs that we'd better penetrate the inner circle fast. One of those warning signs had been the failure to provide my JAG team with body armor. Another was my receiving half the staff I had been promised. Instead of two lawyers and seven paralegals, we had one lawyer and three paralegals.

Not being in the loop was also how I found myself scheduled to give ROE briefings to sleepy soldiers in the middle of the night. After five months in Iraq, I still worried about the fallout from those late night briefings. So far, so good. I prayed it would stay that way.

The Rules of Engagement, or ROE, are basically the guidelines for how to defend yourself in a war zone. They are also one of several briefings soldiers are required to hear before they deploy to Iraq. An important briefing in my estimation, ROE was invariably scheduled last. Scheduling, it turned out, was done alphabetically by subject. So while soldiers' energy levels soared during "mail, medical benefits, and property," they dropped off precipitously by the time I took the floor. Having me brief at that point often felt like a begrudging concession. It was always, "Okay, JAG, get in there and make it quick," as though it were a bathroom break. Make it quick? Please, these guys aren't even awake and now I'm supposed to quickly explain when they can kill someone?

Ten minutes into my presentation, the soldiers were usually completely silent, save one or two adjusting their duffel bags for better back support. Twenty minutes in, and it was easy to spot a few soldiers dozing openly.

Arriving early one evening, I spied a fellow briefer reviewing his Power Point presentation on soldiers' voting rights. Thrilled not have to go last, I sat back and imagined what it might be like to deliver my briefing to an alert audience. Finally, the army's poor logic would work to my advantage. The voting guy could do the graveyard briefing. At least that's what I thought until I saw him scurrying to the front of the gymnasium.

"Hey, what are you doing? You're 'voting'—V. You're not up yet."

Without stopping, he looked over his shoulder and smiled. "Sorry, captain. Absentee Ballots fall under 'mail'—M." Foiled again.

Resigned to my graveyard shift, I knew I had better spice up my briefing. My JAG colleagues at Fort Carson seemed sincerely baffled as to why I would want to make the briefing more interesting. "Did one of your commanders say you had to change it?" they asked. One person forwarded an ancient PowerPoint presentation. Another offered, "Most soldiers won't remember what you say anyways. They just have to check the briefing off their list."

Just check it off the list, huh? Like milk and eggs and butter, right? Just check it off the list.

I was prepared to concede defeat on the issue until Maj. Robert Love arrived on the scene. Love headed the section that prepared Fort Carson soldiers for deployment. Early on in my military career, I discovered that the integration of women into the army produced two types of male soldiers. There were the soldiers who avoided all eye contact, choosing instead to look just to my right, presumably addressing my second head. And then there were guys like Major Love, who punctuated all of his sentences with lingering eye contact.

As I waited to deliver my ROE briefing one day, Love approached, leaned in closer than necessary, and informed me that he wouldn't have a computer for my PowerPoint presentation. "You're okay doing it without slides, right?"

"Sure," I said. I didn't have much of a choice. It was a mandatory briefing and this infantry battalion was taking off for Iraq in less than twenty-four hours.

"Good. Good," Love replied, treating me to his signature wink-smirk.

On the heels of a riveting briefing on "property storage," Love bounded to the front of the room and told the crowd that only one more briefing stood between them and sleep. Groans all around. Hardly the cheers Love was expecting as he stood, palms out, ready to tamp down the whoops of delight that never came.

Undeterred, Love continued, searching for the line that would provoke some cheers from the soldiers. Around this time, I started debating the ethics of condensing my briefing into a tight twenty-minute talk. When I detected what sounded like a pleading quality in the usually irrepressible major's tone, I gathered my notes and stepped forward.

Clapping his hands together, Love grinned broadly. "Okay everyone, I know you're hot and tired, but you have to hang in there. Your final briefing is on ROE, and I've got a very special briefer who I know is going to WAKE YOU GUYS UP!" He paused dramatically. "She's definitely a lot better looking than those last few guys, so everyone make her feel welcome." Jackpot. Hoots. Hollers. The room erupted in cheers. Satisfied, Love wink-smirked in my direction and slithered off into the crowd.

Disbelief and horror washed over me as I realized I was expected to deliver on this buildup. Shuffling forward, I chastised myself for not waking up early enough that morning to apply some makeup. Stammering a bit at first, I launched into the most tedious briefing ever. I droned on and then droned some more. Love's mortifying introduction had paralyzed me with self-consciousness. He had the soldiers expecting va-va-voom akin to Marilyn Monroe bringing love to our boys in Korea. With my hair slicked back into a bun and my uniform hanging off me, I barely qualified as "va." Still, as the energy level in the room plummeted, I had a revelation. Love, with all his lewd innuendo, knew how to motivate soldiers. He understood that a bit of showmanship went a long way. I was done with doing things the hard way. From now on, I would sell ROE.

I would come up with a pitch and sell the ROE like people sell vacuums, computers, and cars. Sure, I never imagined I would need to sell ROE, but then again, it hadn't occurred to me that I might need to buy my own holster or body armor either. The only thing I needed now was the perfect slogan, something that would seal my pitch. I auditioned dozens of them. "Do the right thing" was over-used and too tied to the movie.

The Golden Rule was too wordy, too schoolyard, and definitely not sexy enough.

Things were looking bleak on the slogan front until one evening, shortly before I deployed, I heard "it" while on the phone with my father. I was venting my frustrations about the army, specifically a recommendation I'd made that had been ignored. He didn't let me get far.

"Listen, Viv, you are going to fight a lot more of these little battles out there." He paused a second before adding, "Of course, it's the ones you don't win that you always remember most."

Great. "Okay, Dad, so why should I even bother?"

"Viv, it will bother you more if you don't fight those battles."

"Dad, but I spend so much time . . ."

"Of course, it always feels better to win them," he said with a laugh, "but some circumstances are beyond your control." He cleared his throat before continuing. "Viv, don't lose sight of the bigger picture here. Even with all that chaos around you, you aren't powerless. It's your choice how you respond to things. When this is over, you want to return with your honor intact, knowing you did the right thing regardless. So those battles you'll lose may be hard to swallow, but you'll walk away with no regrets, even thirty years from now."

It made sense, probably more so because it came from him, a man who spent twenty-three years in the army, including two tours in Vietnam. "Thanks, Dad. I'll remember that."

"Hey, on another topic, any luck getting some armored vests?" he asked.

"No, that's a whole other conversation."

"Okay, I'll see what I can do, Viv."

A quick phone conversation with my father and I had it. I certainly hadn't expected it to come from such a casual conversation, but I was pleased nonetheless. I had something I knew the soldiers would hear. With this gem in my back pocket and a fresh coat of lip-gloss, I was ready. The basics were first: how to identify a threat, steps of response, and the self-defense rule, if you feel like your life is in imminent danger, you have the right to respond with lethal force. A few easy-to-remember mnemonics followed, and if I timed it right, I would break out my slogan just as my audience was reaching maximum restlessness.

8

"Hey, guys, I know it's a lot of information, but keep your ROE card on you and remember that ultimately you want to make decisions you can live with, so you return with honor."

Return with honor. With these three simple words, I had their attention. I knew what soldiers liked. I knew the scene. Every soldier did. Their family's beaming faces and outstretched arms, welcoming them home as heroes, against a blurred background of flags and people as the final notes of the national anthem lingered in the air.

I gave them a second to feel it, to lock it in, the memory of their proud chests, their noble chins, and the warmth of the sun on their backs. And then I repeated it: "Complete your mission and return with honor."

Would it be enough when the shit hit the fan? Would it be enough when they realized "real blood" was spewing from their buddy's chest? Would it be enough when they found the nose of their M16 trained on the head of some Iraqi? Who knew? Did it really matter? It was all I had.

Clearing my throat, I resisted the urge to add, "Don't be stupid." Not that it would have mattered. They wouldn't have heard me. They were dazed, completely transfixed with their own homecoming fantasies.

Shameless, I realized, but if it took lip gloss and slogans to sell them on their own valor, I would deliver lip gloss and slogans. I didn't even mind the sometimes outrageous hypothetical questions that now followed. They were listening. They were asking questions. As far as I was concerned, it was just a good investment in the future. If they didn't do anything stupid, I didn't need to bust my butt to prove otherwise.

If I had known then how my year in Iraq would turn out, I wouldn't have stopped with slogans and lip-gloss.

By design or default, Lt. Col. Paul Welsch operated like a David Allen productivity model. His intake and processing of information was streamlined: actionable or inactionable? If actionable, by whom? To execute himself or delegate? His output was similarly, and irritatingly, streamlined. As the brigade's executive officer (XO), it was Welsch's job to be the "detail guy" to the commander's "big picture" guy. It was a good fit because the brigade commander, Col. Frederick Rudesheim, did not want to be bothered with the mechanics. Welsch had the unenviable job of enacting Rudesheim's vision while handling

9

logistics and all of the other day-to-day business. A necessary stepping stone to a command position, it was a thankless job that you hoped to cycle through quickly in garrison. It was Welsch's bad luck to get stuck doing the job in Iraq.

Hours later, in Welsch's office, he filled me in on the runaways. Privates Jason Datray and Thomas Cobb, both from 1-8 Infantry Battalion, were arrested overnight by soldiers from 1-68. 1-68 had stopped an Iraqi civilian vehicle for being out after curfew. Soldiers surrounded the vehicle and ordered the occupants out. To their surprise, two American soldiers, not Iraqis, emerged from the car. Cobb and Datray had one M16 and a knife on them when they were stopped. Welsch also told me that back at 1-8, the soldiers' absence had gone unnoticed until 1-68 reported the arrests.

With these facts established, we had finally arrived at the 64,000 Dollar Question: what did this mean to me?

Laying the papers in his hand down, Welsch looked directly at me. "Vivian, the colonel wants you to handle this. He wants you to bring charges against these guys."

He paused and then added, rather forcefully, "If there's a trial, he wants it to happen here, not back home."

That wasn't surprising; it was, after all, my job. Still, prosecuting criminal charges in Iraq was an entirely different matter. Welsch examined my face for some sign of recognition. "Do you understand?"

Meeting his eyes, I replied, "Yes sir, I do. I will get on it right away."

"Good," he said. With that, his gaze drifted to the captain waiting behind me in the doorway. I could almost hear Welsch's brain chime, "Next, please."

Not so fast, Welsch. You can't just lob this hot potato at me and not help me out with some sort of transportation. Well, of course he could, but I wasn't leaving without trying to nail something down.

"Sir," I said, a little louder than necessary.

With his attention back on me, I continued, "I need to get out to the units to speak with the arresting officers and any witnesses."

There it was, that thorny logistical matter: transportation. I wanted, I mean, I needed a convoy. I couldn't gather evidence or figure out what happened without one. Trying to get detailed information over the tactical phone was nearly impossible. I had to talk to soldiers in person, and Welsch was one of the few people who could make this happen. If he didn't, I would be at the mercy of every random convoy, pleading with them to make room for me in their vehicles and then drop me off outside their scheduled route. If he didn't, there was a good possibility that I'd never be able to bring charges. And if I brought charges late, the charges would be highly susceptible to dismissal. As soon as Cobb and Datray were arrested, it triggered their right to a speedy trial, as well as their right to have their confinement reviewed within forty-eight hours. Without more information about what happened that night, the reviewing authority could order them released back to their unit. While I still didn't have the facts to back it up, I suspected that this would create a dangerous situation back at the unit, not to mention that everyone would think that I blew it. No one would remember that I didn't have any resources.

Welsch pondered my request for a second before responding. "Okay, go get on the TAC phone with 1-68."

He directed his attention back to the captain in the doorway. Classic Welsch. Actionable. By me. And as far as how? Apparently the hard way. A quick phone call or an order for transport from Welsch could save me hours of aggravation. Interviewing soldiers on the TAC phone was impossible. TAC phones crackle worse than boots on dry autumn leaves. Completely ridiculous. Getting information from soldiers was difficult enough in person.

At the JAG desk, Spec. Benjamin Carter was helping a soldier amend his will. As the soldier spelled out his newborn's name, Carter typed it into the computer. He nodded hello and pulled his metal folding chair forward so I could squeeze by.

Carter was my youngest and most reliable soldier. He was lean with intelligent green eyes and razor sharp cheekbones. A small-town boy from Wisconsin, his first time on an airplane had been our flight to Kuwait. He lived for long runs and worshiped Steve Prefontaine, the running legend whose signature was to run full speed from the pop of the gun. Smart, athletic, and disciplined, Carter was the sort of kid army recruiters dream about. As we were packing up to deploy, he tossed a handful of books about positive thinking and "peak performance" into the communal trunk, explaining as only a bright-eyed twenty-year-old could, that the books would help "keep us motivated."

That seemed like ages ago. After five months in Iraq, Carter's angular face had taken on a haunted quality, and there was an unmistakable weariness about him. Had I pushed him too hard? Should I have told him to pace himself? Whatever the answer, I couldn't get through a trial without him.

Back home, I could count on the Criminal Investigations Division (CID) or military police to flush out the basic facts in a potential case. The findings usually arrived on my desk in a tidy file folder for review. I had left CID a message requesting their help in interviewing Cobb and Datray but wasn't holding my breath. I'd heard that the discovery of mass graves up north was tying up the two CID agents responsible for our section of Iraq. It seemed inevitable that we would need to do a lot of the legwork ourselves, all of us: me, Carter, Philibert, and (sigh) Kolb.

Staff Sergeant Michael Kolb, my senior noncommissioned officer, was a continual source of frustration. Instead of being a reliable second in charge, he was a thorn in my side, my Achilles heel. What may have started as simple personality differences was now a substantial rift; Iraq's inhospitable sand proved incredibly fertile ground for resentment. He viewed my push to keep the JAG section "front and center" with the brigade's leadership as needlessly overextending our skeleton staff to further my own interests. Worse still, he rarely confronted me directly about it, opting instead to follow orders, although always a touch reluctantly. With Kolb, it was death by a thousand cuts, daily.

Nearly six feet tall with sandy, close-cropped hair, Kolb had a gentle, unhurried demeanor. No one, it seemed, was more relaxed or willing to lend a hand than Sergeant Kolb. His warm blue eyes and easy smile could calm the most anxious soldier. This cheerful good will, however, did not extend to me. Intelligent and perceptive, he was unusually determined to ignore my need for his support.

"Sergeant Kolb, did you reach Captain Smith about the file?"

"He wasn't there."

"Did you leave a message?"

"No."

"Did you try calling back?"

"Uh, yeah. I will, ma'am."

It was an effective strategy. Too tired to battle even indirectly, I stopped relying on Kolb for anything but the most basic tasks. Today's development would force some sort of resolution of a conflict I had already declared a lost cause.

"Ma'am, I'm done here if you need to get on," Carter said. Finishing with the soldier, Carter slid out from behind the laptop and struggled to tuck the chair back in using one smooth motion. The chair's uneven legs caught on the gravel surface beneath the tarp floor, forcing Carter to shove it inelegantly.

"Thanks, Carter, but don't rush off if you need to finish something."

"No, ma'am, but did Colonel Welsch find you? He was looking for you."

"Yeah, I just talked to him and I want to, well, I need to talk to everyone about what he said. Where are Sergeant Kolb and Sergeant Philibert?"

"Comms are down, so everyone left for chow. I think they're still there, ma'am."

"Lunch at 1030?" I asked, incredulous.

Carter grinned in reply, forcing me to laugh.

"Well," I continued, "I want to talk to all of you at the same time about my meeting with Welsch."

"Uh, oh." Carter pursed his lips and shook his head dramatically. "This doesn't sound good. What now, Captain G?"

What was that supposed to mean? Had Kolb gotten to him?

"So, what's this about the comms being down?" I asked instead.

"Something to do with the heat. You can't send any e-mails, either, ma'am."

"Great, that's great news," I said, falling into a metal chair.

Kolb and Philibert returned from lunch in good spirits.

"Hey, ma'am, you hear about those guys from 1-8 yet? Ya know, Thelma and Louise?" Kolb asked.

I nodded as he continued, "Man, what the hell were they thinking? Crazy stuff."

"Not to mention that if they were captured, we would have had to rescue them," Philibert injected. "Remember those two soldiers who were kidnapped down near Taji?"

Drowning In The Desert

When two soldiers had gone missing several weeks earlier, all units in Iraq were ordered to suspend operations to search for them. Suspending operations was tricky business. Efforts that had taken weeks to enact could be undone in the course of a day.

"Hey, guys," I started tentatively, "Welsch called me in this morning and briefed me on this whole situation with the two 1-8 soldiers. The colonel isn't happy and he wants me to look at possible charges."

"Yeah, like carjacking!" Philibert joked.

"The thing is," I continued, "Welsch said if there's a court-martial, the colonel wants it to take place out here, not back at Carson. You know, make it clear that these guys don't just get a plane ticket home."

Kolb's and Carter's faces were inscrutable. Philibert looked as though he were fixating on some detail.

Colonel Rudesheim was right to be concerned about the two alleged deserters. Military history was filled with tales in which a single act of betrayal triggered a wave of dissent that destroyed a unit. Knowing that another soldier had long since abandoned the cause could have a toxic effect on a soldier's will. *What is this all for? Why am I risking my neck when these guys got off easy?* Even if a soldier never acted on the feeling, his commitment to the unit's mission may be irreparably compromised.

CHAPTER TWO

Sand Trap

WHAT ACTUALLY HAPPENED THE NIGHT Cobb and Datray ran away? The answers to this question were spread across the Sunni Triangle. Balad. Mashahidan. Ad Duluyiah. Ad Dujayl. There was a getaway car, a gun, and a knife. The crime scene crisscrossed and followed long stretches of Highway One. Witnesses from the arresting soldiers to 1-8's battalion commander were equally far flung.

At the JAG workspace, Carter and I studied a map of the Sunni Triangle, specifically 3rd Brigade's area of operations. A day and a half had passed since Cobb and Datray were arrested and I was still no closer to knowing what had happened the night Cobb and Datray tried to slip away from the army. To determine some basic charges, I wanted to know if the car was stolen, what other items they had with them, and whether they said anything at the time of their arrests. I still hadn't been able to reach anyone at 1-8 or 1-68 headquarters to discuss these questions after playing phone tag with both units all morning. By noon, a sandstorm had effectively shut down all communications in the area. The fine sand granules choked the phone lines and disrupted satellite signals. Welsch's suggestion that I use the TAC phone had turned out just as I predicted: poorly.

The longer I waited the greater the likelihood that Cobb and Datray would get off easy because I never secured the evidence. So, while the communications folks scrambled to get the system back up, I moved to Plan B: go out and get the answers myself.

Carter tapped a spot on the lower portion of the map before placing his index finger firmly over Forward Operating Base (FOB) Animal, home of 1-68 Armor Battalion's Alpha Company. "So, you want to go to Animal first, right?" Carter asked.

"Right. That's where they were arrested, right outside Animal," I answered. "I need to talk to the guys who stopped them that night, before they forget everything."

Camp Animal was located twenty-five yards off of Highway One, in an abandoned Iraqi municipal building. While the total distance between brigade headquarters and Animal was only about fourteen miles, it wasn't an easy trip by any means. More RPGs and mortars had hit Animal in the past month than any other installation in Iraq.

"While I'm there I need to find out what happened to the car they were driving."

"I have a few guesses," Carter said, rolling his eyes. "Air conditioning, radio . . . always beats a Humvee."

"Yeah, tell me about it," I said. "Fingers crossed that no one got any funny ideas."

Early on in the war, many units had adopted a broad definition of "mission essential" seizures, eagerly snapping up any new or late-model Iraqi pickup truck or vehicle they came across. As we were making our way into Iraq, it wasn't unusual to find these new acquisitions sprinkled in among the convoys. Even a casual inquiry from me about such a vehicle always produced the same response: "The vehicle belonged to an Iraqi government official and was looted by citizens after they fled." Even the greenest soldiers could dictate the bona fide-owner rule. The last thing I needed now was for the key piece of evidence to become some soldier's new ride.

"After I finish at Animal, I need to get to Eagle and see if they know anything about how these two guys got out there in the first place." Looking back at the map, I traced a path from Carter's finger still covering Animal, northward, past our location at Anaconda, and then east a short distance, before stopping at Forward Operating Base Eagle, 1-8 Infantry Battalion's headquarters in Balad.

"Captain G, this is a huge crime scene," he said stepping back from the map.

No kidding. I grabbed my Kevlar and flak jacket. "Hey, I'll be back in a few minutes. If comms come back up, call 1-8 and 1-68. Try to confirm Cobb and Datray's location and also where the car is."

Carter nodded and I headed for the exit. I didn't slow down until I was a good distance from the tent. Between phone tag with the units and the sandstorm that confined us indoors, I was feeling restless. I needed to move my legs, walk around a bit. I needed to think about how to proceed if things continued this way. Outside, a few billowy puffs of dust still lingered in the air hours after the sandstorm had ended. While the sandstorm had lasted only forty minutes, it had packed a wallop. It was as though a mammoth wheelbarrow of powdery sand and dirt had overturned on Anaconda. My first experience with whirling sand was on our convoy trip into Iraq, and it had been a harrowing one. The seeming merger of ground and sky was disorienting and deadly, responsible for some of the division's earliest casualties.

In the distance, I watched as soldiers struggled to brush sand out of their Humvees. They belonged to one of the several corps-level support units that also resided here at Camp Anaconda, the site of an old Iraqi Air base just forty miles north of Baghdad.

Noting the sun's low position in the sky, I knew my chances of escaping Anaconda today were slim. Even if I were able to reach someone at Animal or Eagle this afternoon, it was doubtful there would be a convoy leaving within the next hour. Having sufficiently tortured us for the day, the Iraqi sun was beginning its slide into the horizon. The heat, however, was slower to retreat, lingering long after the sky grew dark. The heat was inescapable and nuanced while our hours of daylight were precious and few. Day-to-day brigade business was generally confined to daylight hours. After sunset, the focus always turned to "the fight." First the heat, then the sand, and now the sun. It was as though nature was conspiring to ensure that the investigation was off to the worst possible start.

News about the two escapees had spread quickly through the 4th Infantry Division. Soldiers from Balad to Tikrit were relishing the chance to talk about something besides death and danger. The fact that the two soldiers belonged to 1-8, one of the more "hooah" units in the brigade only added to the intrigue. 1-8 had made a name for itself as the "go-to" unit whenever infantry muscle was needed. The notoriously tight-knit unit was hunting for insurgents and Saddam loyalists in some of the hottest pockets of resistance in the Sunni Triangle.

It didn't take long for the chatter to shift to anger. Cobb and Datray had not only betrayed their fellow soldiers, they had introduced a new level of uncertainty. If you couldn't count on your fellow soldier to be there for you, whom could you count on?

Rudesheim's instincts were correct: soldiers wanted and needed to see Cobb and Datray prosecuted in Iraq. Unfortunately, with the escapees on everyone's mind, soldiers and commanders alike were constantly asking for an update. I couldn't turn a corner without someone asking about Cobb and Datray. "They're not going home, are they?" Or, "Hey, captain, what's the latest?" "Working on it," I'd say without stopping. It was my new standard response.

To many of the soldiers, Cobb and Datray were guilty, caught red-handed, game over. They weren't interested in the fine details of evidence collection and eyewitness interviews. Served me right. I'd spent months trying to raise the profile of the JAG team and build my credibility within the brigade. Now, when everyone was finally looking to me to deliver, I was going to let them down.

Kolb was leaning back on the hind legs of a folding chair when I returned. His right elbow rested on the table for support and he was holding a sheaf of papers. Looking up from the papers, he smiled widely.

"Well, captain, it's all been a big misunderstanding," he drawled, his eyes glimmering mischievously.

"Excuse me?" I asked, confused.

"You see, Datray wasn't really trying to escape."

I waited for him to explain.

"He was just joyriding," Kolb said, reading from the paper in his hand. "Just blowing off some steam," he said, letting the chair fall forward.

"It's Datray's statement, ma'am," he said shaking the papers in his hand. I smiled, relieved at the news. CID had been able to interview the soldiers, one of the few arrangements that had actually worked out. When questioned, Cobb had requested a lawyer and refused to speak. Meanwhile, Datray waived his rights and spoke freely.

"Did you just get those?" I asked, pointing to the sworn statement forms he held.

"Hot off the presses," Kolb said, handing me the papers. "The agent left a message saying she would try to reach you later."

I scanned through Datray's statement, wishing it were longer, but feeling grateful nonetheless. "Hey guys," I said, holding the statement up, "this reminds me of a guy who went AWOL but left a note that said 'I went for a walk.' In court, I asked him, 'So, do you always bring a packed duffel bag every time you go for a walk?'"

Carter and Philibert laughed. Kolb shook his head knowingly.

"Just a little joyriding, just blowing off some steam," Kolb trilled.

Philibert leaned forward from his seat on the large black trunk that separated our work area from the communications section, eager to continue the conversation.

"Were they trying to get themselves killed? Who escapes and then drives on Highway One?" he asked. Highway One was the main road running north from Baghdad; it was also the most direct route from Balad to Samarra and then Tikrit. They could not have chosen a more IED-infested (improvised explosive device) route if they tried.

"Your guess is as good as mine," I said flatly, reminded of all the questions I still needed answers to.

As Kolb and Phil combed the statement for other amusing bits, I could feel my mood darkening. I still had no idea what really happened and couldn't even confirm if Cobb and Datray were being held at Animal or if they had been sent back to Eagle. A series of scenarios flashed through my mind, each more grisly than the next. Both options were ripe with potential for abuse. For starters, it was never a good idea to return soldiers to a unit that they just abandoned. Beyond that, 1-68 was stretched thin. They had been attacked more times in the month than any other unit in Iraq. The last thing I wanted was tired, stressed soldiers guarding anybody. It was a constant worry with detainees, but two guys who abandoned their fellow soldiers? Well, that was just asking for trouble.

"Sergeant Kolb, did we get his rights waiver along with the statement?"

Kolb nodded and pushed back on the chair's hind legs again.

"Hey guys, I'm going to need your help finding a convoy to get out to 1-68 or 1-8 as soon as possible. Start asking around about any outgoing convoys—supply runs, chow delivery, anything—because once comms are up, I might not have enough time."

"No chance, ma'am. Comms have been down all day," Kolb replied smoothly.

Again with the cuts. "I realize comms are down," I said, trying to keep the acid out of my voice, "That's why we need to start looking for a convoy. I need to talk to both units as soon as possible to locate the evidence and identify the witnesses. Whether that happens in person or over the phone, I don't care. It just needs to happen."

"Okay, ma'am, but it's going to be hard finding a convoy this late in the day," he said.

"Got it, Sergeant Kolb."

Kolb nodded and changed the subject, seemingly oblivious to the fact that I wanted to kick the back legs of his chair out from under him. "The mail came today, ma'am. Did you see your package?" He pointed to our trunk. Next to Philibert was a large brown box.

I recognized Mike's narrow, jagged handwriting instantly. He had addressed the package to "Captain Vivian Happy Gembara." He had also drawn a smiley face over my name. Unlike the other playful monikers he'd added to some of my previous packages, "Happy" is in fact my middle name. While I wouldn't go as far as to say it is ironic, it has been a source of great amusement to my friends my entire life.

Kolb and Philibert were watching me expectantly. Even Carter had turned away from the laptop. I had the distinct feeling that there had been some discussion, maybe even a bet placed. *Happy? Her? That can't be her middle name. Cranky or even Killjoy—definitely. But Happy? Impossible.*

"That's one unique middle name you got there," Kolb ventured.

"Yes, my middle name is Happy. Weird, I know." Softened by the sight of Mike's familiar scrawl and careful packaging, I added, "It's also my mom's first name."

Mike and I met at Notre Dame, while we were both studying abroad in London. We didn't start dating seriously though until we were in law school. Every other weekend, I either made the trek to see him at Yale or he came down to see me at William and Mary. Although Mike knew about my ROTC commitment from college, neither of us expected that my final year in the army would be spent in Iraq. He had relocated to Denver, which is just an hour north of Colorado Springs and Fort Carson, because we were planning to get married in June. That is, until I deployed.

"Captain G, comms says the phones are up," Philibert said. Captain Matt Provost, the assistant communications officer, flashed a thumb's up and headed toward the front of the tent to notify the guys manning the operations desk. From the operations desk—two long banquet tables set at a right angle—the battle captain and battle sergeant tracked the war via computer and radio reports they received from the brigade's outlying battalions. Today, the sandstorm, and its ramifications on travel and comms, meant little radio traffic; just a few squawks and beeps that occasionally roused the battle sergeant from his magazine.

All right, let's give this a go. I lifted the receiver and pushed hard on the rubbery button labeled "3." A split second of crackling was followed by the encouraging and now slightly unfamiliar dial tone. Bingo. I hurriedly dialed the remaining numbers. Ringing. Ringing. We have contact. Sort of.

The specialist who answered at 1-8 was quick to tell me that their S1 battalion personnel officer wasn't around. I asked for a few other people who were also nowhere to be found. Running out of names, I shuffled through the papers in front of me. Where the heck were those unit rosters I had asked Kolb to get?

"Are they expected back any time soon?"

"You just missed some of them, ma'am. If you want to leave a message . . ."

"Specialist, this is my fourth call to your unit today. I have left more than a few messages."

"Ma'am, like I said, I can make sure he gets it."

"Okay, well, since I last spoke to you has anyone there figured out where your unit is holding Privates Cobb and Datray?"

"Um, ma'am, I am not sure where they are right now. 1-68 caught them, so . . ."

"What do you mean you aren't sure where they are? These are your guys." Pausing, I gave him a second to offer something more reassuring.

"They might be here, but the battle sergeant said he didn't think so. I'm not sure."

I had seen more than one case go up in smoke because an overzealous commander or first sergeant decided to take it upon himself to punish the accused. One frustrated first sergeant had forced a soldier to live in a small tent outside the barracks, complete with a sign identifying the crime the soldier was accused of. This was before he went to trial. Worse still, the first sergeant and the unit were upset with *me* because I had to drop some of the charges after learning about the pup tent. Courts frown on pretrial punishment, their little hang-up about being "innocent until proven guilty." I had said it a million times: trust the legal system.

"Listen, specialist, I am leaving a message, but this time I want you to deliver it to your commander. You need to deliver this to Lieutenant Colonel Sassaman, do you understand?"

"Yes, ma'am."

Pleased to finally have his full attention, I continued more slowly, "Tell him that JAG from brigade called and that I am dropping the cases against your soldiers until I get support for the investigation."

Abort. Abort. Abort. The frantic warning from my brain arrived at the precise moment I was delivering the last part of my hostile message. It was followed by tightness in my chest. Dear God. Tell me I didn't just throw down the gauntlet to a senior officer, a commander no less. The buzzing sound of the disconnected line answered. I replaced the receiver clumsily in its cradle.

Had I lost my mind? Threatening a senior officer? Making demands? My belligerent tone still resonated with me. What the hell was I thinking? So much for playing it safe.

Lieutenant Colonel Nathan Sassaman was 1-8's dashing young commander. Sassaman had been on a trajectory for military greatness since his West Point days. He was a "fast tracker" that few doubted would wear at least one general's star on his shoulder. Within weeks of his taking command, he had transformed 1-8 into an infantry powerhouse. While outsiders marveled at 1-8's dramatic turnaround, Sassaman took the changes in stride. In the context of his life, it made sense. At West Point, Sassaman had led Army to its first ever appearance in a college bowl game, and marshaled his Black Knights to a stunning, against-the-odds, 10-6 victory over Michigan State in the 1984 Cherry Bowl.

I doubted Sassaman would take kindly to a threat from a junior JAG officer. Maybe he would assume it was a miscommunication. Surely, nobody would be so foolish as to threaten a senior officer. Would he respond himself? Or would he call Tikrit and tell the division JAG to rein me in? More importantly, would Sassaman get the message before the Battle Update Briefing (BUB) in two hours?

Around me, soldiers bantered with one another, oblivious to the turmoil I had just invited. All of them, every last one, seemed so carefree. Even those complaining about the heat did so in a sunny, jaunty way. What I wouldn't give to roll down the shades, lock the door, and return after this ugly situation resolved itself. Fast forward. Fast forward. Better yet, eject.

A hand flashed just a few inches in front of my face; at least, I thought it was a hand.

"Hello in there. Hellooooo."

"Oh, hey Sergeant Phil," I said, startled to find him less than a foot away from me.

"Hey, Captain G, are you okay?"

"Yeah, why?"

"You were just staring into space."

Affable, as malicious as a golden retriever, Sgt. John Philibert, pronounced "Phil-a-bear," had joined us several months into our deployment. He was a replacement for a sergeant who had to leave because of a family medical emergency. Relentlessly cheerful, the thirty-six-year-old Californian possessed a host of little habits that could get a man in a war zone killed by his own men: whistling, gum smacking, and nervous fidgeting. When he wasn't swinging his key-chain in large circles, allowing it to wind and then unwind around his fingers, he was consumed with some form of correspondence. Philibert spent so much time writing postcards and e-mails that we were baffled as to what he might actually have to say in them.

Dear Jim Bob Joe, I spent the day writing e-mails and postcards. I may tackle some longer letters tomorrow. Best, Phil

Phil was the only one of us with children. He had a daughter, a beautiful little girl with a megawatt smile, clearly the best thing to come out of his short-lived marriage. He doted on her and looked forward to taking her on a Disney cruise when we returned. In the neighborhood of five feet seven inches, Philibert was tan, bald, and obsessed with improving his run times. Copious notes about his workout regimen and run times, which he kept attached to a clipboard, suggested a meticulousness I had yet to see applied to our JAG mission. Still, as maddening as his density could be, the round-faced sergeant's perpetually sunny disposition made it difficult to stay angry long.

With one shoulder trapping the phone receiver to my ear, I listened for the dial tone.

"Hey, Sergeant Phil, if Cobb and Datray were sent home to Carson, how do you think the JAG office would handle it?" I asked for fun.

Looking up from the postcard he was writing, Philibert placed his pen down carefully and struck a pose of contemplation.

"Mmmm. Well, ma'am, they'd probably chapter them out or," he tilted his head and smiled, "they would wait for you to return and try the cases."

"Great." Just as I feared. Hearing Philibert confirm it made my stomach turn. The last thing I wanted was to see these guys get off easy because no one wanted to do the work back home. Yet, if the investigation continued as it was going, that was a very real possibility. If I didn't secure the evidence and bring charges soon, I would have no choice but to recommend sending Thelma and Louise back to Fort Carson.

Being "chaptered out" is an administrative procedure that ends a soldier's contractual commitment to the army. From a JAG perspective, weak cases were likely candidates for chaptering. The problem was that having the less work-intensive chapter option available meant it was frequently overused. Why exhaust yourself bringing charges and building a criminal case when you could aim a little lower and just move the guy out? It was the path of least resistance, the Fort Carson way.

Even more distressing was the idea of prosecuting the case when I returned. Nothing weakens a case more than delay. There is truth to the adage, "Justice delayed is justice denied." The passage of time creates opportunities for testimony to change, memories to fade, evidence to disappear, and for the aggrieved parties to lose their will. Sure, I had argued cases with weak evidence, but time-weakened evidence was a different thing entirely. It almost guaranteed failure.

Another failure. The prospect was almost too much to contemplate. Time had done little to remove the sting of my last performance review at Fort Carson. "Mismanagement" was the primary criticism, something my superiors had said contributed to my "not resolving cases quickly." They said I took on more than

I could handle. They dinged me for missing several morning physical training exercises, but failed to note that I was up to my elbows in a date-rape drug investigation. As petty as their criticisms had been, their suggestions were far worse: "You have to listen to your commanders. They'll tell you what's important, what they need from you," they said, emphasizing the word "listen."

The message was clear all right: don't make things complicated, and don't make more work for yourself. They had even appropriated without question or pause the army axiom Keep It Simple Stupid (KISS). Apparently, I was the stupid one who made things sticky. Thanking my superiors, I had offered a weak promise to do better and then quickly departed the building. I didn't worry about adding an angry or defensive rejoinder. Their suggestions had killed all the fight within me.

Only when I was in my car, hidden by the darkness of Colorado's early evening sky, did I find it again. How is justice served when you only take on the easy cases? When you don't ask questions? Didn't we take an oath to uphold the law, the Uniform Code of Military Justice, and not to simply take cues from commanders? I knew from experience that by the time most commanders decided they needed legal input, the problem was already too far gone.

Iraq was going to be different. It was my second chance. With a new set of JAG bosses in theater, I was determined to show the Fort Carson JAG office that their passive approach benefited no one. As part of my effort to be full service, I tried to keep the JAG desk manned nearly twenty-four hours a day. If a soldier or commander needed legal guidance, I wanted it to be available to them. With over three thousand soldiers to watch out for, it was good bet someone, somewhere, was in need of counsel and, more often than not, a sympathetic ear. It didn't matter if their questions were about use of force or a child custody battle; our goal was to reinforce the practice of consulting with JAG *before* pursuing an irreversible course of action.

As JAGs, or at least as the competent, effective JAGs we strived to be, it was our job to scan the road ahead for legal landmines. To do that well, we had to be vigilant and accessible to the soldiers. More effort and knowledge on the front end and we might be able to deactivate that landmine or, at the very least, identify it and minimize the damage. Because once that landmine went off, it was guaranteed to take down everything and everyone around it.

* * *

My plan was to intercept Sassaman before the nightly Battle Update Briefing began. With only a few minutes remaining before 1700, Sassaman's seat was still empty among the designated commanders' seats in front. Was his entourage here? I didn't see any of them. I needed to catch him before the meeting. Afterwards, commanders were in a hurry to leave; no one wanted to be on the road at dusk. Dusk favored those who knew the lay of the land intimately. For that reason alone, the BUB started precisely at 1700.

Sassaman arrived just as the briefing began. I spent the majority of the briefing studying the back of his head, trying to gauge how quickly I could close the twenty-five to thirty feet that separated us when the BUB ended. At best, I had a five-minute window to make my move. It didn't look promising. As soon as Welsch called dismiss, Sassaman was surrounded by a sea of captains and majors.

That same instant, a determined private first-class pounced on me, clearly more skilled at tracking his prey. He pushed some file folders forward with an expectant look. Frantic, I tried to move past him, hoping to spot Sassaman's head again among the crowd. Confused, the private stepped directly in my path, like a human speed bump.

"Ma'am, the first sergeant wanted me to bring them back signed. Ma'am?"

Shoot. I lost him.

Taking the files, I said, "Tell your first sergeant that the files won't be ready until tomorrow, no exceptions." Irritated, I had failed to notice that Sassaman was waiting to speak to me.

"Captain Gembara, I got your message," he said stepping up to the table.

Your message. That induced a wince. "Sir, I'm sorry if I sounded abrupt, it's just that—" Was I whining already?

"Vivian," he said, cutting me off. "I want Cobb and Datray tried out here. I need you to make that happen, so whatever you need, let me know, okay?" Sassaman nodded determinedly and waited for me to say something.

"Yes, sir," I said mirroring his nod and still digesting the unexpected turn of events. He wasn't angry?

"I don't want these guys sent home to Carson. Get in touch with Major [Robert] Gwinner right away. He's my battalion XO," he clarified. "Make him your point of contact. Let him know what you need to make this happen."

"Yes, sir," I said nodding more vigorously. Jubilant, I repeated myself, "Yes, sir, I understand. I'll talk to Major Gwinner right away."

"Good." With that he turned and headed for the door. I watched him wave to a few of his fellow commanders before exiting with his entourage, and my gratitude.

Help had finally arrived. Perhaps there was something to the buzz surrounding this young commander. I had heard it said on more than one occasion: Sassaman possessed the Midas touch.

I should have slept well that night. Sassaman's surprising support should have calmed my nerves. Somehow, sleep still eluded me. I'd settle into one position just long enough to figure out that I needed to be in a different position. I'd make the proper adjustment only to discover my limbs weren't buying it. I didn't dare look at my watch. I'd cycled through all the plausible positions enough times to know it had to be after 0200.

It wasn't the usual suspects either: heat, insects, and itchy skin, days overdue for a shower. I just couldn't get comfortable. Searching for the right position was in itself exhausting. Considering the state of the cot, it seemed particularly futile. Months of use had caused the cot's initial tautness to give way, leaving it slack, more like a hammock. Most nights, I didn't notice. Most nights, I fell right to sleep.

Tonight, my brain was heeding no messages from the rest of my body. It ignored my raw eyes and my parched, unrested skin. Not content to just chill, it insisted on reviewing the day's events. When that grew old, my thoughts turned to the next day and the day after that. If I was going to bring criminal charges against Cobb and Datray (carjacking, assault with a deadly weapon, and desertion) I'd be spending a lot of time on the roads, particularly Highway One.

That would mean exposing my men and others in our convoys to IEDs and a host of other roadside fun. What if something happened to Carter or someone else in the convoy? Could I live with myself if one of my men was killed or injured because we needed to gather evidence? How much was a limb worth? Philibert had a daughter. Would his little girl understand if her father were killed in the pursuit of *evidence*? Kolb had a wife. Would she understand? Would she think it was worth it?

Drowning In The Desert

But what if I didn't investigate? What if these two yahoos got off with a slap on the wrist?

We all hated it here. Every day was the same. Sand. Heat. Stress. Long hours. Crappy food. Insects and rodents. Insurgents out for our blood. Day in, day out, the constant shifting between tedium and anxiety was exhausting.

Life in Iraq sucked. It sucked, and we knew it, and yet we all did our best to drag ourselves out of our cots each morning. Why should Cobb and Datray be any different? They had jeopardized their fellow soldiers' safety by leaving their posts. What if something bad had happened to other 1-8 soldiers?

"Ma'am, your son is dead because the guys who were supposed to protect him got antsy and went on a joy ride." Bastards.

CHAPTER THREE

Joy Ride

SASSAMAN MADE GOOD ON HIS pledge of support and many of the logistical hurdles fell away. I had the convoys, translators, and soldiers I needed. Within days, I had a better understanding of what Privates Cobb and Datray were trying to achieve the night they set out on Highway One. I also learned what they were leaving behind.

Staff Sergeant Bryant Adams of Alpha Company, 1-68 Armor Battalion was one of the few people to see Cobb and Datray that evening. Adams and his men were in the middle of their nightly hunt for IEDs and curfew violators. Battling exhaustion, Adams forced himself to focus on his surroundings. It wasn't long after that, he noticed headlights coming toward them on Highway One. Two weeks earlier, Iraqis driving a pickup truck passed them on the road just before raining rocket-propelled grenades (RPGs) down on their compound. Tonight, he wasn't taking any chances. He gave the flash checkpoint signal to his men and their convoy of Humvees crossed the median. They surrounded the civilian vehicle and forced it to come to a stop.

Weapons trained on the vehicle, Adams yelled to the driver, "Get out of the car and keep your hands in the air!"

Nearly forty-five seconds passed before two men emerged.

Drowning In The Desert

When Adams and his soldiers noticed that the two men were wearing U.S. Army desert uniforms, they instantly went "red tight," meaning they chambered rounds in their weapons. They had heard rumors about insurgents wearing American uniforms to fool coalition forces. Adams kept his weapon trained on the driver as he approached.

Cobb and Datray were eventually brought to Alpha Company's main building where they were questioned by the company commander. As Adams passed the room where the two men waited, he heard one of them say he had purchased the car for $200.

Amar Hussan, the owner of the vehicle Cobb and Datray drove that night, remembered it differently. The twenty-six-year-old auto mechanic from Balad said he was on his way home from Baghdad when he made the mistake of stopping to help a man on the side of the road. Within seconds of stopping, two American soldiers appeared, one pointing an M16 at him. The soldiers, Cobb and Datray, commandeered Amar's car and held him hostage for several hours before he was able to escape on foot.

Just hours after the incident, Amar informed the Iraqi police that his car had been stolen. When they did nothing to help him, he knew he would have no choice but to approach the American base directly. The next morning, swallowing his fear and several antianxiety pills, Amar forced himself to make the long walk up to Camp Eagle's front gate. Every few steps, he reminded himself that they had already stolen his car and threatened his life. It wasn't enough to calm his nerves, but it did keep him moving. He told himself that the worst they could do was call him a liar and send him away empty-handed.

Camp Eagle was a thorny presence in Balad that deserved journalists' comparisons to the fictional Fort Apache. Located on the grounds of an old elementary school, its mile-and-a-half perimeter was defined by a wire fence and concentric layers of concertina and barbed wire. Within the fence, there were berms on all sides, offering yet another layer of insulation from the outside.

I met with Amar at Eagle a few days later. Slim and small in stature, he was trembling inside his oatmeal-colored tunic when I approached. His dark eyes continuously darted from me to the translator. He repeatedly clasped and unclasped his hands throughout our entire meeting. We took several breaks during the interview so Amar could smoke and regain his composure.

In the shade outside the building's main entrance, Amar glanced nervously at the soldiers milling about. He brought a cigarette to his lips with fingers that still trembled slightly. I leaned against a cement pillar nearby, admiring the latest improvements to the building and tried my best to appear relaxed and unhurried. He was skittish enough as it was.

No place was 1-8's "hooah" spirit more evident than in the old school building that served as the battalion's headquarters. A bulletin board just inside the entrance showcased 1-8's "Play of the Day," a typewritten account of particularly courageous acts, close calls, and, in some cases, humorous incidents. Surrounding it were countless photos of soldiers meeting with locals, posing in front of weapons caches, or simply standing in the hatch of a Bradley Fighting Vehicle. Past the "brag board," the building's main hallway was draped in state flags. Sassaman had encouraged his soldiers to write to all of the state governors requesting state flags as a sign of their support for the unit. As the flags came in, they were added to the growing collection. Blank spots along the wall were left for states that chose not to participate, their denial letters prominently displayed instead, along with a note encouraging soldiers hailing from the dissenting state to solicit other state politicians. Brilliant and multicolored, the flags did more than just dress up a bland hallway, they were reminders to the soldiers of who was behind them.

My peaceful survey of the building was interrupted when a handful of soldiers passing through spotted the sword and pen JAG insignia on my collar. "Hey ma'am, are Cobb and Datray gonna get off?" "They'll definitely go to jail, right?"

"Working on it," I said smiling, hoping the soldiers' excited banter and volume wouldn't unnerve Amar any further.

In the split second I had looked away, Amar was approached by two broad-shouldered soldiers dressed in their full "battle rattle"—armored vests covered with ammo clips and gadgetry, Kevlar helmets with night-vision goggle mounts, weapons in hand, and the reflective sunglasses that 1-8 soldiers seemed to favor. One of the soldiers swiveled his head robotically, surveying the immediate area for Amar's escort.

"Hey guys, he's with me," I said hurrying over. Sandwiched between the two robo-soldiers, Amar looked frail and defeated. "I was sitting right over there," I explained. God, this place was efficient.

31

"Oh, okay, ma'am," replied the taller soldier, a specialist. "But, you know, he has to be escorted at all times," he said, pointing at Amar, who was now standing behind me. The specialist kept his finger trained on Amar.

"Yeah, I got it," I said sharply, holding up my palm so he would lower his finger. "Thank you, specialist."

Several hours later, I gave Amar $40 to cover the cost of several taxi trips and a visit to his doctor for antianxiety medication. He was still vibrating with tension as I watched him walk toward the gate. Despite my assurances, he believed that Cobb and Datray would come after him. His faith in Americans was shaken.

"So, did you get what you need?" Major Gwinner asked, approaching from behind. Having just stepped out from the lobby area, he wore no Kevlar or body armor.

"Yes, sir," I replied. "Thanks for the help coordinating today. I could not have . . ."

"Good, good," he interrupted, "just let us know what you need and we'll do our best. We just don't want to drag it out." His gaze shifted from me to the front gate, where he watched expectantly.

Seizing on the offer, I continued, "Thanks, sir. Actually, I'll be back here in a few days and again next week." I hesitated then, uncertain whether I should wait to ask for more help. My requests would feel less burdensome if parsed out over time.

"Well, you're always welcome," Gwinner said. "It's just good to see you getting outside the wire."

Too tired and just relieved to be done with my first interview, Gwinner's little dig barely registered. Watching the sun disappear between several small buildings in the distance, I felt a growing sense of weariness. The logistical assistance, though invaluable, was only part of it. One interview had consumed my entire day and I still had to draft a sworn statement, have it translated, have Amar read and approve it, and have the final version translated again. The physical evidence also had yet to show up. Where the hell was it? I debated momentarily whether I should mention my other needs to Gwinner now or introduce them a few at a time. What the hell, may as well strike while the iron was hot.

"Sir, I've also had problems securing the items they found on Cobb and Datray that evening, and the stuff they left behind. It's important evidence I need to support charges of AWOL or desertion," I said before rushing to my last request, "and the guys working with Cobb and Datray at headquarters before they left. I need to speak with them too."

A look of irritation flashed briefly across Gwinner's face, but he caught it before it could settle. In the signature move of a field grade officer, he delegated the matter.

"Lieutenant Francis Blake can help you, just talk to him about what you'll need. And," he said with emphasis, "let me know if there's a problem."

As I thanked him again, a convoy of Bradley Fighting Vehicles pulled through the main gate and roared up the dirt road toward 1-8's headquarters, a storm of dust surrounding them. It was unusual to see an entire convoy of Bradleys, especially during the day. Bradleys were usually reserved for nighttime operations.

"Who is that?" I asked.

"Oh, it's the colonel's convoy. He's just returning from some meetings in town," Gwinner explained, still watching their approach.

"What's with all the track vehicles?" I asked, shielding my face as they drew near.

Eager to educate me on the dangers of war, he said, "It's too dangerous for him to travel around in a Humvee. These insurgents have a price on his head now. Apparently, they learned which Humvee was his because he's always in town. The Bradleys provide a lot more protection from an attack." He paused, before adding, "I swear, they're tracking him like an animal."

Unsure how to respond, I said, "Thanks again, sir," and made my way over to my piece-of-junk, soft-skin Humvee for the anxious ride home.

At brigade headquarters on Anaconda that evening, I began transcribing my notes from Amar's interview. It was just past 2200 when Carter returned to the workspace and reported he was unable to secure a translator. Then the TAC phone rang.

"Hey, ma'am, 1-8 is on the phone. Lieutenant Blake, 1-8. He wants to speak to you right away." I rounded the desk and took the receiver from Carter, wondering what urgent matter had transpired since I left Eagle just a few hours earlier.

"Hey, Vivian, another hajji came by and said our soldiers had attacked him. I'm pretty sure that he meant Datray/Cobb because it's the same night and he said they stole a car. I already sent him away once, but he keeps coming back."

"Wait a minute," I said, confused, "you're not talking about Amar, are you? This is a different guy?"

"Yeah, a different hajji." Blake continued, "When he came back, I gave him some money because he gave us some intel on a mortar attack, but he wants more for whatever happened. Want me to get rid of him or what?"

"Wait! What money did you give him for the mortar attack?" I asked, distracted by the mention of a payment for information. I didn't bother questioning Blake about why I was just learning about this man now.

"Hey, don't worry. It's my own money. Just ten bucks. I just had a hunch he was telling the truth, seemed real eager, ya know?"

Never mind that you're the comms guy. "Well, was he telling the truth?" While fully aware that we were completely off subject by now, I was pushing to change the current prohibition against paying locals for information.

"Oh yeah, yeah, he showed us where they launched from. Sure glad he came back, eh?"

"Definitely," I said, pleased to hear they found the site. "Money didn't hurt, either, did it?"

Blake described what they had found, how surprised his colleagues had been when he told them, and how they shouldn't be so dismissive of him in the future. I wanted to say that I understood how infantry officers could sometimes be patronizing when you offered them advice or input, but I didn't. Despite his gripes, Blake was a loyal member of 1-8, which meant he was sensitive to anyone else's criticism of his team. So I just listened, reminding myself to take it easy. Blake was, after all, just a lieutenant—promotable, still a month or two away from pinning on his captain's bars.

"Hey, about this second hajji, do you believe him? Is he still there?"

"No, he already went home," replied Blake. I could feel my shoulder muscles tighten as he explained why this guy probably was telling the truth.

A second victim? My clean, open-and-shut AWOL case was growing messy. Just how much trouble did Cobb and Datray get into on their joy ride? Interviewing Amar had already been a feat of logistics. Like most Iraqi civilians, Amar didn't have a phone, which meant we contacted him by relaying our messages through three different locals. After Amar had agreed to an interview, we still had to arrange the convoy to 1-8's headquarters and line up a translator.

A three-hour interview took the better part of two days to plan and execute. Now I had a new guy claiming he had been kidnapped. I would need to repeat the process all over again.

"Do you know where he lives? Or how to get in touch with him? How do I get a message to him?"

"He's practically here every day. I see this guy so much—"

I cut Blake off. "Hey, can you tell him to be back there at Eagle TOC on Thursday, around 1400? I'm still trying to arrange a ride out, but I need to talk to this guy."

"Can I tell him you'll pay him then? I've already sent him away a few times," Blake asked.

The immediate issue was money. I hesitated. This was a common dilemma when trying to build trust with the locals. Money talks, especially now with so many out of work and their lives turned upside down. They see the money we're shelling out to build our own bases and they think we're all swimming in it. Understandably, there's little incentive to deal with U.S. soldiers without money involved, especially with the recent upswing in violence against Iraqis pegged as collaborators. It was common sense really; my father had said as much.

When I told him that my unit had received deployment orders, my father's first response had been, "Make sure to get your funds squared away."

"What?" I asked, wondering why he was worried about my bills at a time like this. Perhaps he'd missed the part about me going to Iraq.

"Start getting your funds together, the cash," he emphasized, hoping I'd catch on. "Viv, you're going to need to have cash available for dealing with the locals. You'll never have enough, so you need to start the process of securing those funds through your chain right away. Trust me, you'll need it for everything: intelligence, building goodwill, you name it. Trust me."

By now, I considered my father's words a roadmap for survival out here. From the extra flak vests he insisted I bring to line our soft-skin Humvee, to the old special forces pamphlet on Arab customs that arrived in the mail shortly before I deployed, even his minor tidbits of advice were grounded in a foresight that had proven eerily accurate.

If I hadn't had some money readily available to compensate Amar, he would have had little incentive to continue cooperating. And yet Amar never mentioned anything about a second Iraqi man being in the car that night. Lost in translation, perhaps?

"You still there?" Blake asked.

"Yeah, let him know that he will be paid for his damages. Make sure to say 'damages,' okay?"

"Got it, I'll tell him. Thursday at 1400. He's all yours, so you better be here."

Blake was pushing it. "Lieutenant Blake, is there anyone else I need to know about?" I asked with a tense voice. "You do realize that if this guy is credible, he is going to be a witness. His testimony will be considered to be evidence." I was tempted to go on but held my tongue. I hoped that this was the last of the surprises.

"Hey, how was I supposed to know? Everyone at the gate is looking for money. Everyone at the gate now seems to be my business," Blake whined.

I was still annoyed, but I had to admit that Blake was also in an unenviable position as 1-8's claims officer. Claims are the method by which the army compensates locals for any incidental property damage or personal injury resulting from our operations. In his capacity, Blake investigated and filed claims specifically for 1-8. I didn't need to even look at the file to know it had been a busy few weeks for him.

"Okay, Blake, see you Thursday." A quick look at the claims folder showed we had a little a less than $200 and two other battalion "claims days" before Thursday. Not good.

Kolb smirked as he leaned back in his chair, his weight balanced on the chair's two back legs. He had overheard the last part of my conversation with Blake, and Kolb didn't need to review the ledger to know that we had a serious cash-flow problem.

"Ma'am," Kolb drawled, "unless we get more dough, we're gonna have some unhappy hajjis these next couple days. Did I mention that Samarra is one of the claims days?"

"How much are we talking?" I asked.

"You approved $320 for Samarra, disapproved about $250," he replied smoothly, his chair still on its back legs. Balancing there, he waited for me to digest the information before slamming his chair back down and standing up.

"I'll go ahead and cancel claims day in Ad Duluyiah, but Lieutenant Colonel [Jeffrey] Springman won't be happy, so heads up at the BUB," Kolb added.

Unfortunately, Carter overheard this.

"Ma'am, I don't want to go to Samarra if we're not paying anyone. No way. That place is crazy!" Carter protested as he dropped our weekly allotment of water bottles on the ground. We waited for the swirl of dust and dirt to settle back down.

Unsure what to say, I wiped my face to buy some time.

"Okay, guys, nothing has changed for claims day in Samarra. You'll definitely be paying people; it's simply a matter of how much. I just need to set aside a little for Thursday's trip to 1-8."

Carter said nothing in response. His jaw was tight as he flipped through the claims book. Better he brood than protest again. I could hardly blame him. In every town we conducted operations, we would establish a claims day. This involved distributing claim forms to the locals, explaining the evidence required to support a claim, and listening to countless grievances against 3rd Brigade's soldiers. Claims days were a headache even when we had enough money. The meeting room was always sweltering and packed with disgruntled locals vying for your attention.

Just as our claims money was nearly depleted, so were my guys. They were exhausted after five nonstop months in theater. From our first day in Iraq, it was clear we had joined a mission teeming with legal landmines. There were clearly marked problems like ROE, and plenty with the lightest coating of sand obscuring them. Our workload had mushroomed and we scurried to get ahead of every issue we suspected to be explosive.

The strain of all this vigilance, however, was apparent in my team. The most indefatigable of the JAG team, Carter's mounting frustration was especially worrying. Unfortunately, I had little energy or spirit to rally Carter or the others. I was also at loss for how to motivate them. I knew what my father would say. He'd tell me to listen more. "You have to hear them before you can lead them," he would say.

My father had led elite soldiers for years, and trained foreign armies all over the world, teaching the best of the best how to lead. To my father, there was no better way to figure out how to motivate soldiers than to listen to them.

Drowning In The Desert

Applying his approach, I tried to imagine what each of my guys might say. I knew they were tired, but were they tired because they felt unappreciated? Or tired because they needed more variety? Or tired because they needed more of a challenge?

Carter would probably tell me he felt like he did more work than the others. Philibert, I imagined, would say he was bored. And Kolb, I imagined Kolb was tired of what he considered to be my micromanaging. Hell, I was tired of having to micromanage, so we were even. Just speculating on what might be on each of their minds, however, gave me some perspective. As to what I planned to do with the information, turning this morale situation around seemed too daunting at the moment. I already was running on fumes.

This excuse, of course, would be little deterrent for my dad. He would have figured out how to turn around this desperate situation, as he always had.

Still, faced with a cloudy legal forecast and zero hope of receiving more staff, I knew something had to change. While I suspected it might have to be me, I settled for a stop-gap measure and outsourced. That night I asked Mike to send a care package to Carter. For the meanwhile, encouragement and acknowledgement by proxy would have to do.

A convoy delay the next day meant we were two hours late to meet with Cobb and Datray's alleged second victim. By the time we arrived at Camp Eagle, it was midafternoon. An Iraqi man was squatting to the left of the guard booth as we drove in. He held papers over his head to ward off the blazing afternoon sun.

First Lieutenant Blake greeted me with a snide remark about timeliness after we parked in the makeshift dirt lot outside the building's main entrance. "What happened to 1400?" Blake asked. "He's been waiting around here all day. Where were you?"

Ignoring his question, I asked, "Are you talking about that guy at the gate? Why didn't you let him wait inside?"

"Look, if I let him in, then I would have to babysit him all day," he answered shortly.

Swallowing my irritation, I started over. "Hey, sorry about being late. Thanks for coordinating this. I know it has been a pain."

Mollified, he led me to a room I could use inside. "You're lucky. Colonel Sassaman said you could use his room for interviews today since he's headed back into town."

"Wow, that's great." It certainly wasn't every day that a unit accommodated a JAG visit like this. "Wait, does that mean Tina . . ."

"Yeah, she's headed over here right now."

"That is wonderful news!" I said, grinning.

Professional, flexible, and fluent in Arabic, Tina was an excellent translator. She had been a godsend in helping me calm the skittish Amar. An Iraqi-American civilian from Redford, Michigan, she had volunteered, along with her sister, Thanna "Donna" Azawi, to serve as translators in Operation Iraqi Freedom. Their only condition was that they did not want to be separated.

Despite our late start, it definitely looked like things were turning around today.

I regretted my optimism the moment I met Murtdadah Fadel, the second Iraqi victim. Murtdadah did not so much tell me about what happened, but reenact every detail of the evening. Three hours later, my head was pounding.

"Calm down. Calm down! Tina, please tell him to stop talking and sit back down."

Murtdadah repeatedly grabbed his chest and thanked Allah. "Shukran. Shukran," he said in Arabic, meaning "Thank you. Thank you." It had been weeks since his encounter with Cobb and Datray, but his fear had not subsided. He recalled the evening in rapid-fire bursts, using his arms to demonstrate how he had flagged down Amar's car. He jumped up to demonstrate the soldiers' aggressive posture and showed us how he was pushed to the ground. Up and down. Back and forth. He revisited different parts of the evening as the details came flooding back to him. The rustling in the courtyard. His confusion. The M16 pointed at his head. The irritable Americans.

"Tina, he can't keep jumping around like this. Please, tell him to just answer my questions. I need to know the chronology," I pleaded.

Tina widened her eyes and gestured as if to say, "What else can I do?"

Murtdadah's story was that he had walked out into his family's courtyard to investigate a rattling sound. Soon, he was on his knees pleading with what appeared to be two American soldiers. One had wavy, dark hair and the other had straight, lighter hair. They yelled at him in English. He repeated the only English he knew. "Good Morning. Good Morning." Frightened, he put up his hands in a gesture of surrender and fell to his knees. This seemed to appease them somewhat. He watched as one of the soldiers disappeared into the house. He was alone. What did they want?

The soldier who had gone inside returned to the courtyard, held out his arms, and pretended to drive. Ah! The Americans were looking for a car. Or, perhaps their car had broken down? Maybe they were lost and needed a ride? Either way, Murtdadah didn't have car, and he didn't know how to fix a broken one. With the other soldier's gun still trained on him, he pointed to the empty dirt path leading up to the house. He tried to explain that he didn't have a car, or a house for that matter. This was his parents' house.

The Americans seemed agitated again. Get up, the darker-haired one signaled with his M16. When Murtdadah was on his feet, the soldiers held the rifle to his back and directed him down the street. They needed a car and they wanted him to find one for them. Murtdadah's neighbor stared at him in bewilderment. She explained to him that her husband had taken the car out earlier that evening. Her words trailed off as she noticed the two figures lurking behind Murtdadah. Before she could continue, Murtdadah straightened up as one of the Americans pushed the nose of the gun into his back.

If Murtdadah couldn't borrow a car for the Americans, he would have to flag one down, or at least that's what they seemed to say as they nudged him toward the road. Murtdadah scanned the road for headlights, occasionally turning to indicate that no cars were coming their way. From their hiding place in a ditch several meters from the road, the two Americans yelled at Murtdadah to pay attention and keep watching for cars. Minutes passed before he spotted a car and began waving his arms, urging the driver to stop. As the driver, Amar, slowed to examine the flailing spectacle, the soldiers emerged from their hiding place and pointed the weapon at his head. Murtdadah looked at Amar apologetically and began to explain in Arabic. They are Americans. They just need a ride to their base.

The Americans piled into the backseat of the maroon Chevy Caprice and directed Murtdadah to the front passenger seat. The dark-haired American pointed the gun at the driver and ordered the man to drive. Minutes later, they were nearing an army base. As the base's perimeter became clearer, the Americans began yelling at Amar. Amar pointed to the base, searching for the right words to explain that this was where the Americans lived.

The Americans continued to yell and motioned for the driver to turn the car around. "No. No. No!" they said angrily until Amar made a sharp turn away from the base. Confused, Amar headed toward the nearest police station, the only other location where he had ever seen American soldiers. They drove for several minutes before the police station came into view. The Americans recognized the station's police cars and became angry again. The light-haired American leaned forward from the back seat and held a knife inches away from the Amar's right ear. Without turning his head, Amar asked, "No police?"

"No police!" the American hissed. When Amar drove past the police station, the Americans slid down in their seats to avoid being seen.

A mile from Camp Eagle's perimeter, the Americans ordered Amar to stop the car and made him and Murtdadah get out. The Americans were angry and yelled at them. They pointed to the road and tried drawing a map in the dirt, but Murtdadah didn't understand. The soldiers began arguing with each other. Sensing his opportunity, Amar broke into a sprint and disappeared into a neighboring orchard. One soldier ran after him but gave up quickly and returned to the car.

Murtdadah cursed his own cowardice. He should have run, too. He should have at least tried. If he had run, they might not have caught him. Now, he was sure the soldiers would kill him. Sickened, he collapsed to the ground and waited for the bullet. Nothing. A door slammed, but Murtdadah didn't dare look up. The Americans were leaving. The sound of the engine grew fainter. Murtdadah still kept his head to the ground. Minutes later, he finally looked up and confirmed that he was alone. Praise Allah! I have been spared!

Again, Murtdadah leapt from his chair to demonstrate. Ignoring our protests, he hurled himself to the ground, putting his forehead to the floor. Prostrate, he showed us how he listened for movement before daring to lift his head. Turning his head robotically, Murtdadah raised his head slowly, his eyes wide open, his face resembled a fright mask.

Following the incident, Murtdadah was picked up by Iraqi police, who arrested him for helping two Americans steal a car from a fellow Iraqi.

Drowning In The Desert

Murtdadah's cries of innocence went unheeded, and he spent twelve days in the local jail before Amar agreed not to press charges. Amazingly, Murtdadah seemed unfazed by his brief stint in jail.

Murtdadah possessed none of the wariness toward Americans I'd experienced with other Iraqi civilians. He seemed to relish the opportunity to discuss his night with Cobb and Datray, as well as a laundry list of other things on his mind. He boasted repeatedly about greeting soldiers in English, saying "Good morning." We learned about his illnesses, his family, and the daily challenges facing farmers in Balad.

After the meeting, I said to Tina, "I don't know, I'm just hoping he comes out of his shell."

We both laughed, me a little too loudly. The language barrier was the least of my concerns. Murtdadah was a prosecutor's nightmare. Highly excitable. Easily distracted. And chatty. Defense counsel would have a field day with him on cross-examination.

CHAPTER FOUR

Warning Signs

AT CAMP EAGLE, THE SOLDIERS had discovered that when the lights on the local mosque began to flicker, mortars were forthcoming. A keen guard in 1-8's observation tower took note when he saw faint flickering just moments before a mortar exploded near Eagle's perimeter. Days later when the same curious flickering was followed by the ominous whistle of an incoming mortar, others were alerted to watch for flashing neon lights across Balad's dusty skyline. It seemed the insurgents were using the lights to warn civilians and, some speculated, as a visual guidepost to help their folks on the ground target the base. The heads-up gave the soldiers at Eagle a thirty-second warning, at most. Just enough time to scramble for shelter and try to launch a counterattack. Or, in the case of some soldiers, just enough time to make a decision they might later regret.

Arriving early at Camp Eagle for a follow-up meeting with Murtdadah, Kolb and I found soldiers gathered around the freshly charred frame of a supply truck. Less than twenty-four hours earlier, insurgents had pulled off their most impressive strike yet, landing a mortar next to the vehicle within thirty feet of 1-8's headquarters building. All morning, soldiers had filed by the wreckage, their eyes drinking in every inch of the twisted metal heap. They alternated between gawking and chatting breezily about the nature of the damage. They had seen dozens of scenes like this one. Still, in spite of everything, few of the soldiers had experienced the exquisite violation of being mortared right at their doorstep.

"Ma'am, here's where it penetrated," a young soldier explained, pointing out the various points near the driver's seat that shrapnel had penetrated. The truck's body was rocked by dozens of angry gaping holes, tears so violent you would have thought the vehicle was made out of fabric, not steel. The driver's seat was splattered with blood, as was everything else in the cabin. Dark-brown stains were also visible on the ground outside.

Examining the bent metal, I couldn't help but wonder how valuable any warning was to twenty-two-year-old Spec. Roy Gray. Did he hear the warning? Had it made any difference? Gray had been part of a convoy delivering hot meals to soldiers in outlying posts. He had just parked the truck when the first mortars landed. Gray suddenly had a decision to make. Should he stay or go? The truck's cabin was made of steel, but not reinforced steel. The headquarters building had a hard roof and offered better protection but it was a significant distance away. He could stay and hope the truck's minimal protection would be enough or he could make a run for it and hope he reached the building in time. Weighing the benefits of a semi-secure shelter against the possibility of being hit out in the open, Gray stayed put. The mortar landed on the ground some fifteen feet from the truck. The force of the blast left pockmarks on the rear wall of the headquarters building and the wooden porta-potties nearby. It rained pieces of metal across the entire front of the vehicle. Gray's face was battered with shrapnel. One sliver shot upward, penetrating the flimsy metal driver's door and Gray's seat before lodging in his upper thigh. Severing a major artery, it caused so much blood loss that it was still unclear whether Gray would survive.

A soldier came over to escort Kolb to the spot where he would meet with soldiers in need of legal assistance. The growing demand for legal assistance services at outlying units was forcing us to maximize our trips to nearby bases. Although I could sometimes knock out some part of the investigation and a few legal questions in one trip, that wasn't always the case. It also wasn't fair to soldiers with serious legal concerns to feel rushed to squeeze in their question before my convoy took off. In my effort to hear my team's concerns and therefore lead more effectively, I decided to give Kolb some of the autonomy I knew he craved. Asking Kolb to handle some of these legal assistance house calls was

44

risky. It was a lot of responsibility, and considering our recent disagreements, I wasn't sure he was up to it. When he said "yes," I resisted the urge to advise him on how to handle things. Instead, I left it up to him. So far, the feedback from the battalions about Kolb was positive. I kept my fingers crossed it would continue that way.

"Captain, I see you've made it."

I turned to see Blake ambling towards me. The morning sun hugged the outline of his sturdy frame and dark hair, adding an almost ethereal quality to his appearance. Smiling and more relaxed than usual, Blake seemed almost pleased to see me. Curious.

"Yeah, got here early. This looks pretty bad," I said, turning toward the wreckage.

Blake nodded and gestured for me to walk with him. He wanted to talk about rewards payments. In addition to seeing Murtdadah today, I had also agreed to meet with yet a third Iraqi who claimed to have been victimized by Cobb and Datray. Blake, however, wanted to discuss the rewards payment for Murtdadah.

"Don't worry, I've got money for him."

"Well, can you give him some more because he showed us another site?" Blake said.

"Another site? What are you talking about?"

I turned to examine the thin smile on Blake's lips. "Blake, what's going on?"

"Mortar sites. He showed us where the mortars were launched from again."

"He did?"

"Yeah, he knew exactly where they were, again. As usual, everyone thought he was just being crazy."

Murtdadah had all of the ease of an anxious puppy. Hyper and clamoring one moment, nervous and agitated the next. He hardly inspired confidence.

"I told him no, but after this latest attack, I said screw it, and took the Humvee out by myself. Sure enough, he was right."

"You went out by yourself?" I asked, trying to hide my alarm. It was never easy to go out on the heels of an attack, and here the smoke was still in the air and Blake was venturing out with an Iraqi he hardly knew.

"Yeah, but he took me right to the spot," Blake said, smiling.

"Hey, just don't make it a habit, okay? These guys have to believe . . . him now." I had almost said "you."

"Yeah, I think so," he said dismissively. "You know how crazy he is. I figured I might as well . . ."

I hurried to assure him, "Yeah, I know, he's really erratic, but then you realize he's telling the truth."

Blake nodded, suddenly self-conscious. He added, "Who knows, he probably *is* playing both sides."

"What do you mean?"

"Helping us. Helping them. You've seen his hands, right?"

I shook my head. I hadn't even noticed his hands. The man never stood still long enough.

"His tattoos—take a look at the ones on his hands. He's Fedayeen."

"He's Fedayeen?" I repeated incredulous.

"Yeah, he was an artillery guy. That's how he can figure out where the mortars are launched from. That's what he claims anyways."

Thanks, Blake, I thought. *I'm heading into the trial of my life and you're only now telling me my key witness is a possible insurgent.*

The Fedayeen Saddam was a paramilitary organization that had served as a personal militia for Saddam Hussein when he was in power. Numbering between twenty thousand and forty thousand irregular soldiers, they provided the former president with a reliable force against domestic opponents. After the invasion of Iraq, many of the Fedayeen who survived had reportedly joined guerilla groups that formed the insurgency.

I spent the first twenty minutes of my meeting with Murtdadah staring at the three small dark tattoos on the inside of his wrist. Crude and barely visible against his tan skin, it was difficult to distinguish what they were. Murtdadah wasn't quick to explain them either. My first few questions garnered little more than confused looks from him. It wasn't until he sensed that he might be falling out of favor that he launched into a rambling explanation of his past involvement with the Iraqi Army.

Before leaving, he lifted his shirt repeatedly to show us a large wound near the center of his chest. It happened years ago, when he was in the regular Iraqi army. The injury was so bad that it ended his days as a soldier. He was sent home to his parents and expected to die. It was Allah's will, he explained, that he recovered. Still, while Murtdadah admitted to once being a soldier, he avoided answering whether he was once Fedayeen. "I am not Fedayeen," he said repeatedly, feigning confusion.

I tried to get him to specify the time frame for his Fedayeen service, but he refused, sticking with his standard response. "2000 to 2001?"

"I am not Fedayeen."

"2001 to 2002?"

"I am not Fedayeen."

Turning to the translator, I finally said, "I give up."

Murtdadah wasn't crazy. He knew exactly what he was doing.

Even in a place as neutral as the recreational room, there was no mistaking that I was at 1-8 Infantry Battalion's headquarters, home of the "Screaming Eagles." The rec room was covered with fliers reminding soldiers of various "Eagle" events. The 1-8 crest was stenciled on a large sign in the corner. Amid this "Eagle Spirit," I waited for Cobb and Datray's latest victim and wondered if I should get a sign with the JAG insignia for our workspace. Was that the secret? Did my men need a reminder that we were on the same team, working for the same goal? Wasn't it enough that we wore the same uniform?

It might be a nice touch for the new place. We had recently moved our workspace out of the tactical operations tent and into the brigade headquarters building. It was part of Welsch's grand plan to eventually move all workspace indoors so he could permanently pack up the tents. Due to limited space inside the building, an outdoor courtyard between two hallways had been refashioned into a new wing. The long, rectangular space, complete with concrete benches protruding through the new plywood floor, was now the brigade's Administrative and Logistical Operations Center, or ALOC. Battle tracking continued in the Tactical Operations Center next door, while logistics and support operations centered in the ALOC. Altogether, the ALOC would be home to the S1 personnel section, the S5 civil affairs section, the public affairs officer, combat camera, JAG, and several others throughout our deployment.

At the back of the hall, Welsch had walled off one room for use as a library of sorts, for book and magazine swapping. The remaining space was separated by a walkway with various sections allocated room on either side, like booths at a craft fair. We scored a large area in the left rear, with the library wall on our left, and a concrete bench separating us from another section. The idea of some paint and wood identifying our workspace sounded perfect. And, if it would get my guys moving a little faster, who was I to argue?

I looked up to see Blake shepherding into the room an elderly Iraqi man with white hair and a distinct limp. Standing behind the man, Blake mouthed, "This is the guy." An elderly Iraqi woman and young boy followed close behind.

Jumping to my feet, I pulled a few white plastic chairs forward for the three of them.

"You set?" Blake asked from the doorway.

"Yeah."

A translator joined us and we sat down for what I was certain would be another disturbing discovery about Cobb and Datray's night on the run. Thirty minutes later, I wasn't sure what to make of the old man's story. He claimed that he and several family members had been sleeping in the fields on his property when two soldiers came across them. The soldiers were startled to encounter a half dozen Iraqi men sleeping among the stalks, and one of the two soldiers panicked and fired a gun. He was a neighbor of Murtdadah's, so it was plausible that Cobb and Datray had crossed his property. It also wasn't unusual for Iraqis to sleep in the fields to protect their crops from thieves.

It was the next part that left me doubtful. The old man claimed that when the soldier fired his weapon, the bullet grazed him. He pushed back his sleeve to reveal a dry, almost scaly patch of scar tissue on his forearm. Pointing to the healed and obviously ancient wound, identical in color to his skin, he insisted it was where the bullet had grazed him. Unwilling to meet his eyes, I stared at his arm a little longer than necessary, weighing my options.

The medic I called in to examine the scar shot me a look that said, "You're kidding, right?" The elderly woman and young boy sat behind the old man, their anxious faces watching mine for some indication that I was buying the old man's story. Leaning forward, the woman added that the shot had left blood everywhere. Pleased to have contributed, she sat back in her chair and watched with large hopeful eyes.

Taking one last look at the wound, I wished their story were even slightly more plausible. It felt terrible to say no to old people. Their wrinkled and weather-beaten faces were evidence enough that they had gotten a bad deal in life, though not from Cobb and Datray. And the young boy who hid behind the woman's skirt? He was looking at the same bleak future.

I rested my chin on my chest for a second before giving the man another chance to amend his story.

"Are you sure that the bullet didn't graze something else?"

He wasn't budging.

Turning toward the translator, I asked, "Is he sure it didn't hit . . . maybe something on his property?"

Come on, man. Work with me. Say something. Say it killed one of your chickens or shattered your window. Give me something I can pay you for. Anything. Just stop showing me that wrinkled old scar.

"Ask him again," I urged the translator.

Not getting the answer I needed, I had little choice.

"I'm sorry, but this scar looks too old to have been caused just a month ago. We can't pay you," I said finally, more to the translator than to the old man.

The three faces before me fell as I stood to signal that they were ready to be escorted out. Returning to my seat, I pulled out the notes from my meeting with Murtdadah and flipped blindly through the pages. I waited to hear the door close behind them.

Heading back to Anaconda that evening, Kolb and I were both quiet. He was focused on keeping up with two turbo-powered Humvees dispatched to escort us back. It wasn't until we sat idling in the line of vehicles waiting to enter Anaconda that Kolb brought up the old man. Turning away from the window, I suddenly regretted telling him what had happened.

"You know, I hate saying no to old people. It's the worst," I said, my guilt still fresh and close to the surface.

"Everybody's looking for money," Kolb said.

"I mean, why couldn't they have just said that the guys killed one of their goats or something?" I said, voicing the dialogue I'd been having in my head all afternoon. "A chicken at the very least," I said, tucking my right leg under me as I waved off the peddlers gathering by the side of our Humvee.

"It's a good thing you didn't pay them, because then we'd have everybody in the world showing up." Sighing dramatically, Kolb repositioned his hands on the wheel.

"Yeah, but I just feel so bad."

"They were lying, ma'am."

"I know. I know," I mumbled, turning to look out the window. Images of the old man sleeping in a field kept gnawing at me.

"He made it up. You saw the scar," Kolb added, struggling to make me feel better. "It was probably from the Iran-Iraq war. I mean, c'mon, you think Iran paid claims?"

Now he was just talking crazy. Turning, I found Kolb sporting a big cheesy grin, "What the hell are you talking about, Iran?" I asked, now fighting back laughter.

"I don't know, ma'am, I don't know . . ." replied Kolb, before erupting into laughter.

Back at brigade headquarters, I went in search of Colonel Rudesheim's translator, Donald Dawood. He had graciously agreed to translate several of my documents, but I hadn't seen him in days, which worried me. I did a loop around the building before checking a few of his favorite smoking spots. The division JAG office wanted a copy of both of the Iraqis' final sworn statements. What was I going to do about Murtdadah? With no sign of Donald loitering near the back door, I headed for the ALOC.

Several soldiers, including a guy I recognized as one of Philibert's friends, were gathered around the JAG workspace table. Behind the table, Philibert and Carter appeared to be holding court.

"Hey Sergeant Phil, hey Carter," I said louder than necessary. "Sergeant Kolb went to fill up the Humvee."

Hearing my voice, several of the soldiers dispersed.

"Wow, ma'am, you'll be glad to know that the showers aren't working again." Philibert said, eyeing my matted hair and the grimy fingers I used to push it out of my eyes.

I wouldn't have had time anyway; the BUB started in twenty minutes. No doubt, young gloomy-faced soldiers were already busy setting up metal folding chairs in the Tactical Operations Center while others worked hard at sweeping the tarp floor, causing whirls of dirt and sand to fill the tent's air. Just remembering it made me grateful, again, for our new workspace in the Administrative and Logistical Operations Center.

Meanwhile, Carter and Phil wasted no time donning their gear to leave.

They would still be at the chow hall when the BUB ended. And the last thing I wanted was to be left on my own to figure out everything that wasn't accomplished during the day.

"Hey guys, don't leave yet," I said to Carter and Phil "I just need to send a quick e-mail to Colonel Barnes." Lt. Col. Tracey Barnes was the division's senior ranking JAG, otherwise called the Division Staff Judge Advocate (SJA). It was my job to keep him, and the division JAG office in Tikrit, informed about anything important brewing down here at the brigade.

Taking Carter's seat in front of the laptop, I banged out the first few lines of my e-mail. Studying the screen, I considered what else to include. Should I explain what I'd learned today? *Hey sir, about that second victim. Well, it turns out he's Fedayeen, but no worries, because he's helping us locate the mortar launch sites, okay?*

Was it even worth it to involve division at all? Their handling of my last request didn't inspire much confidence. After hunting down a defense attorney to represent Cobb, I had requested their help finding representation for Datray. There were at least six available defense attorneys in Tikrit, so it didn't seem unreasonable to ask them to assign one to Datray. Their response was to offer me the name of a captain in Kuwait. No phone number, e-mail address, or additional information, just the guy's name. The e-mail address Carter eventually located for the captain was one that had to be accessed from a nonsecure network.

Out of the corner of my eye, I saw a soldier lean across the table toward me.

"So, the legal beagle has been away all day, huh?"

I didn't have to look over to know who it was. The cajoling tone alone was enough to let me know it was Capt. Tom Roughneen.

"Hey Tom. Sorry, I'm rushing to get this out before the BUB," I said, tapping loudly on the keyboard to underscore the point.

"Yeah, yeah, I know you're *always* busy, but I need to talk to you."

"Okay. Just wait, okay," I said, still preoccupied with how to handle Murtdadah.

A reserve civil affairs officer, Tom and his team of three civil affairs soldiers had done a stint in Kirkuk before joining 3rd Brigade a few weeks ago. They were assigned to work with 1-8 in Balad. Tom was in his early thirties, tall

51

with a handsome, freckled face and sapphire blue eyes. We became fast friends, though his instant familiarity could be both charming and abrasive.

Tom moved so that he was looking over my shoulder. "Still slave-driving, huh?" he said pointing at Carter and Phil, who sat patiently waiting.

Holding up my finger, I urged him to give me one second.

"Aww, come on, captain, why don't you let these poor lads go to chow?" he said in a deep Irish brogue as he gestured toward Carter and Philibert. Philibert chimed in with what sounded more like an Indian accent.

Ignoring Tom completely, I looked directly at Carter and Philibert. "Sorry, guys, go on ahead. I am definitely not going to finish this e-mail in time," I said. I waited until their gear-laden figures disappeared through the ALOC's double doors before turning back to Tom.

"Hey, Tom," I said, trying to sound casual, "I'd appreciate it if you didn't make comments like that around my guys in the future. I'm already short four guys, and making me out to be a villain isn't helping on the morale front, get it?"

"Well, if you'd give them a break some time . . . ," he began.

"Tom, what do you want? What can I do for you? I have a lot on my plate right now, so what is it?"

"That carjacking case?" Tom continued, ignoring my question. "If you need someone to talk it over with, I have some experience in the courtroom."

I studied his face, uncertain whether he was serious or setting me up for another one of his jokes.

Suddenly too tired to care anymore, I said, "Look, Tom, I'm sorry I was so short with you. Today has been a complete nightmare and everything about my case keeps changing, so it's really no use explaining it right now, okay?"

It sounded harsh even to my own ears. Undeterred, Tom replied, "Vivian, believe it or not, I do know a little about criminal law."

Did this guy ever give up? "Tom! I never claimed to be an expert at anything. I'm the only lawyer out here. I'm just trying to figure out what I can do." All efforts to keep the tension out of my voice had been aborted. "What makes you such an expert on criminal law?" I asked, shrugging my shoulders dejectedly.

Tom smiled. "District attorney. New Jersey. Seven years." Now beaming, he added, "I thought I told you."

Stunned, I wasn't sure if I wanted to hug him or hit him.

I could feel the corners of my mouth rising to form a smile.

"For God's sake, you never told me. How many times have you heard me complaining about this case, the investigation, and . . . you never told me and you know it."

Tom just shrugged. I was too relieved to argue. I finally had someone to discuss the case with.

"Tom, meet me outside after the BUB. It will be quick. I need your opinion on the case."

Tom sat behind two trays piled high with a little bit of everything. Lucky for Tom, he had the metabolism of a hummingbird to go with the appetite of a bear. Holding a burger in his hands, he examined it for a few seconds before taking a large bite.

He chewed heartily, swallowed, and offered a satisfied grin. "Well, why haven't you retraced the route?" he asked. "That's the best way to show their intent that night," he said between bites.

"Tom, what do you mean, retrace the route? This is Iraq, remember? I'm trying to *avoid* being a target. Do you think slowly trolling the roads in a convoy, trying to retrace a route that supposedly goes in circles is such a good idea?"

"You're right, it's safer to travel with less vehicles. That's what I do," he said, grinning. "But really, you're out there every day already. Why so safety conscious now? How else will you show their intent? You can't just rely on these Iraqis."

After all the time and effort I'd spent on Amar and Murtdadah—on their sworn statements and the interviews—hearing Tom, a seasoned prosecutor, confirm that it just wasn't enough was hard to swallow. I reluctantly agreed. He was right. There really wasn't much I could do about Murtdadah. He would either combust on the stand or not. No amount of worrying would change that. I needed to prove Cobb and Datray were actively trying to escape and that they weren't just lost. If I showed their route that night, I could establish their intent.

Still, was it worth tracing the route, endangering other soldiers, my team? If they didn't already think I was crazy, once they learned that I wanted to retrace the route, they might revolt. Things with Kolb were strained enough already after I'd told Welsch that we would process the temporary weapons card applications for the brigade's area. Losing me and Phil to another day on the road wasn't going to improve Kolb's mood either. Hadn't Tom just finished telling me how he traveled to Balad by himself a lot? For the time being, I changed the subject.

"Tom, what's the latest between you and Sassaman?

"Nothing. Nothing's changed on that."

"What do you mean nothing's changed? Have you tried talking to Major Gwinner? It's better to work something out. You'll have more support for civil affairs in the long run, trust me."

The civil affairs section was located across from us in our new workspace. I'd overheard enough conversations to know that Tom was clashing with 1-8 over his civil affairs projects. After working relatively independently in Kirkuk for months, Tom couldn't seem to accept that as long as civil affairs relied on the units they worked with for convoys, security, and logistical support, the civil affairs mission would remain secondary.

"It may take some time, but I'm sure things will smooth out between you and 1-8."

"It doesn't matter at this point, Vivian. Sassaman doesn't like me, and everyone there knows it," he said flatly. According to Tom, Sassaman had even gone so far as to denounce Tom during a recent 1-8 staff meeting. Apparently, Tom supported working on a project with some locals whom Sassaman distrusted. The public display of disdain by Sassaman had set the tone for the rest of the soldiers. In the wake of the meeting, Tom found himself with virtually no logistical support or transport.

Listening to him describe the incident made me uncomfortable. Tom was matter-of-fact, and even accepted blame for part of it, but Sassaman's reaction seemed unduly harsh. Had I missed something? I wondered if Tom's direct manner and trusting nature with Iraqis had rubbed some of 1-8's senior officers the wrong way.

While Tom went on to complain about the shortage of translators, I was still digesting the details of his conflict with 1-8. I was struck by how people seemed to crave Sassaman's approval, myself included, and suddenly felt grateful that I wasn't in Tom's shoes.

Jerking his head up suddenly, Tom fixed his gaze on me. "Hey, aren't you the ROE person? Aren't you supposed to monitor what they do over there? Were you aware that 1-8 arrests every Iraqi that even looks at them wrong?"

If Tom intended to hit a sore spot, he succeeded. For months I had pushed for better training and more accountability of soldiers' search, seizure, arrest, and detention procedures. The success I'd had was still modest compared to the brigade operations I'd seen in Kirkuk, when I visited Capt. Brian Hughes, a fellow JAG. The 173rd Airborne Brigade had divided Kirkuk into sectors, worked closely with the local police force, and had a clear detention plan and hearing process. I'd left there inspired, convinced that I'd finally found the answers, especially those that concerned detainees. Convincing 3rd Brigade's leadership was another matter. Tom's frustrations echoed many of my own, but like many soldiers who'd been out here too long, I took Tom's accusing questions personally. How was he qualified to judge me?

"Tom, you've been here for what? Three weeks? I think you spent too much time in Kirkuk. I was there, and it's a different world. There are phones and trained police, and the brigade commander is tracking his detainees as closely as he tracks the battle. Trust me, Brian Hughes toured me around Kirkuk in his civilian Jeep. It's a different world here. You're just too used to life in Kirkuk."

Located in Iraq's Kurdish northern region, Kirkuk was an oasis of calm and prosperity compared to Balad, which was experiencing a spike in insurgent activity. I did, however, glean some good tips from Hughes, the first of which was to get our brigade to task one of the less active battalions with handling the majority of detainees. With six battalions in 3rd Brigade—two mechanized infantry, one armor, one combat engineers, one field artillery, and one forward support—I was able to convince Colonel Rudesheim to task the field artillery battalion, commanded by Col. Jefferey Springman, to run the detainee operations. While the other battalions might bring in detainees after a raid and hold them temporarily, having a brigade-designated facility handling the detainees and processing the evidence they arrived with went a long way to preventing abuses. Expecting the stretched-too-thin battalions to do their regular jobs in addition to maintaining Geneva Convention-abiding detention facilities, was beyond naïve.

"I don't think you realize what 1-8 is up against here," I said, carefully measuring my tone in the hope that Tom might reveal what was really bothering him.

Instead, he lobbed it back to me. "You're just lucky they're behind you on this case. I mean it, just tell them you need to retrace the route."

Ignoring him, I continued, "Well, I think you just rubbed each other the wrong way. Do you want me to say something to Gwinner about how important your civil affairs work is? You know, something like that?"

Tom smiled and shook his head reassuringly. "No, I'd much rather you attend a meeting I've set up with the judges in Balad tomorrow." He tilted his head, feigning confusion at my discomfort. "I saw them again today, and they said you still had not returned."

God, I was starting to understand why 1-8 didn't like him. One of five children, Tom was adept at all manner of teasing and cajoling. All four of the Roughneen boys had found a way to serve their country. Two of Tom's brothers were Blackhawk helicopter pilots and the other flew C-130s. Amazingly, Tom was considered the diplomat of the group.

The judges were another sore point, a constant reminder of my own futility. At first, it was exciting to think I could help rebuild Iraq's judicial system. At each new location, I eagerly met with the judges, conducted the requisite review of their caseloads, expedited the finances for facility repairs, and ensured the courts were up and running. I would relay all of their concerns to division and inevitably we would hit a wall. Division would stop responding to my requests for this or that, and their lack of response had a ripple effect. With few answers to the judges' mounting concerns, the meetings seemed to only compound their frustration. Tom was right. I was definitely avoiding the judges.

Guns. Guns. Guns. It didn't matter what corner of Iraq we were in, the number one issue for the judges was their personal safety. Having relinquished their weapons as part of one of Coalition Provisional Authority's ill-conceived "weapons turn-in" program, the already unpopular judges felt particularly vulnerable. Adding to that was the fact that many of them had lengthy commutes. Under Saddam, judges had been prohibited from working in the same town in which they lived, to deter collusion and maintain control. As a result, they were easy targets for locals seeking to exact revenge for past injustices. A spate of recent attacks on judges in Baghdad and Mosul only added to their worries. My last meeting with the judges in Balad had been dominated by talk about security issues. Speaking with the judges the next day would be no different.

* * *

As soon as Tom and I arrived, we were ushered into the chief judge's office where several other judges waited expectantly. Closing the door behind him, the chief judge took a deep breath and exhaled dramatically before beginning.

"From the moment I leave my house to the time I get back, I am scared," he said. "It's not fair to have to be here with no security. I can't do my job. I can't do anything."

The three other judges nodded in agreement.

Stifling the urge to kick Tom's foot and say, "See, I told you so," I promised the chief judge I would look into getting the judges an exemption from the CPA's weapons policy.

"I'm afraid someone is going to try and kill me every day," the chief judge continued.

"I know. I know. It's not right," I responded weakly.

"You don't understand how many checkpoints there are just to get to work," he pushed on. The judge was aware of the latest insurgent tactic: setting up fake checkpoints to trap and kill your target.

I shook my head sympathetically. "It isn't right. I will do what I can to get that weapons ban changed."

It continued like that for most of the afternoon, until the judges sensed I was running out of ways to say I would look into it right away. Abandoning the security issue momentarily, they expressed concern that U.S. forces were arresting Iraqis and holding them without any sort of accountability.

"It would help if we could just get a list of the people you are holding," the chief judge said. The other judges chimed in immediately.

I didn't bother looking at the translator. Instead, I whispered to Tom, "He wants a list? Do you know how long I have been after the units to keep records? We're lucky we even have a central detention facility in the brigade." Tom nodded solemnly.

On the trip back to Anaconda, Tom drove as I fought against the often unmentioned enemy, fatigue. The mixture of hot wind and sand pelting my face and piercing every exposed crevice on my body was usually enough to keep me alert, albeit irritated. The judges, however, had sapped my energy with their pleas for assistance and grave predictions of the future. Adjusting my sleeve to cover a nasty cut on my wrist, I attempted to focus on the enemy outside, the one that hid bombs in the debris and garbage alongside the road. Instead, my head bobbed under the weight of my Kevlar as I became mesmerized by the monotonous landscape blurring by at increasing speeds. Closing my eyes for just a second, my head finally succumbed, pitching forward before I jerked violently awake just inches from kissing the door. Unfortunately, Tom's hawk eyes missed nothing.

"Hey, JAG!" he yelled over the engine. "Wake up, this ain't no taxi!" Tom's cackling continued even as I assumed a decidedly more alert position.

Exhausted and now embarrassed, I considered ignoring him but yielded to a more hostile instinct.

"Hey Tom, what exactly did we accomplish today by seeing those judges?" I asked pointedly. "Didn't I tell you what they would want, and that we couldn't help them?

"For God's sake, we just wasted the whole day. The whole day," I repeated angrily. Shaking my head, I turned my attention back to the landscape whizzing by. I was definitely awake now.

Tom said nothing in response, and we spent the rest of the trip in silence. Whether he was angry wasn't clear, but as we passed through the gates of Anaconda, I knew he had every right to be. I owed him an apology. Just inside the gate, we pulled over to clear our weapons and Tom released the other vehicles in our convoy. As I watched him get back in, Tom beat me to the punch.

"Hey," he said smiling, "sorry today's meeting took so long, but I promised the judges I would bring you back."

"No, Tom, you were right, I'm a jerk for waiting so long," I insisted, grateful he wasn't angry. "Thanks for making me followup. I just wish I had some answers for them."

"Well, I think just voicing their concerns made them feel better, don't you think?" I nodded as Tom continued, "and they did have some valid issues, especially with 1-8's conduct."

Tom was starting to sound like a broken record. I knew his casual comment was anything but. "Tom, you're fixating a little, don't you think? I swear, if you'd just let me talk to Gwinner for you . . ."

"Viv, I mean it, don't bother." Tom paused before continuing, "Just pay attention. There's a lot going on with 1-8. You don't want this to blow up in your face."

CHAPTER FIVE

Mortarville

CAPTAIN TOM WESTIN WAS IN hot pursuit. He had already spotted me sitting on the steps in front of the headquarters building. His thin, wire-frame glasses were trained on me as his round form negotiated the rocky path.

Where the heck was Philibert? It shouldn't take this long to gas up the Humvee. Damn, Westin was doing better on the rocks than I expected.

Seeing Philibert pull up behind the rest of our waiting convoy, I hurried over to the Humvee, circling my index finger to indicate that we were all here and we needed to get on the road.

"Hey, Vivian!" Westin yelled.

I'd tell him that I didn't hear him. Plausible deniability, you know, Humvee engines are really loud. I was in no mood for Westin's whining today.

At the Humvee, I struggled to wedge my backpack on the floor behind my seat, between a sandbag and the seat bottom. Satisfied, I turned to get in front and glimpsed Westin drawing closer in my periphery. Because the outside handle was jammed on the passenger door, I reached through the window and grabbed the inside handle to release it. The door sprung open and I moved to sit down, one eye still tracking Westin.

Drowning In The Desert

Too busy worrying about Westin, I slammed my head into the steel support bar over the door frame. Oooowww. The pain registered a full second after impact. My Kevlar took the brunt of it, dulling the jolt that coursed down my spine. Reaching through the flashes of light, I tried to steady myself. When Carter and Kolb had built the roof for the Humvee back in Kuwait, they had mounted it about six inches too low. Like so many other things, the too-low bar was a hassle we had grown used to, sort of.

Still dazed, I struggled to close the door behind me, but Westin had since caught up. "Hey," he shouted, "hey, Vivian," his voice as thin and piercing as the whistle on a teakettle. "You should have already cleaned out that trailer! I need your stuff out of there today!" He waited for me to say something, but the pulsing in my head was too loud for me to even form a response.

Suddenly aware that three vehicles filled with soldiers were watching him, he didn't move to close the several feet remaining between us.

"Move into the female tent!" he said with less conviction.

I nodded listlessly, fighting the impulse to tell him what he could do with the "female tent." Didn't he have anything better to do? Standing out here and making such a scene over a stupid trailer.

My home, or "hooch," was a spare wagon trailer parked one hundred or so yards behind the brigade headquarters building. The tiny rusted wagon with a canvas cover measured only seven feet long and four feet wide. It wasn't tall enough to stand up in, but squatting didn't bother me because the trailer had the one thing I craved more than anything else: a touch of privacy. I acquired this little hideout months ago, when our headquarters company wasn't using it and needed a Humvee to tow the trailer. Fed up with calling attention to myself each time I had to change my shirt or pants, I volunteered to tow the trailer and began using it as a quick changing area. No more "heads-up, I'm changing over here," a call that had a tendency to attract, rather than deter, soldiers.

Westin was the Brigade Headquarters and Headquarters Company (HHC) commander. A whiny but generally harmless figure, he had been sent on this mission by a fellow who was far from benign: HHC 1st Sgt. Jerry Hodson. Hodson was Westin's senior noncommissioned officer. A cantankerous guy with a talent for building and fixing things, Hodson bore a striking resemblance to Popeye. Together, Westin and Hodson were responsible for the day-to-day management of brigade headquarters, the two hundred soldiers who worked here, as well as the facilities; overseeing the construction of living spaces, workspaces, and latrines at each location where the brigade took up residence. Above these two, Lieutenant Colonel Welsch was still the architect.

Hodson resented the fact that I always tried to get my guys excluded from tedious labor details, like stirring the burn pit in which our company disposed of human waste. As the only section at brigade headquarters operating with less than half of the soldiers we were allotted, I could hardly afford to have my guys stirring burning feces, or hauling water, while other over-staffed sections had surplus soldiers sitting around doing nothing. Our history of clashes over my JAG team's share of labor details, and Hodson's disdain for constructing latrines at each new location, kept things interesting between us.

Recently, Welsch had refused my request to build a small addition onto my adopted trailer. "Look," Welsch had said, "I want you out of there and into the new tent with the other females. I don't need it looking like a shantytown out there."

I gave up on building an addition and laid low for a while, hoping Welsch would forget about the whole thing. Hodson, I suspected, was keeping the issue front and center, with loud declarations that he needed my trailer urgently to haul stuff around Anaconda. There were plenty of available trailers for Hodson's use, of course, but he needed *mine* urgently.

Feeling my gaze, Philibert asked, "So what did Captain Westin want, ma'am?"

I pretended not to hear Phil and kept my eyes on the list of soldiers that I planned to interview after our convoy reached Camp Animal. Only days away from the trial, I couldn't afford to spend an afternoon moving my living quarters. I needed Welsch to put the kibosh on my eviction, at least for a week. Recalling how well my last special request to Welsch had gone, I knew I had to consult an expert.

Captain Noel Pace was not a doctor, but he had the sort of bedside manner that made commanders and brass swoon. He knew when to cry "hooah," and when to say, "No problem, sir, too easy," and when to just pump his fist in agreement. In his capacity as the brigade's preventative medicine officer, Noel could easily have remained off the radar of Welsch and Rudesheim, but Noel was not one to toil in obscurity.

Tall, with a muscular build and sandy hair, Noel's job was to identify health risks to soldiers and devise plans to mitigate the risks through vaccinations, insecticides, and so forth. Aggressive, informed, and completely fluent in brass-speak, Noel had succeeded in making his personal agenda part of the brigade's official agenda. Noel and I had initially bonded over a shared dislike for Hodson, the one person who seemed immune to Noel's charms. When I protested Hodson's decision to park a convoy on the side of a major Baghdad highway, other soldiers and officers, including Kolb, just shrugged their shoulders and averted my gaze.

Noel, however, knew a bad situation when he saw one and didn't hesitate to back up the female JAG, informing Hodson that he was making us the biggest target on the road. Noel and I had been friends ever since.

That night, outside my rusting trailer-hooch, Noel listened thoughtfully as I explained my predicament.

"I just want to stay in the trailer," I said, lovingly patting the metal frame of the trailer beneath me. "I'd rather stay here than move into a cramped tent."

Seated on an overturned bucket in which I washed my clothes, Noel nodded before offering his assessment.

"Forget the trailer, Viv. You need to move into a hard-top building."

"Noel, look, I already know that Welsch doesn't want soldiers in another building," I said. "He wants to keep our footprint small, remember? Let's not debate this." Sighing, I continued, "I just want to stay in my trailer. How do I get Welsch to agree? What would you say to him?" I pleaded.

Noel rolled his eyes and shook his head. "You're crazy, you know that?" He stood up forcefully and the bucket fell over. "We're getting mortared almost every day out here. They just hit us over there, remember?" he asked, pointing to a spot about a hundred yards from brigade headquarters. "Don't you get it? Don't even bother asking Welsch about moving, just move. To a building."

Perched on the open side of my trailer, I watched him pace back and forth, surprised by his fervor.

"The colonel and Welsch could care less, don't you see? They live in that building! They just want it to look nice and neat out here. If Welsch really cared about living conditions, he would put us all somewhere safe, like in a building. Like the building they live in!" he cried, jabbing his finger accusingly in the direction of the headquarters building. With the exception of about two dozen soldiers sharing two rooms inside, only Colonels Rudesheim and Welsch and the sergeant major were permitted to live there. Pleased with how the ALOC had turned out, Welsch was renovating the remaining space for meeting rooms and more workspaces for other sections.

"Vivian, you're fungible. Don't you get it? They'll ship you home in a body bag, and Fort Carson will have a replacement in by next week."

"From Carson? Try next year," I said returning to one of my favorite rants. Carson wouldn't even send me a new battery for the antique digital camera they had issued to my team for the deployment. I received more support and supplies from my fiancé's law firm than I did from Carson.

With two weeks remaining in his tour, Noel was suffering from short-timer's syndrome. As the preventive medicine officer, trained to identify risk, his anxiousness was especially bad. Short-timer's syndrome afflicted soldiers whose departure from the field was imminent. It was characterized by a preoccupation with safety and a fervent desire to minimize all unnecessary risks. Short-timers almost always started scaling back trips outside the wire.

Intelligent, tall, and handsome, Noel knew fortune owed him little. He also knew that a better life was waiting for him at his next duty assignment, in Miami. That is, if he could just get through the next few weeks unharmed. These days Noel was wearing his armored vest constantly and perpetually berating me for not demanding body armor for myself. Grabbing a meal at the chow hall or even watching a DVD with friends, it wasn't unusual to look over and see Noel red faced, sweating in his armored vest, insisting, "I'm fine. I'm fine." Someone even suggested that Noel was showering in his vest, although no one volunteered to confirm it.

The housing issue had plagued Noel for quite a while. Among the dozen of us squatting outside the headquarters building, he was scornful of the "if it happens, it happens" attitude that most of us had adopted. A week earlier, when a unit vacated a nearby building on Anaconda, Noel didn't hesitate to move himself in. Tonight, our conversation renewed his insistence that I check out his new home and consider it as an alternative to my preferred wagon-trailer and the female officers' tent. Noel continued the safety lecture as I followed him to his new home.

"You can't wait for anyone to approve this," he said. "Viv, consider your options. They're just going to move you into a tent otherwise. A tent!" he repeated incredulously.

"I know. It's ridiculous." A tent, with its soft sides all around, offered no protection from mortars. From a safety perspective, it was definitely a step down from my trailer, which had three metal sides.

"Noel, the problem is that it just wouldn't look good. Come on, two officers, a guy and a girl, squirreled away over here in our own building?" There, I'd said it. My move undoubtedly would have started rumors. As the brigade's legal officer, I was supposed to be the moral compass. I needed to be above reproach and avoid even the appearance of impropriety.

"Whatever," Noel said, shaking his head.

"Easy for you to say, you'll be out of here in two weeks. And besides, you're a guy," I said, referring to the undeniable double standard in the army. A female officer rumored to be carrying on a relationship with a fellow officer would be judged more harshly than the guy she was involved with.

"Hey, if you're still alive, you can deal with it then," he replied dismissively.

Noel's new home had at one time been used by the Iraqis as a cafeteria for the airbase. In one of the large rooms off of the entrance, you could still see the wooden rails that kept the lunch line orderly.

"Home sweet home," Noel said proudly, weaving through breaks in the wooden railing until we reached an open area on the other side of the room. "And, here we are," he said sweeping his arm in the direction of what appeared to be a mound of debris. Closer examination revealed that it was actually several wooden benches stacked on top of each other and positioned in a semi-circle. Half a dozen planks of wood had been laid across the top of the semi-circle forming a wooden igloo-like structure. Eyes beaming, Noel pointed to the opening of his makeshift wooden hovel.

"My cot is right in there," he said.

Short-timer indeed. *Okay, Viv, don't say anything.* Swallowing hard, I pretended to inspect the structure by moving slowly around to the side. With Noel out of sight, I pressed my lips together tightly, fighting to stave off laughter.

"They left these benches, so I use them as cover," Noel explained earnestly, pounding his fist on the wood for emphasis.

Noel wasn't making this easy.

"Wow, Noel. This is . . . something," I said, searching for a neutral spot in the room to focus on as the laughter raced to escape my throat. Directing my gaze over Noel's shoulder, a safe distance from his open, unabashed face, and his wooden fallout shelter, I willed the corners of my mouth to stay down.

Cheerfully defiant, he said, "I know. I know, it looks a little crazy, but I don't care," then disappeared behind the woodpile.

I walked around to the other side, and found Noel preparing to demonstrate the technique he used to enter his beaver lodge. Seated at the end of his cot that protruded from the opening, he laid back slowly, explaining how he had to be careful to avoid hitting one of the benches stacked overhead.

"You see," he said between shallow breaths, "once I'm in, it's pretty roomy." Fully horizontal, Noel began to shimmy his body further up the cot, his torso disappearing in the tunnel. By the time he was through, only his shins and feet were visible as they rested on the exposed end of the cot.

Hearing a weird noise, I looked around to see where it was coming from. It was Noel, still talking inside the hut. His sunny explanations, now muffled, had continued without pause. He was a regular Harriet the Homeowner, prattling on about the joy of living inside a hive of wooden benches.

Finally, it was too much. A tidal wave of laughter rocked my body and I surrendered to it. No use fighting it, not after Noel's inchworm routine into the MRI-like tunnel. Had it come to this? A Matryoshka-doll fortress within a fortress? My cheeks ached and I was heaving, every breath disrupted by another wave of laughter. Turning, I braced myself against the railing, unable to watch his inchworm routine in reverse.

"Noel, c'mon, this is crazy!" I gasped. "I'm sorry, I know I shouldn't be laughing."

"I know it's a bit ridiculous," he said good-naturedly.

"Yes, it is. But the really crazy thing is that," inhaling, I tried to steady my breath, "you're now safer than me!" Unable to resist, I perched on the end of the cot and leaned back, pretending to get lost in the wood planks overhead. "Seriously, I think you have too much time on your hands lately," I said, knocking a beam by accident. "Please, just promise me that you won't add any more wood to this fortress or I'll be forced to bring in other people to check this out." The thought triggered another round of laughter.

Two weeks later, we dropped Noel off at the airfield to catch his flight home. He hugged me with such intensity that I wondered if he knew something I didn't. Almost a month later, Anaconda would earn the nickname Mortarville.

If the definition of happiness is having a place to work and a place to live, September in Iraq offered me little in the way of either. On the verge of eviction from my trailer, I was still looking for a place to hold Cobb's trial at Anaconda. (Datray would have to be tried separately, at a later date, to allow each soldier to put on a complete defense at trial without potentially prejudicing the other's case.)

"Well, ma'am, I'm not sure what you're looking for, but I think you might like this," First Sergeant Cunningham said as he led me into the tent.

Located near Anaconda's perimeter, the khaki-colored tent wasn't much to look at from the outside. Inside, however, I discovered it possessed a high-pitched ceiling, windows for ventilation, and more than enough space to conduct a trial, 2,500 square feet. The stale air could be fixed with a few fans. Cunningham led me to the far right corner of the room and pulled back another tent flap to reveal a small side room. There was an identical room on the left side. The side rooms could easily function as the judge's quarters and a jury deliberation room. The massive tent had been designated for the headquarters company's recreational purposes, but the sparse furnishings indicated little, if any use. Wandering back into the main tent, I envisioned the judge's bench, the witness chair, the jury panel, and where I would give my opening statement. Having already seen my fair share of heinous venues, I was falling hard for this khaki canvas marvel.

"This looks perfect, first sergeant," I said excitedly, "absolutely perfect!" After spending the past few weeks coordinating complicated and risky trips to gather evidence, I had let finding a place to conduct the trial fall by the wayside. The original proposed venue, a chapel that would do double-duty as a house of worship and courtroom, was still under construction. The alternative was to move the trial to Tikrit, which Lieutenant Colonel Barnes still favored, especially since division JAG had just finished transforming a palace room into a state-of-the-art courtroom. Taking one last look around the empty tent, I was satisfied that Barnes would not object to this venue.

"Hey, Vivian, do you approve?" Captain Kevin Ryan, 1-8 Battalion Headquarters and Headquarters Company commander, called out as he joined us in the tent. This tent belonged to 1-8's HHC.

"Completely. It's great," I said holding up my thumb.

Ryan grinned appreciatively.

"So, any chance you have some additional furniture?" I asked.

"What are you looking for exactly?"

"I don't know, chairs, a few tables, stuff like that."

"Yeah, that's no problem. We have almost anything you need." Motioning toward the side room, he added, "Hey, we even brought in our own stars."

I followed his gaze to the corner of the tent where I notice that the tent's khaki-colored ceiling was speckled with dozens of white dots, varying in size and shape.

Confused, I walked over for a closer inspection.

"Mortar, ma'am," Cunningham explained. "Landed right outside, not too long ago. Lucky no one was in here."

"Wait, what?" I asked, searching Ryan's face for the mirthful smile that indicated he was joking. Ryan and Cunningham looked at me quizzically.

"Those holes are from the shrapnel," Ryan confirmed, pointing to the ceiling.

Shrapnel? I strained my neck for a better look at the ceiling. The white dots I had assumed were paint were, in fact, dozens of punctures in the tent fabric, backlit by sunlight. As it turned out, my ideal venue was also a frequent target of insurgents' mortars due to its location at Anaconda's perimeter. Several feet outside the entrance to the tent was a shallow crater, dug out of the earth by the most recent mortar attack.

"So?" Ryan asked expectantly.

There was nothing more to consider. I could never gather the division's senior leadership for jury duty in this death trap.

"Can't do it."

"No?"

"It's just too dangerous," I explained, pointing dejectedly at the ceiling. Recent mortar attacks were a deal breaker. Taking a final, wistful look at the tent's majestic main area, I thanked Ryan and Cunningham for their help and hurried to catch the ice truck headed to Eagle.

Wearing an ill-fitting armored vest I had borrowed from the chaplain, complete with a large, embossed cross on the front, I could only imagine how lawyerly I must have looked perched on a mammoth slab of ice in the back of the truck's cargo area. Every turn or bump sent me sliding across the slick surface and into the sidewall. The ice skating routine continued until I discovered that I could brace myself better if I stretched across the block of ice and curled my fingers around the ends of the blocks next to me. It was a smoother ride, and, conveniently, the vestiges of my dignity had already melted around me.

Splayed across the ice blocks, I recalled a friend's recent e-mail. Lamenting her long hours at the office, she wrote, "Your job sounds so exciting." *Exciting? Skydiving is exciting. Skiing is exciting.* Peeling my ear off the ice to shake the water out, I braced for the big swinging turn into Camp Eagle. *Humbling is more like it.*

The ice truck was the answer to my growing concern about needlessly exposing my guys to too much danger. With the Cobb trial coming up quickly, I found I needed to be on the road almost daily. After discovering the ice truck made almost daily runs from Anaconda to the battalions, I started arranging my meetings to fit with the delivery schedule. That way I didn't have to worry about endangering one of my guys or an entire convoy. It wasn't pretty or even that convenient, but at least I could sleep at night.

Finding a suitable venue for the trial was proving harder than I had anticipated. The first potential venue I considered on Anaconda met all the physical criteria but was controlled by a reserve unit that was hardly accommodating.

Slightly less desirable was a room I found in a building located in the center of Anaconda. The corps-level support unit that controlled this second potential venue was extremely amenable. They even warned me that, depending on the time of my trial, I might have some noise to contend with. When the soldier showing me around had checked the room's availability on October 29, she paused in consternation.

"What is it?" I asked. "Is it not available?"

"No, ma'am, it's available. It's just that there's a video teleconference scheduled next door the same day."

Video teleconferences between deployed soldiers and their loved ones back home were one of the perks of war in the new millennium. They were also one of the numerous advantages of being in a fixed location. Because of the hassles of coordinating logistics on both ends, the teleconferences were infrequent but could last for hours at a time.

"That shouldn't be a problem, should it?" I asked.

She pointed to five-inch gap between the top of one of the walls and the ceiling.

"It can get pretty loud next door," she warned.

Sensing that her words had not penetrated, she elaborated, "Ma'am, these teleconferences always turn into one big cry-fest. You might hear a lot of crying."

"I see. Thanks for that," I said. Wailing soldiers were a major deal breaker.

Around this same time, soldiers at Camp Eagle were digging in for an extended stay. New watchtowers had been added to 1-8's perimeter, and they reinforced the front gate. About ten white trailers were stacked near the unit's main building. While most soldiers—including myself—would have been eager to claim one of the new aluminum trailers, they remained wrapped in plastic. Dubbed "aluminum coffins" by 1-8's leadership, the trailers were off limits until they could be fortified. The attention to detail extended beyond just security. Sassaman's staff installed an Internet café and a weight room, perks that went a long way with the soldiers.

I was at 1-8 to meet with Sassaman to discuss his impressions of Cobb and Datray. Due to his packed schedule, he suggested that I accompany him as he checked in on the battalion's various companies. It was a good suggestion, and I jumped at the opportunity to make some headway on the case.

Arriving early for my meeting with Sassaman, I headed for 1-8's lounge to see if I could answer some legal questions for soldiers who had missed me on my last trip out. What I discovered behind the main building filled me with shame and anger. At least a dozen Iraqi men were squeezed into a concertina-wired holding pen. Dressed mainly in traditional tunics, they were packed so tightly that it was difficult to see where one person began and another ended. A few men stood, but the majority appeared to be sitting on the ground, resting on one another in what looked like a human patchwork quilt. Several held their hands over their faces, trying to escape the morning sun.

Closing my eyes, I looked again to make sure the sun wasn't playing tricks on me. Every foot or so, a dark head bobbed above the crowd of detainees. I looked away, shame burning my cheeks. What the hell was this? I had spent months advising the units on how to process, treat, and confine detainees. What wasn't clear? I racked my mind trying to recall the last time I discussed these issues with 1-8. Had I not been diligent enough?

With Sassaman still yet to arrive, I raised the subject with Gwinner, who assured me it was a temporary situation, a result of limited space. "This is an isolated incident," he said. "We're just waiting on transport to take them to division's holding facility in Tikrit."

"Sir, they've clearly been here for a while. They're crammed in that pen with no cover or water that I can even see," I said, trying to maintain an even tone. "Geneva Conven . . ."

"I know. I know. We're taking care of it. They're leaving as soon as we get the transport," he responded quickly.

"Sir, one of your guys said that they were crammed together out there to teach them a lesson," I said, quoting the smug staff officer who had laughed when I asked him about the situation.

"Trust me. It was an oversight. We're on top of it."

"Uh, okay, sir," I finally said, unsure what else I could say without offending him. He had been nothing but helpful to me. I had no reason to doubt him.

By this time, a small group of us were waiting together for Sassaman to return from a meeting in town. Watching his convoy pull through the gate, I felt like a groupie waiting for her favorite rock star. Exhaust fumes and clouds of dust didn't prevent the crowd from surging forward as Sassaman's convoy came to a stop. Straightening my shoulders, I tried to make eye contact with Sassaman as he emerged from the haze. With the trial looming, I was worried he might have forgotten about our plans. Several soldiers were at his side instantly, all of them clamoring to ask him a question or offer him an update. Standing apart from the group, I watched him systematically work through the throng. Focused and decisive, he made eye contact with each soldier and offered answers on the spot. There was no limp "get back to me later," or worse, "let me think about it." Each soldier seemed to bloom in Sassaman's presence. Eyes bright, they were both inspired by, and determined to impress, the man in front of them.

Sassaman possessed that rarest and most complicated of military virtues: true leadership ability. It was the kind of leadership that extended beyond the right schools and the right awards, the sort of leadership that rang true to the lowliest enlisted soldier who knew better than to put too much faith in pedigree.

On paper, Sassaman *was* impressive. In person, the ruggedly handsome commander crackled with competence and charisma. Few who met him doubted that this was the sort of man soldiers would follow anywhere.

Sassaman's magnetism was not limited to the soldiers who scrambled to execute his orders. Journalists covering 1-8's operations often lingered after a mission was complete, content to remain within his orbit. They sensed there was something different about this battalion commander, and produced story after story saying just that. Objectivity was sometimes thrown out the window; their desire to please him bordered on slavish. A lengthy *New York Times Magazine* profile hailed Sassaman as the "warrior king" and read like an open love letter by journalist Dexter Filkins.

Spotting me off to the side, Sassaman said, "Hey, Captain Gembara."

The soldiers turned to see whom Sassaman was addressing.

"Hi, sir. You didn't forget that I was joining you today, did you?" I asked brightly.

"No, I didn't. Go ahead and grab a seat. I'm heading back out in a minute," he replied, before turning to talk to a staff officer.

Not seeing an obvious spot in the convoy, I lingered near Sassaman's Bradley Fighting Vehicle. I was in no mood to start browbeating soldiers to make room for me in the cramped troop carrier. When he was finished with the last soldier, Sassaman turned toward the convoy, saw me, and pointed to the backseat of a soft-skin Humvee in the lineup.

"They'll make room for you in here. Are you okay with that?"

No problem. I headed for the Humvee, grateful that it was *his* order that set the soldiers scrambling to clear a seat.

At one of our first stops, Sassaman was scheduled to present awards to a combat engineer company that had been attached to 1-8 since June. He was honoring Bravo Company, 4th Engineer Battalion, for their support fortifying 1-8's bases and assisting with patrols.

At a hulking six feet six inches tall, the blonde-haired, blue-eyed Capt. Eric Paliwoda was the engineering company's larger-than-life commander. In what may have been a deliberate contrast to his outsized appearance, Eric was quiet, humble, and thoughtful. His company's effectiveness was evident throughout 1-8's bases, especially at Camp Eagle where Eric's team had built berms, guard towers, and other reinforcements for Sassaman's men. Eric understood the threat facing 1-8 and used the bulldozers and concrete at his disposal to try to minimize it.

Eric was waiting in the doorway of the company's main building when our convoy pulled up. Ruddy cheeked and eager, Eric hurried over to greet us. Sassaman patted Eric on the shoulder warmly when he reached us. Both West Pointers and former college football players, the two were clearly friends as well as colleagues.

"Good to see you, Vivian," Eric said turning to give me a hug.

We knew each other from his days as a staff officer at brigade headquarters. I had seen him just a handful of times since he took command of Bravo Company several months ago. As we pulled apart, I took stock of the dramatic physical transformation he had undergone recently. Since taking command in May, he'd shed at least fifty pounds, reducing him from a big, beefy guy to a lean and compelling presence. His pinkish skin had warmed to a golden brown that accentuated the contours of his face.

Reading the surprise in my face, Eric's smile deepened, and he spread his arms wide before slapping his stomach. "I couldn't go home fat," he said. He explained that wearing his armored vest around the clock was his weight-loss trick. "Just sweating it off," he joked.

"You look great. It's great to see you," I said, suddenly grateful that I had picked today to shadow Sassaman.

He beamed and then excused himself to get his team ready for the awards ceremony.

I watched Eric talk with his soldiers as I waited for Sassaman. Modest, principled, and immensely capable, Eric personified the best of the army. He was precisely the sort of soldier the army needed more of.

Understand that combat engineers have always had dangerous jobs: building land barriers, fortifying living areas, mine recovery, and destroying ordnance and weapons. But under Paliwoda's leadership, his company had performed these tasks and so much more. Because his company has been attached to one of our infantry battalions since he had taken command, they ended up performing many missions right alongside the infantry soldiers. That's a lot to ask of soldiers who had been trained to do engineering tasks and defensive-type operations. In order to motivate these soldiers to switch to effective offensive operations, it took quite a leader. Eric was the rare individual who could do it. His soldiers respected him, trusted him, and followed him. I witnessed it each time I had visited his company.

During those early months when I struggled to be in the loop, Eric had been my ally. He was generous with information and resources when he didn't have to be, when others in the same capacity were territorial and haughty. While Eric's operational knowledge and ability won him the respect of soldiers in all units, it was his generosity and inclusiveness that distinguished him in my eyes. Eric was above the cliquishness and condescension I had begun to think was inherent to West Pointers.

Sassaman joined me by the Humvee and we watched the soldiers get into formation.

Turning to face me, Sassaman extended his arm and opened his palm.

"You know what these are, Vivian?" he asked.

I scrutinized the rocks in his hand and tried to imagine how an infantry soldier might describe them. Projectiles? Shrapnel?

I finally said, "Well, they're rocks, sir."

Sassaman snapped his palm closed, forming a fist around the rocks.

"They're more than just rocks, Vivian. These are part of 1-8's history, our legacy." He squeezed his fist tighter. "I gathered them from the beaches of Normandy myself, where 1-8 soldiers landed and fought for their lives against an entrenched German army."

Understanding the unit's history and past sacrifice, he explained, was crucial to instilling pride and inspiring soldiers today. With that, Sassaman turned and walked toward the formation. Why did I always blow these moments? A well-timed nod would have been acceptable. Noel would have let off a perfect "hooah." But me, I just stood here like a mute toad.

Leaning against the Humvee, I watched the awards presentation with mild disinterest until Sassaman stepped forward and ordered the soldiers to stand at ease. Pulling the rocks from his pocket, he walked back and forth in front of the formation.

"Can anybody tell me what these are?" he asked. Again, he explained that the seemingly innocuous rocks were reminders of the courage and honor of 1-8 soldiers from previous generations. The soldiers listened, riveted as he recounted 1-8's triumphs, beginning with Normandy and up to the present day.

I had entirely forgotten that the soldiers he was speaking to weren't officially a part of 1-8, until Sassaman raised the issue himself.

"So what does 1-8's history have to do with you?" He waited a few beats before explaining that the engineers' work had contributed significantly to 1-8's mission. Because of that, he said, the engineers were part of 1-8's history of success in Iraq.

"Bravo Company, 4th Engineer, is no different from any other company within the battalion," he declared. Moments later, Sassaman straightened his posture and called the company to attention. A soldier stepped forwarded and announced "attention to orders" for the awards presentation to begin. Standing at attention, I waited.

This was the part where the unit usually would be presented with some sort of plaque or medal. Instead, a soldier stepped forward and handed Sassaman a guidon, a small, swallow-tailed pennant affixed to a pole, which is used to identify a company-sized unit. Turning back to the formation, Sassaman thanked the engineers for their bravery and their tireless work in support of 1-8's mission. He told them that he was honored to present the engineers with their very own guidon as Delta Company of 1-8 Infantry Battalion. Flicking his wrist, the guidon pennant unfurled as it caught in the wind. It bore 1-8's crossed-rifle insignia and a large black "D," signifying the engineers' unofficial designation as 1-8's Delta Company.

While clearly well intended, the gesture was highly unusual considering the sensitive nature of unit integrity within the army. Why honor them by calling them Delta Company, 1-8? It diminished the importance of their official unit, Bravo Company, 4th Engineer Battalion, and struck me as condescending, as if to say Bravo Company had earned this new, better designation, almost like a higher rank. The standard practice was for a battalion to present the "slice" units attached to them with the battalion's colors, usually an embroidered wall hanging of their coat of arms. For the 4th Engineer soldiers, however, the feelings appeared to be mutual. They felt at home with 1-8 and hollered their approval of this new honorary designation. Beaming with pride, Sassaman raised the guidon above his head.

* * *

En route to our next stop, Sassaman told me that this wasn't the first time he'd had problems with Cobb or Datray. He had counseled both of them for various infractions before their botched escape, but had given both soldiers opportunities to improve. When Cobb claimed that he wanted to quit the army, Sassaman had counseled him on the importance of honoring the oath that Cobb had sworn, to defend the country. During his session with Cobb, Sassaman had even shared excerpts from a letter Sassaman carried, written by his grandfather during World War II. Sassaman wanted Cobb to understand that today's hardships paled in comparison.

Pushing off the table, Kolb swiveled around to greet me. He was sitting in a dark blue office chair, complete with castors and a padded back.

"Check it out, ma'am. It's our lucky day," Kolb said hopping out of the chair.

"Where did you get it?" I asked, sinking into the chair. Cushioned and supportive, it was leagues above our metal folding chairs. The back support alone made it worth any favor we might owe our benefactor.

"Lieutenant—I mean Captain—Gebhardt brought it by. He said you mentioned needing one a while back."

Captain Brian Gebhardt was the one bright spot among the Brigade headquarters company's otherwise dismal leadership. Gebhardt struggled to placate both Westin and Hodson while getting the real work of the company done. While Westin and Hodson were often petty toward the JAG section, Gebhardt always endeavored to make it up to us, and to other sections that Westin and Hodson viewed as "hangers-on." The office chair was just the latest example. Months earlier, it was Gebhardt who loaned us the wagon trailer after watching us load our sagging Humvee with equipment during a move. Moreover, Gebhardt had skillfully mediated a near-fatal argument between the first sergeant and me over the fair distribution of supplies at our previous location.

Since moving to Anaconda, I had seen less of Gebhardt. In an act of self-preservation, Gebhardt helped the company settle into our designated area, and then moved his own living area, along with the motor pool he oversaw, to a separate part of Anaconda. He needed the separation, he explained, to mitigate the likelihood of his being charged with disrespect, or worse, toward Captain Westin.

Drowning In The Desert

Although it was too late for Gebhardt to intercede on behalf of my trailer, I was delighted by his thoughtfulness. Spinning around in the chair was a nice distraction from the other issues I'd failed to resolve today, namely, securing a home and a trial venue.

"Are you losing it, JAG?" Tom asked from across the table.

"Tom, what are you doing here?" I asked, spinning around to face him. I had not seen him in days and was excited to tell him that I had successfully retraced Cobb and Datray's route. With Philibert behind the wheel, Amar, Thanna the translator, and I retraced their steps from the spot where Murtdadah had stood waving for a car to stop, to where Amar was forced to pull over and eventually escaped.

Tom was dusty and disheveled, but the look of urgency on his face suggested that he had more pressing concerns.

"Is everything okay, Tom?"

"Yeah, yeah. I just need to know where the showers are."

Curious about his sudden appearance, I walked outside to point him in the right direction. Tom provided a quick explanation. Sassaman's dislike for him had effectively spread to the rest of 1-8, creating a hostile living and working situation for Tom's civil affairs team. Convinced that their situation was only going to get worse, Tom and his team packed up in search of greener pastures at Anaconda. At the moment, they were waiting for approval to move into a building currently occupied by several civil affairs teams, he explained. He remained committed, however, to continuing his civil affairs projects in Balad.

"I'll have a better chance of putting together a convoy from the units here on Anaconda anyways," he added, before rushing to the showers.

Tom's hasty relocation reminded me of my own housing woes. After watching him depart, I made a beeline for Welsch's office. Welsch, as it turned out, had a solution for both my lack of a courthouse and my pending eviction from the trailer.

"You and your guys will help build both of them," he said flatly before returning his attention to his computer screen.

A man of finite resources and limited time, Welsch maximized his use of both. A water shortage in Kirkuk had Welsch collecting the remaining contents of discarded water bottles in order to wash his clothes. After discovering one of the combat photographers was also a talented painter, he commissioned her to paint massive brigade signs, complete with the outline of Iraq in the background. Knowing Welsch, he probably ate apples, core and all. Talent. Space. Materials. It didn't matter what the resource was, he found a way to repurpose it. Everyone did double duty.

And now my team would be swinging hammers to help get the chapel to serve as a courthouse, and to build new living quarters. It made sense to Welsch, but I took issue with the division of labor. We were already struggling to stay on top of our workload. It seemed unfair that my team should have to try the Cobb case on top of our regular work while also helping build the chapel and living quarters.

As Welsch made quick work of an e-mail, I was formulating my response. Wasn't this the building crew's job? I was already down four men. It wasn't like I asked anybody to help me try my cases.

Anticipating my concerns, Welsch got right to the point. "Listen, Vivian, that's the best I can do. You're going to have to help these guys build it because they're already grumbling about a separate female living area," he said.

My new living quarters were going to be part of a new "female wing" Welsch envisioned being built in the last of four courtyards off the headquarters building. Although it was technically the building crew's job to build all of the structures, Welsch's insistence that my team help out was strategic. The one resource Welsch couldn't afford to alienate was his building crew.

Days later, we broke ground on the new cubbies. As promised, I turned up and went right to work hammering in parts of the cubby frames. My mind, however, was on the evidence against Cobb that I was still missing. One item in particular, something described as a "knife with a compass" on the inventory sheet provided by 1-68 Battalion, which listed the items found in Cobb and Datray's car when the soldiers were stopped. Murtdadah and Amar also had described the knife used by the lighter-haired soldier as unique, with some sort of dial on it. For me, the knife was critical to proving that the two soldiers were doing more than just joy riding, that they had planned to escape Iraq. Caught up with the whereabouts of the elusive "knife with a compass," I landed the hammer squarely on my thumb.

"Damn it!" I clenched my fist around my thumb, trying to numb the pain.

A soldier working near me set down his hammer to see if I was okay. Satisfied that I would survive the ordeal, he proceeded to school me on the fine art of hammering nails.

CHAPTER SIX

The Trial

THE COURT REPORTER, SPEC. WILLIE Weatherspoon, needed a cot. Not a bedroll or a poncho, but a proper canvas sheath stretched across a metal frame some two feet off the ground. Had it just been General Jones, we might not have had a problem. Unfortunately, Judge Stephen Henley, Capt. Magda Prystulska from the division JAG office, and a whole host of other soldiers, whose accommodations were my responsibility, also had the irksome habit of sleeping. The supply sergeant said it would be at least two weeks until the next shipment of cots came in. Having bartered and borrowed four cots, we still needed one more. Carter hugged the sleeping bag under his arm defensively, waiting for some acknowledgement of his efforts.

"Has anybody tried calling over to the civil affairs guys to see if they have an extra cot?" I asked Kolb and Carter. Specialist Weatherspoon and Captain Prystulska had flown down from division headquarters in Tikrit to help us. Captain Prystulska was a last-minute addition who would serve as my assistant trial counsel, and I'd been lucky enough to find her a space to sleep. I didn't need Weatherspoon griping about sleeping on the floor when he returned to division.

"You mean the crazy CA house?" Kolb asked.

Drowning In The Desert

"Yeah, maybe Captain Roughneen has one." Tom, of all people, would know how to locate a cot, I thought desperately. I already had my hands full trying to locate a pair of boots and an extension cord for Weatherspoon's recording equipment.

"Remind me again why we have to handle all of the arrangements for every single person coming to Anaconda?" Kolb asked.

No, remind me, I thought bitterly. Three years of law school, plus JAG school in Charlottesville, Virginia, had not prepared me for the very real possibility that a cot and a pair of boots would keep me from preparing for one of the most important cases of my JAG career. In JAG school, the instructors made it abundantly clear that the government's trial counsel was responsible for "hosting" the trial, and had cleverly pitched that as an advantage. You control the stage, you command the room. What they never mentioned was how time-consuming it could be to orchestrate every logistical aspect of the trial. "Hosting" the trial is one thing, but having to make sure everyone involved—the bailiff, the judge, the witnesses, the court reporter, and the accused—all have transportation, know when to arrive, actually do arrive on time, and are properly dressed, is another thing entirely. Being in Iraq added a new level of danger and uncertainty to an already complicated equation. Because Cobb would be the first trial of a U.S. soldier in Iraq, we also had no template to follow.

One of my recurring nightmares featured the accused showing up at the trial wearing an orange jumpsuit and shackles. If that happened, it was grounds for a mistrial. Counter-intuitively, it was *my* job as the government trial counsel to ensure that the accused was dressed properly when he faced a judge or jury. In garrison at Fort Carson, it was a detail I always stressed leading up to the trial. "Class A" uniforms are so seldom worn by most soldiers that ensuring that I had all the proper pieces for my own uniform was a challenge. The various patches and insignia on a uniform also meant there was a good chance that I'd overlook the one ribbon or patch that the defense counsel insisted his client wear on the day of the trial.

For courts-martial held in Iraq, the standard attire was the more casual desert camouflage uniform. I had mistakenly assumed it would be easy to out-fit Cobb because that was all he had worn out here. Now, as we scavenged Anaconda for boots to fit Cobb, I found myself worrying that my nightmares would come true.

"Hey Carter, we need boots, but Cobb has his uniform, right?" I asked.

"I think so."

"He should be wearing it," I said, trying to prompt a more definitive response.

"Don't worry, Captain G, he's got it."

"Okay." I grabbed my Kevlar. "Then, let's go check out the chapel."

The chapel was a one-room wooden building located right next to brigade headquarters. Keeping with Lieutenant Colonel Welsch's edict, Kolb, Carter, and Philibert all helped construct the rectangular, windowless structure. Final touches were applied a week earlier, just enough time, it seemed, for the chaplain to get territorial about our using the building as a courthouse. A series of "urgent" meetings at the chapel had prevented us from getting inside and setting up the courtroom until the night before the trial. By the time we finished bringing in counsel tables, chairs, and the judge's more formal nonfolding table, it was well after 2100.

Standing at the front of the chapel, Kolb and I assessed the oddest-looking courtroom we'd ever seen. A narrow center aisle ran from the entrance to the front of the chapel. Cheap, white, stackable plastic chairs were set in neat rows on each side of the aisle. Beneath them, several large, intricately designed Persian rugs were overlapped to cover every inch of the chapel floor. Even dusty, the elaborate rugs were beautiful and strangely comforting. They reminded me of rugs my parents have, rugs they acquired in Tehran and Afghanistan in the 1970s. Growing up, those rugs had seemed gaudy, especially in contrast to the more colonial trappings of my friends' homes. Tonight, however, the rugs were a welcome sight, a comforting reminder of home, though it still felt wrong to tromp across them in my dirty boots.

Less welcome was the congestion at the front of the chapel. The two folding tables we had set up as counsel tables were cramped and felt unsteady on the rugs. Counting the steps from the tables to the judge's bench and witness chair, I wondered if there was enough open space for me and the defense attorney to question witnesses without it looking as though we were badgering them. And where would the translator sit?

"Anything else, ma'am?" Kolb asked from the doorway. "I still have to go check on the cot for Weatherspoon."

One glance at my checklist confirmed that I should let him go. Kolb had been on top of things all week. Micromanaging him now over logistical crap wasn't going to help me write my opening and closing arguments, or finish drafting my questions.

"Hey, just let me know where we are on the boot hunt before you turn in. Oh, and we need to put up a flag somewhere, probably behind the bench." Kolb's eyebrows rose in response.

"Okay, let's just do that in the morning," I said. Kolb smiled.

As he left, the spring-hinged chapel door banged against, but did not quite fall into, its frame. From the outside, Kolb pulled on the handle to try and force the door into place. When that didn't work, he wrenched the door upward to align it. Once the top of the door was properly situated, he let go of the door and it fell noisily into position. Watching this, I made a mental note to assign someone to monitor the traffic in and out of the courtroom. Judges hated a ruckus, and the door's clanging would be enough to make one irritable.

Planting myself in a plastic chair, I tried to envision the room as it would look tomorrow. Visualize the soldiers, the accused, the judge. Willing myself to stay positive, I imagined delivering a smooth opening statement. No hiccups. No snafus. The visualization ended there. I still had to write my opening. Exhausted, I stood, did a final scan of the room, and headed to the computer lab. According to my watch, it was just after midnight.

The following morning boots and cots were the least of my worries.

It began with an error on the charge sheet. The judge, Col. Stephen Henley, seized on the error immediately and informed Cobb's defense counsel, Capt. Clinton Campion, and me in the gravest of tones. Although most judges would have mentioned the error to the lawyers in the customary chambers meeting before the trial began so that the lawyers could fix it once the court convened, Judge Henley was not like most judges. Apparently a fan of the "gotcha" approach, the judge made it clear that he wanted us to figure it out on our own. Glancing quickly at the full house behind me, I scanned the charge sheet praying the error would announce itself. When it didn't, I requested a recess.

Between Prystulska, Campion, and me, we couldn't figure it out, so we called Lieutenant Colonel Barnes in Tikrit. When that yielded nothing, we reexamined my battered copy of the Uniformed Code of Military Justice, futilely searching its pages for an answer. Ten minutes turned into twenty. Unaware of how slow and unreliable our Internet connection was, Campion went to the computer lab hoping to find the answer online. The next time I looked up, over an hour had passed. One less hour of daylight for soldiers who had to drive back to their units before dark. I had the painful realization that the trial would have to be postponed. Solving the charge sheet problem was suddenly less important than trying to mitigate the loss of a day's work for the courtroom of waiting soldiers.

The trial had been a logistical impossibility made possible by dozens of favors called in, wily bartering, and endless hours of planning, pleading, and reminding. The stars were never aligned to hold a trial "in theater." It was risky, dangerous, and complicated. Heading back to the courthouse, I struggled to channel some calm. All I found, however, was rage. Outrage, that is, over the fact that the judge valued a lesson to the lawyers more than the fact that many of these soldiers had risked their lives to be here today and were fully expecting a trial.

To the soldiers, it would be their expectation of justice that I'd failed to deliver on. I loathed telling them that there would be no trial today. Any delay or postponement of the trial affected their ability to conduct patrols and other operations.

Outside the courtroom, the judge was kneeling in the shade as he chatted with a few soldiers. Seeing that he wore no Kevlar didn't improve my mood. Didn't he notice that every NCO that passed him blanched at the sight of his bare head outside, and then, seeing his rank, resisted the urge to correct his oversight? It was Army 101, when outdoors, in uniform, that uniform includes your "cover." Have some respect for the uniform, sir. No wonder Judge Henley didn't have any qualms about wasting so many soldiers' time for a legal lesson on technical drafting of the charge sheet. *I should just walk right past this guy, just ignore him completely.* Not far from the door, I chickened out, and mumbled a greeting with a half-hearted salute.

It wasn't until I told the judge that I needed to dismiss everyone if there wasn't going to be a trial, that he finally offered a clue to the charge sheet mystery. He said that the issue involved the use of the phrase "in a time of war." Sadly, that was all it took. The problem was that by charging the offense as one that occurred "in a time of war," the potential punishment was greater and included the possibility of the death penalty. The accused could not waive his right to a jury when facing charges that carried a potential death sentence. The "error" was that Cobb had waived his right to a jury panel in favor of being heard by the judge alone. Essentially, the lawyers needed to strike "in a time of war" from the charge sheet to prevent the technical error from voiding any resulting judgment. If I didn't amend the charge sheet, we would have to convene a jury panel.

Because the commanders and I had never even considered seeking the death penalty in this case, it was an easy decision. We amended the charge sheet and began the trial twenty minutes later.

"Counsel, are you prepared to proceed with opening statements?" the judge asked.

"Yes, your honor."

He motioned for me to begin. Checking that my holster was securely strapped to my right leg, I approached the front of the chapel. At long last, it was show time.

The one-room chapel swelled with the breath, sweat, and anticipation of nearly ninety soldiers. They had seen fellow soldiers and friends killed and maimed in circumstances that caused them to question the existence of God. Today, they filled every plastic chair and open spot along the wall of the courtroom. The space was packed so tightly that most had no choice but to wear their armored vests, balance their Kevlar helmets on their knees, and hold their rifles by their sides. Sweltering in the cramped, poorly ventilated chapel, they had come to learn the fate of a soldier who had abandoned his post. After everything these soldiers had experienced, they needed to know whether justice, in fact, existed.

"Your honor, mortars, RPGs, and IEDs: this is life for soldiers of the 1-8 Infantry Battalion, 3rd Brigade Combat Team, 4th Infantry Division, in Balad, Iraq. Their mission is to defend their area, secure the city of Balad in Iraq, and free the Iraqi people."

I stood at an angle so I could address the judge and the crowd of soldiers toward the back of the chapel.

"Private Thomas C. Cobb was part of this battalion at one point, part of the band of brothers here," I said gesturing in the direction of the soldiers.

Mention your central theme early and often. That is a law school axiom that I was trying to abide by. Trusting judges (or jurors) to discern innocence or guilt from complicated and sometimes disjointed bits of evidence was dangerous. People need to know the short story: a wronged husband seeking vengeance, quiet loner turned stalker, disgruntled worker without a conscience. All the evidence in the world was useless if you couldn't distill it to a story that would resonate with the judge or jury.

Having settled on "misfit soldier abandons his band of brothers," I called my first witness, Lt. Col. Nathan Sassaman, to the stand.

In the back of the chapel, Sassaman stepped forward from a wall of desert camouflage. Broad shouldered, his face tanned to a deep nut-brown, Sassaman moved with remarkable grace despite wearing nearly thirty pounds of armor and gear. There was none of the clunky, unconscious adjusting of equipment or the constant rediscovery of a weapon. Everything was fluid, as though his body had adapted to life at war by seamless acceptance of the ever-present Kevlar, vest, and weapon. It was a point noted by the roomful of soldiers who watched, transfixed, as Sassaman approached the front of the chapel: the steady, even quality of his steps, and the way he carried his Kevlar under his arm, balanced at the top of his hipbone. As he turned and stood in front of the witness chair, I felt the crowd relax back into their own chairs, eager for the story to unfold.

Watching him take the witness chair, I exhaled for what felt like the first time in weeks. For a moment, I forgot about the minutiae that threatened to derail the investigation at every turn, the impossible logistics, and my own gnawing self-doubt. If nothing else, I knew I had made the right choice in putting Sassaman on the stand first. My first order of business was establishing the climate in which Cobb's crimes were committed. This was no pedestrian AWOL in garrison. We were in a war zone. Lives were at stake. If I couldn't establish that, then Cobb's crimes and the cost of those crimes would not resonate with the judge.

With the introductory information established, I asked, "Could you describe for us the threat level in your area?" With that, Sassaman and I were off and running.

"Since we arrived on 9 July we've had 129 attacks, so it roughly averages out to a little over an attack per day. In the week leading up to—just to give you an example—in the week leading up to the 20th and the 21st, we had eight attacks in that week. Two were RPG ambushes, and two were IED ambushes."

Credible. Smooth. Sassaman's description of the challenges facing 1-8 riveted the courtroom. He described a world of consequence, one so unforgiving and dangerous that every precaution had to be taken. For the soldiers, there was the satisfaction of hearing the amorphous terror of their lives distilled to chilling statistics. It gave weight and substance to the fear that had stalked them for months.

My first exhibit was an enlarged map of Balad and the surrounding area. Philibert had traded in a few favors for the map with an engineer unit he found on Anaconda. Carter and Mendoza had helped Phil glue the map to a massive wood board they had scavenged from another neighboring unit.

Sassaman pointed out the terrain under 1-8's responsibility, an area covering over 750 square miles. He described how his unit patrolled the area despite a chronic shortage of soldiers—646 instead of the authorized 702—and how losing just one soldier to an attack, as they had experienced several times already, compromised their entire mission.

Midway through Sassaman's testimony, Philibert, who sat in the first row just a few feet behind me, passed up a folded note. Scrawled inside was, "Don't forget to admit all your exhibits into evidence."

It could only be Tom, my secret weapon. After helping me prepare for the trial earlier in the week, Tom had disappeared for a few days, busy opening a girls' school in Yathrib, a small town outside Balad. It comforted me to know Tom was here now watching the proceedings from the back of the room. Sandwiched between two 1-8 soldiers, he flashed a thumbs up when I turned around to acknowledge his assistance.

Several minutes later, there was another note: "Keep up this pace."

During the first recess, I returned to the JAG workspace feeling over-caffeinated and eager to confer with my guys.

"Hey, Sergeant Kolb," I said excitedly, "man, what was up with the judge? Is it me or is he the crankiest judge you've ever seen? Did you see his face when the door kept opening? Thanks for remembering to fix it, because I almost had a heart attack watching it swing shut."

"No problem, ma'am," Kolb drawled, his relaxed demeanor a stark contrast to my own. He was thumbing through songs on his MP3 player, his latest paperback novel open face down to the left of the keyboard. Kolb was never far from these two items. With a face full of mischief, Kolb set the MP3 player down and looked toward the entryway of our workspace to see who was close by.

Satisfied that no one was within earshot, he said, "I think the judge got a little shaken up coming up from Camp Victory. I heard his convoy came under some small arms fire."

"Really? Huh." All the more reason why he shouldn't have delayed this morning, I thought, still bitter. These soldiers are on the road every day. "Nobody was hurt?"

"No," he said, shaking his head slowly as he searched his memory, "not that I heard, but you know how it is for people who have never been out here." Then, having reached his serious quotient for the day, Kolb smiled broadly. "Plus, he probably thought he was going to be staying in something a little more comfortable."

We had gone to great lengths to ensure that the judge's trip was as smooth and as painless as possible. We had even set him up with a private cubicle, complete with a cot, chair, and a small army-issue collapsible chaplain's table. We had focused on the little details, bringing in an additional clip lamp and making sure the judge's room was stocked with water bottles and rolls of toilet paper. We didn't want a JAG colonel wandering around asking soldiers for water or toilet paper. We were proud of the effort we had made to lubricate the judge's time in Iraq. As the official host of the trial, we felt responsible for all of our guests', especially the judge's, comfort during their stay.

"More comfortable?" I puzzled. "Like what? The Ritz? Geez, I forgot to get the name of that hotel from the Department of Justice attorneys in Kirkuk." I was punchy from too little sleep, running on coffee and an acute fear of failure.

Recalling the high-maintenance visit by several Department of Justice attorneys several months earlier, Kolb started laugh. About two months after we had arrived, the war had calmed down to the point that government folks back home thought it might be fun to visit us and notch their own little war-zone anecdote. Ahead of their visit, the DOJ attorneys sent us a list of demands so fussy that we were too busy milking its comic value to be annoyed.

"They will need two or three rooms," I said between breaths.

"They won't stay more than forty-eight hours, but arrange for them to tour every courthouse and meet with all the Iraqi judges," recalled Kolb with glee.

"Wait, ma'am," he said, still trying to catch his breath, "wait, remember, the group is not physically fit, so they will need lots of water and want to avoid extreme heat!"

"Oh God, I forgot about that one," I said, panting now as ripples of laughter rocked my body. Extreme heat! At the time, in the heart of the desert summer, we had been living on a frying pan. Our hooches literally sat on a large tar-based blacktop surface. All of the muscles in my face felt sharp and sore from the strain of laughing so hard. It felt wonderful.

"And they don't want to travel at dusk or later," I added, slamming my hand down triumphantly on the desk. I wiped tears from my eyes as our laughter subsided.

"Well, ma'am, I still think it was the convoy that spooked him," Kolb said, flashing me a smirk before turning to greet several soldiers who had just arrived.

I left the JAG workspace to check on Amar and Murtdadah, still discontent with the judge's surly demeanor.

Pale and jittery, Amar was nervously tapping his foot when I found him in the witness waiting area. The translator and Murtdadah hovered nearby, unsure what to do.

Seeing me, Amar said, "I can't do it. I can't do it, not with them here. I have a family." The sight of Cobb and Datray in the courtroom had frightened Amar.

I cursed inwardly, hating myself for not having foreseen this problem. I had Datray flown in for his arraignment hearing and to meet with his defense counsel, but I hadn't expected them to wait in the courtroom. Nor did I expect that Datray would have two attorneys. To my chagrin, the first defense lawyer I'd found to represent Datray, a captain with a thoughtful, reserved demeanor, appeared to have been relegated to an assistant, and a second, more antagonistic lawyer had taken over as Datray's lead counsel. Both lawyers now flanked Datray in the rear of the courtroom, the lead attorney's overconfident face mirroring Datray's smug expression. Until they made a scene though, there was little I could do to have them removed from the courtroom.

Unfortunately, Amar assumed that Datray's presence meant that Cobb and Datray were free to come and go as they pleased.

"They will come after me," he insisted.

"Amar, I promise you they won't. They will never come near you again," I said.

"Captain, I must leave. This is not for me. I have to go," Amar pleaded.

Mindful of the clock and the fact that the judge was waiting, I appealed to Amar's sense of justice.

"Amar, you have been through so much. People need to hear what happened to you if we want to stop soldiers from doing things like this. It's important that you tell your story," I assured him, making sure to look him in the eye.

I knew I was asking a lot. After having his car stolen and his life threatened by two people wearing the same uniform as me, what reason did he have to believe that any of us would be decent? I had hoped Amar's initial fears had been assuaged by our meetings at Camp Eagle.

Amar said nothing. The misery of his predicament was written on his face. Releasing a long sigh and dropping his shoulders in resignation, he allowed me and the translator to lead him to the courtroom.

Adding to the charged atmosphere was the fact that it was Ramadan. Amar and Murtdadah were both fasting. My two key witnesses, one of them as skittish as a kicked puppy and the other easily the most hyperactive person in Iraq, had not eaten since before sunrise. I hoped Amar's empty stomach wouldn't exacerbate another characteristic I had seen Amar exhibit: a short temper. Over the course of our meetings, Amar's anger had flared numerous times. In our preparation sessions, no amount of explanation could quell his visible irritation each time I asked questions that he considered insulting. "How did you feel?" inevitably provoked a terse reply like, "I was scared they would kill me," accompanied by a glare that said, *you idiot, what do you think?* A frightened victim on the stand was one thing, but an irritable victim was not likely to garner much sympathy from the judge.

Drawn and trembling, Amar approached the stand. Settling into his seat, his eyes never left the rows of soldiers. Still, the beginning of his testimony went surprisingly smoothly.

It wasn't until about fifteen minutes into it that Amar went completely silent, his eyes wide with terror. I followed Amar's gaze to the back of the courtroom where Datray sat smirking. I considered asking the judge to order Datray out of the courtroom, but restrained myself because he undoubtedly would erase that smug face before I could get the words out.

A few minutes later, a quaking Amar faltered while identifying Datray. Datray sniggered loudly, then turned and smiled at the soldiers seated around him.

Next to Datray sat his two defense attorneys. Both of them feigned surprise when the judge ordered them to gain control of their client. Fed up, the judge finally ordered that Datray be removed from the courtroom.

Although Amar relaxed a little following Datray's exit, the trial was committed to its own dreadful course. Minutes later, we heard the all too familiar sound of a truck in reverse. Beep. Beep. Beep.

It was the sanitation truck, driven by Murphy's Law no doubt, coming to empty the porta-potties located conveniently close to the courtroom's entrance. The irksome noise was soon forgotten as the stench of human waste enveloped the courtroom. The foul odor settled over the chapel like a heavy wool blanket on a humid summer day. Several soldiers began coughing. Others sniffed and snorted in a futile attempt to clear the putrid smell from their noses.

"We'll take a ten-minute recess," the judge said, glowering at me, the official host of this painful, foul-smelling trial.

When we reconvened, I knew I had to get Amar to the meat of his testimony fast, or the judge's impressions of the afternoon would remain with the stink, rather than anything Amar actually said.

"How often do you see American soldiers?" I asked.

"Driving by, shopping, in the police stations. All of the time," answered Amar.

"Has this experience affected your impression of American soldiers?

"Objection, your honor, relevance," defense counsel Campion interjected.

"Overruled," the judge said.

Amar continued, oblivious to the objection.

"Yes. It has a big effect on me. I was so happy and proud the Coalition forces came up and freed my country, my family, and myself from the dictatorship that was ruling the country. But a few bad people in the American forces and the Iraqi forces make everybody look bad and I don't trust anybody anymore. I'm asking the court today to . . ."

"Objection, your honor," Campion said, unable to contain his irritation.

"Sustained." Turning to me, the judge continued, "Captain Gembara, I know you probably haven't discussed the different philosophies in the criminal justice systems. It might be a good time for you to move on to another area, if you have another area."

The judge's irritation with the slow pace of Amar's testimony, caused by the necessary use of a translator, was palpable. The judge barely looked up at Amar during the remainder of his testimony. And when the judge did glance at Amar, it wasn't out of respect. With Murtdadah up next, I prayed that fasting had zapped some of his energy and curbed his fondness for reenactment.

When Murtdadah's turn finally came, he bounded towards the witness chair, eyes bright with excitement. If we had not been running so far behind schedule, I would have called for a recess that instant.

Murtdadah, being Murtdadah, attempted to bridge the language barrier by physically demonstrating everything that happened the night of the carjacking. He jumped up repeatedly, eager to illustrate not only his experience of the evening but the angry expressions on the faces of his two kidnappers. His antics drew laughter from the soldiers, and ire from the judge and Campion. My clenched-teeth warnings did little to contain Murtdadah. His fervor could not be diminished by the judge's angry admonishments or Campion's repeated objections.

But the greatest victim of Murtdadah's testimony was Donald Dawood, the translator, who had difficulty keeping up with the spastic witness while relaying the judge's repeated warnings and defense counsel's objections. By the end of Murtdadah's testimony, the harried Dawood looked as though he needed a drink. I have rarely felt as relieved as when Murtdadah finally left the witness chair.

Cobb's company commander, Capt. Robert Brown, also took the stand. The handsome captain bore a striking resemblance to the British movie star Jude Law. Another West Point grad, Brown drove home the almost immediate impact that Cobb and Datray's absence had on his unit.

"It's a much greater danger. You have to do more with less. Our area is not shrinking," Brown said. He went on to explain how clearing a building with four soldiers was much safer than trying to clear it with two soldiers.

"You have to change up the weapons systems and guys have to cover more area. It's easier to fight with twenty guys than it is with five," he explained.

Injured soldiers also felt the impact of the company's shrinking numbers. "Are you always able to keep those guys out of the field?" I asked.

"Not as often as we should or want to. Sometimes, there are missions that require those guys to go out there with broken ribs, dislocated shoulders, messed-up knees," Brown said, shaking his head with disgust.

I also looked to Brown to illustrate how the hemorrhaging went well beyond simply losing two men. "I've got five soldiers assigned to escort Datray and Cobb. With Datray and Cobb, it makes it a seven-man squad that [is] effectively out of the fight whenever they move."

When it was Campion's turn, he called 1st Lt. Francis Blake. Through questioning of Blake, Campion showed that 1-8 had paid Murtdadah for information regarding insurgent mortar activity. Presumably, Campion was trying to establish that Murtdadah either had been paid for his testimony or had made up the carjacking story to scam the army out of a few dollars. It didn't matter. The nails were already in Cobb's coffin.

We actually managed to finish the evidence in one day, albeit one long, harrowing day filled with some foul odors and a few other surprises.

After the defense rested its case, I was pleased to find that Tom was still in the courtroom. As my de facto advisor and witness to one brutal afternoon, he said, "Just keep it as simple and as straightforward as possible. Remind the judge how you've proven the elements."

In my closing argument, I heeded Tom's reminder while emphasizing that Cobb's actions not only compromised the safety of his fellow 1-8 soldiers, but were contrary to the unit's very purpose: to win the hearts and minds of the Iraqi people. I also emphasized the impact that such mistreatment of locals could have on our ability to continue working in the area.

Campion's closing argument had two themes: that Amar and Murtdadah's testimony could not be trusted, and that Cobb and Datray were just blowing off some steam, joy riding. You know, a hot night out on the town. In Balad. Where the locals would sooner kill these goons than show them a good time.

The chockfull courthouse reverberated with anticipation following the closing arguments. Despite the late hour, both Murtdadah and Amar also stayed to hear the verdict. They requested cigarettes and water as they waited.

I sat down, praying that I had done my job.

Expecting an immediate judgment and sentence, dozens of soldiers had gathered outside the chapel. I retreated to the JAG workspace with Kolb, Carter, and Philibert, where we rehashed some of the testimony. As usual, I focused on my mistakes, all the stuff I could have, and should have, done better. For instance, we still hadn't found the "knife with compass" that Cobb and Datray had used that night. It wasn't enough to have a description on an inventory sheet.

With the sentencing phase of the court-martial still ahead, the judge was quick with his judgment. He found Pvt. Thomas C. Cobb guilty of AWOL, not desertion. Apparently, Judge Henley found reasonable doubt that Cobb was trying to quit the army and escape Iraq altogether.

I was deeply disappointed. All I could do was stare at the massive map still positioned near the witness chair. With Sassaman's help, I'd ensured that the route Cobb and Datray had driven that night was highlighted, emphasizing how each time that they had found themselves near an American base, or an Iraqi police station, they had U-turned. In stark contrast to the weaving routes around the bases, their route straightened out and continued due south as soon as they had found Highway One. There were no deviations there, no U-turns, no turnoffs. That's where they covered the most mileage. Nearly 90 percent of their joy ride was heading due south, toward Kuwait and, presumably, passage out of this war. If that wasn't ground to find Cobb guilty of desertion in the absence of his admitting it, I didn't know what was.

As these angry thoughts swirled through my head, I forced myself to concentrate on the sentencing portion of the trial. There was still an opportunity to ensure that Cobb didn't get off easy, that he would receive the punishment he deserved.

Emphasizing the detrimental effects that Cobb's actions had on 1-8 and the brigade and that this was no ordinary AWOL, I asked the judge for a dishonorable discharge and at least six years' confinement.

Judge Henley sentenced Cobb to six-and-a-half years' confinement and a dishonorable discharge. Although the judge's findings still bothered me, the sentence recognized that Cobb had endangered his fellow soldiers as well as the lives of two innocent civilians. Given the lengthy term of incarceration, I felt the trial accomplished what I had hoped it would.

"Congratulations, Vivian."

"Good job."

"Nice work."

Leaving the courthouse, I was humbled by the many familiar faces from 1-8, 1-68, and my own headquarters company who congratulated me as I passed by. To the soldiers, the AWOL versus desertion verdict was a distinction without a difference; what mattered was that Cobb would be severely punished for his crimes.

I paused briefly to correct several soldiers' mistaken assumption that Cobb would serve his time at Fort Leavenworth. The minimum sentence for Leavenworth was seven years, I explained, a point many seemed to find interesting.

Back at the JAG workspace, the guys were busy with post-trial paperwork. When I sensed a lull, I gathered them quickly to thank and congratulate them on our shared success. Finally, they would receive some recognition from their fellow soldiers as a result of this most visible display of our JAG mission.

Lieutenant Colonel Barnes, the division Staff Judge Advocate, called to congratulate and inform me that my team would be receiving a new legal specialist. Spec. Kissthopher Mendoza would be arriving the next day. Colonels Welsch and Rudesheim also stopped by the workspace to offer their congratulations. I felt satisfied that my client, the U.S. Army, was happy with the outcome.

I slept until 1100 the next day, oblivious to the mortar rounds that landed nearby through the night. Carter came to check whether I was awake, and alive.

"Also, ma'am," he said loudly, thinking I couldn't hear him through the fabric curtain that formed the door of my cubby, "the new guy is here. I just wanted to let you know. Nothing big going on, so if you want to keep sleeping, that's cool."

"What new guy?" I asked, my head still heavy with sleep.

"From division JAG, ma'am. Don't you remember? Colonel Barnes said he was coming today."

"Oh, yeah. Okay, I'm up. I mean, I'm getting up," I said, struggling to sound convincing. I heard Carter chuckle on the other side of the curtain as vague memories of Murtdadah miming on the stand flashed through my head.

"Any chance the showers are open?" I asked hopefully.

"Oh, uh, sorry, ma'am, I'm pretty sure female time doesn't start until 1700."
What else is new? "Okay, I'll be out in fifteen minutes to meet the new guy."
Specialist Mendoza was a recent college graduate seeking some adventure,
a steady job, and the opportunity to serve his country. Not long out of boot
camp, Mendoza was a meatball of a man, with round full cheeks and large
brown eyes. Still, Mendoza's enthusiasm for the mission was undeniable. Kolb,
Philibert, and Carter took instantly to the jovial Mendoza and his myriad of
quirky interests: drag-racing, chunky gold chains, and sword collecting. When I
realized that my newest team member would need training, Carter volunteered
to take Mendoza under his wing.

Unbeknownst to me, the days after the Cobb trial would be the high point
of my tour in Iraq. Had I known what was in store for me, I would have savored
every minute of that lull.

Two days later, I called my parents to tell them about the trial. My father
congratulated me and said he was proud. It was my mother's reaction, however,
that stayed with me after the call.

"Viv, I don't know, I don't like hearing about soldiers going to jail. He's so
young," she said mournfully.

Incredulous, I fumbled for a response. "Mom, it's not like I'm looking to
put soldiers in jail."

"I know," she said before lapsing into silence.

"Mom, I think you're forgetting that there are thousands of soldiers out
here doing their jobs every day. They want to go home too, but *they* still do
their jobs."

"Yeah, but couldn't you just send him home? Why jail?"

"Mom, you're missing the point. This guy not only ran away, he jeopardized
everyone's safety. We had to catch him, and he still showed no remorse."

No response.

"He also threatened two Iraqis, two innocent guys," I added.

"I'm not worried about them!" she snapped. The stress of my deployment
had clearly gotten to her. My father, sister, and brother each had mentioned as
much in their letters. With nonstop news coverage of soldiers killed or injured
in Iraq, she couldn't bear to hear about a bad outcome for any U.S. soldier, even
if it was his own fault.

"Okay, Mom," I exhaled. "How are things at home?"

CHAPTER SEVEN

Blackhawk Down

TOM LEANED AGAINST THE TABLE, his long legs crossed at the ankles in front of him. It was a decidedly relaxed posture for a man in the midst of an aggressive campaign.

"Viv, you look like shit. You need a day off," Tom said.

"Thanks, Tom, just what I love to hear."

"You've been running around like a knucklehead for months now. The trial is over. Why don't you take some R&R?"

I shot him a look. As much as I enjoyed Tom's friendship, I wasn't in the mood for a protracted discussion about leave. I had three summary courts-martial to prepare, and Datray's trial date was still uncertain. "I'd love to, but it's a little hard to justify."

"What's the latest on your leave situation?" he persisted.

He had me there. "Not good," I replied. "The whole leave policy is going to be a debacle anyways," I added defensively. "And I'm still trying to catch up on the work I put off before the trial."

"I thought you were happy about the leave policy," Tom countered.

I was, at first, but the idea of sending soldiers home for two weeks now seemed ludicrous. On the heels of prosecuting Cobb for trying to escape Iraq, what could we expect the soldiers to do when they were back home for two weeks' vacation? Life-altering events inevitably had transpired, both here and at home, for many soldiers granted leave, and many wouldn't be good. Besides the inevitable DUI arrests, domestic violence incidents, and malingerers, how many soldiers might go AWOL? Having made it this far along, I just didn't want soldiers to go home and implode. To my pessimistic state of mind, sending the soldiers home on leave seemed like an unnecessary risk to their honorably finishing out their tours. God knew that I would not want to return here if I were given two weeks at home. Unfortunately, I made the mistake of sharing these uplifting thoughts with Tom.

"What's wrong with you? So, you'd rather have everyone stay here because you don't trust soldiers?"

"Tom, it's not that," I protested.

"No, that's essentially what you just said."

Defeated, I said, "Look, Tom, I'm probably not going home anyways so this is a moot point."

"Why?"

I kept it brief, hoping he'd give up. "I don't have a replacement, no back up."

Among other obstacles, I knew that Welsch wasn't keen on having a JAG captain from division staff come down to Anaconda to fill in for me. Whether Welsch intended to or not, my exchange with him about leave had left me doubting that I should even want to go.

"But aren't a bunch of the other section leaders on the list?" Tom continued.

I sighed audibly, hoping he'd take the hint. "Yes."

"Aren't their sections covering for them?"

"Yeah."

"And the other brigade trial counsels, don't they get to go home? I know 2nd Brigade's JAG is going and . . ." Tom was now in cross-examination mode and gaining momentum.

"Yeah, I got it, Tom."

Then he surprised me. "But two weeks, what is it, sixteen, or seventeen, days, including the travel time?" Not pausing for an answer, he continued, "Yeah, well, I guess it makes sense that they would want a JAG that they know around."

"Yeah," I said, pretending to focus on the papers in front of me. Didn't Tom have anything else to do? Erect a water plant, build a bridge, something?

"And your guys, you said Kolb and Carter are going home, right?"

"Yeah, but not at the same time."

"Either way, they'd be overwhelmed by themselves here for two weeks, right?" Tom asked more forcefully.

"Well, no. I mean, they would know what to do. They cover all the time when I'm on the road, or visiting a unit," I said a tad defensively. "It's just that there's a lot of stuff they can't do, that requires my signature and review, and well, it would suck for them, and me, because it would all just pile up." So much for the curt replies.

"It is a long time," Tom agreed, and then said in a more wistful tone, "It probably would have been better if leave were only a week. Then they'd probably let you go, right?"

I nodded. Just the thought of sending Mike an e-mail that said "I'm coming home!" made me smile. Or would I surprise him? Or, maybe Mike and I could surprise my parents?

Tom cleared his throat, and I looked up to find him smiling triumphantly. "So, then, you have no excuse for not going on R&R! Just tell Welsch," Tom said more definitively. He stood and reached for his Kevlar. "Qatar is a four-day trip. You just said your guys could handle it. I mean it. You need to tell Welsch that you need a break. It's four days." Tom's voice had taken on a serious tone that made me slightly uncomfortable. He was not smiling either.

I nodded, suddenly feeling like the subject of an intervention. "Okay, I'll talk to him."

A week after the trial I was settling into my five-feet-by-nine-feet living cubicle in the brigade headquarters building, the thrill of being able to stand up as I changed my clothes still fresh. It was the best living situation I'd experienced since arriving in Iraq, but still cold consolation for the bomb that Tom had dropped on me the previous night. He was leaving the brigade at the end of the month. Having done what he could at 1-8, his civil affairs boss in Kirkuk had ordered Tom's team to return north.

This was terrible news, made worse by Tom's rocky ending with Sassaman, who had also refused to endorse an award for Tom, despite the fact that Tom had completed a record number of projects in Balad.

Drowning In The Desert

The constant departure of friends and colleagues was demoralizing. Tom's departure would be the worst by far.

On the heels of all the living quarters and workplace improvements, November seemed like as good a time as any to "pimp our ride." We needed to get our Humvee armored. Weeks earlier, odd splotches of silver and gray, and sometimes rusty brown, metal started appearing on Anaconda's otherwise beige landscape. These were the soft-skin Humvees that had been locally outfitted in the first wave of what was referred to as "hajji" or "hillbilly" armor. No longer waiting for the army to send them armor kits to reinforce their Humvees, the soldiers of several units took matters into their own hands and started contracting armor retrofitting to the locals. The armor used on the first test subjects was clunky, frequently mismatched, and awkward. One Humvee I saw had new armored doors that hinged at the bottom instead of at the side. I observed a lieutenant entering the vehicle by lowering the door to the ground, climbing in, and then pulling on a rope to bring the door back up. Other Humvees were so plastered with haphazardly placed metal that they no longer resembled Humvees. The side windows on one Humvee were covered completely but for a six-inch slit from which I imagined that its sheltered occupants might fire arrows, like medieval sentinels.

While the retro-armoring process had growing pains, I did not want to miss the chance to be part of the second wave. Sgt. Jay Arthurs, my friend and neighbor in the ALOC, was instrumental in making that happen. As one of several reserve civil affairs soldiers attached to the brigade, he worked at headquarters and sat directly across from the JAG section in the ALOC. We had become friends by virtue of proximity and a shared habit of working late into the night. Jay shared my intolerance of bureaucratic paperwork and acquired a reputation for finding loopholes to fund his civil affairs programs. When Jay's team received the green light to start armoring its vehicles, I persuaded him to include our Humvee in their armor budget.

"Okay, JAGs, one of you has to join me at the range today if you want that piece of junk you drive armored," Jay said. Jay and Kolb spent the afternoon firing their M16s at different grades of armor plates to test the metals' strength.

Several rounds of testing and weeks later, my JAG team was the proud owner of a Humvee with pale green metal doors and metal floor plates.

My father, seemingly omniscient about all things war, was the first person to point out the problems that we would have with our soft-skin Humvee. Weeks before we deployed, two massive boxes of Vietnam-era flak jackets had arrived at my home in Colorado Springs.

"Use them to line the floor of your Humvee, and anywhere else they can fit," my father explained. The flak jackets, along with two-quart canteens, desert camouflage netting, and several bayonets, were sent by Mike Gil, one of my father's army buddies and a dear family friend. Gil is a former special forces supply sergeant who had handled logistical support for a special intelligence unit my father was a part of during his second tour in Vietnam. A scrounger extraordinaire, Gil was the kind of soldier who could produce anything, anywhere, a master of obtaining hard-to-come-by supplies.

If you needed a Mitsubishi sedan or a Santa suit in Southeast Asia, no problem. Just give Gil a few days. While the Pentagon was enjoying protracted bureaucratic dialogue about requested supplies, Gil was on the ground, begging, borrowing, and sometimes stealing, so his intelligence unit had the civilian vehicles, weapons, and fake IDs that it needed to complete its mission. He also made sure that they had plenty of liquor and cigarettes to bribe and barter with, my father included. At one point Gil even procured crates of apples, a fruit considered so exotic in Vietnam that the locals preferred to display them as a luxury item, rather than eat them. In Vietnam's tropical climate, a bag of red apples opened doors.

After retiring from the army, Gil put his talents to work for the U.S. Border Patrol. Thirty years later, it was a different war, and a different Gembara, but Gil was still filling in the equipment gaps. While I didn't win a popularity contest when I told my guys that we would need to hump about four hundred pounds of flak vests, along with all of our other gear, the extra layer of protection and peace of mind they provided was invaluable once we got to Iraq. Even with our new armor, we still kept the flak jackets in the Humvee.

That same month, November 2003, Lieutenant Colonel Barnes gave us yet another reason to put our newly armored Humvee on the tenuous road to Tikrit. Maj. Gen. Thomas J. Romig, *The* Judge Advocate General (TJAG), the JAG Corps' highest-ranking officer, was making a morale visit to Iraq. As part of his official duties, the TJAG is expected to make what is called an Article 6 visit to every JAG office worldwide at least once every few years.

Drowning In The Desert

The ostensible purpose of TJAG's Article 6 visit is to inspect the "administration of justice." Because General Romig was making only two stops in Iraq, one in Baghdad and the other in Tikrit, the army's JAG officers and senior enlisted deployed elsewhere in Iraq were ordered to travel to one of these two locations. For Kolb and me, the privilege of saluting senior JAG officers boiled down to more time spent on our least favorite road, IED-infested Highway One.

The next morning, I was on the phone with the division JAG office. Since Barnes wasn't in, I decided to probe Capt. Magda Prystulska, who worked with Barnes every day, for information. She could tell me how "mandatory" our attendance was and whether we'd catch hell with Barnes if we didn't show at the Article 6 visit.

Magda didn't hesitate to kill the no-show idea. I moved to plan B. "Do both of us need to attend?" I asked, hoping I might get Kolb excused. "We're down as it is. How about if I come and Kolb stays to handle things at the brigade?" By myself, I also had a better shot at finding a seat on a helicopter, thereby avoiding the road altogether.

No dice. "Vivian, this is an Article 6 visit," she reminded me, somewhat haughtily, I thought. "*The* Judge Advocate General of the army is going to be here. It's an official visit, so attendance is mandatory for all JAG officers and senior enlisted." Interestingly, it was Magda who had said she would assist me with the Cobb trial only if she were allowed to fly down to Anaconda.

"Got it," I said, hanging up the phone. Resigned, Kolb and I added our Humvee to a supply convoy headed to Tikrit the next morning.

Despite the supply convoy's 0700 departure, a suspicious object in the middle of the road had the IED team concerned. So, while the IED team checked to see if the object was indeed a bomb, the rest of our convoy waited like ducks in a barrel, along the side of Highway One. To stave off the wave of resentment threatening to envelop me, I focused on the latest security report warning: "Be on the lookout for high-end sedans on hills and bridges near major roadways. They may contain concealed spotters prepared to alert others of a convoy's approach to ensure timely detonation."

Well, this was no good. Hell, if Kolb and I saw a Mercedes on a hill, our best bet would be to pray like hell. We didn't even have a radio to alert the other vehicles. Our options would have included firing off a few rounds in the direction of the suspicious car. You know, as a distraction.

Forty minutes passed before the IED team gave us the "all clear" and we were on our way again. It was just past 0900 when we pulled through the gates of 4th Infantry division's main headquarters in Tikrit, located in one of Saddam's former palaces. Once we were through the gate, Kolb and I broke away from the convoy and sped the remaining distance toward the headquarters building. The only thing marring the crisp blue sky over Tikrit was a line of black smoke rising in the distance, perhaps a half-mile away. Seeing the plume, we quit our hunt for a parking spot. Kolb brought the Humvee to a screeching halt in a gap alongside some bushes and we ran single file up the hill toward the palace. Several feet ahead of me, Kolb murmured something, but I couldn't hear him over my own heavy breathing. Reaching a side entrance, Kolb pulled open the heavy palace door and a stream of JAG officers and soldiers rushed out past us towards the patio area.

"Sorry we're late," I started to say, stopping as soon as I realized that they hadn't even noticed us. There were several other JAG soldiers already standing on the patio when we made our way over. They stood near the railing gaping at the dark puffs of smoke over the hill.

"Hey, what's going on?" I asked a young female sergeant standing near me.

She was transfixed by the black column. Lowering her hands from her mouth, she turned to me and said, "They crashed, ma'am. That was the TJAG."

As she spoke, I saw Captain Prystulska making her way through the gathering crowd.

"Magda, what's going on?"

"Vivian, one of the TJAG's Blackhawks just crashed. That's the smoke," she said impatiently, pointing toward the hills. "We don't know what happened yet, but Colonel Barnes wants everyone inside. Now."

Tasked with the unenviable position of herding us inside, Magda repeated herself several times.

Kolb and I found each other as the crowd began moving into the palace. In hushed tones, we compared notes about what we had heard and seen.

"There were two Blackhawk helicopters carrying the JAG Corps senior brass from Baghdad. One Blackhawk crashed, or was shot down. It's still unclear. They're still waiting to hear if the second one landed or not," Kolb said. He paused then and lowered his voice to a whisper. "The JAG Corps' sergeant major and chief warrant officer are confirmed dead. Their Blackhawk was the one that went down. That was what caused all the smoke we saw."

He shook his head in disbelief, but said nothing else. Both of us simply followed the stream of soldiers as it coursed through the palace's hallways, up a winding marble staircase. We eventually arrived at a briefing room where I waited for Kolb to say something else. Kolb remained quiet, impassive. Eventually, I left him in search of a more vocal companion to help me process my rattled emotions. How could they be dead? They were just visiting. Lots of people visit for no good reason. Lately, it felt like we were always tidying up our workspace because some politician was expected to show up.

I felt guilty for resenting the Article 6 visit in the first place. I searched for familiar faces but found mostly new ones among the JAG captains. Only a handful of the original group of officers that I'd deployed with remained in country. Most of the officers had left at the six-month mark to cycle back through Fort Hood and on to other duties.

I forced myself to approach a few of the new captains. Introducing myself, I explained, "I'm at the 3rd Brigade, you know, Fort Carson." By this point, I was familiar with the confused looks from many of the JAGs when I mentioned that I was with the 3rd Brigade and that I was based at Anaconda. The other three brigades from 4th Division were based out of Fort Hood, Texas. With the exception of the three other brigades' trial counsel, most of the JAG captains worked either here at division main (DMAIN) JAG office, or at a second JAG office located on the neighboring compound in Tikrit. The division JAGs had limited contact with those of us assigned to the brigades.

My oscillating feelings about the JAGs in Tikrit moved toward sympathy. Although their location and assignments were safer, they were confined to the palace grounds, save the occasional trip to Anaconda or Camp Victory. Theirs was a narrow experience of Iraq.

Geez, I was beginning to sound like my dad, extolling every challenge as a great learning experience.

Turning back to the conversation around me, one of the newer captains recounted his experience working with Sgt. Maj. Cornell Gilmore, who had just perished in the Blackhawk. Silence followed the captain's description of the amiable, extremely competent head of the JAG Corps' paralegals. There was nothing else to say. This simply wasn't supposed to happen to JAGs.

Once a meeting time was set for that afternoon, Kolb and I left in search of a TAC phone to call Philibert and Carter, both of whom had been trying to reach us since hearing the initial radio reports that several JAG personnel had been killed. With time to spare, we also took advantage of division's Internet connectivity.

"Please let us know you're alive" was the subject line of the first e-mail in my inbox. It was from my sister, Debbie, a journalist. In our last conversation, I had mentioned that I might try to catch a helicopter ride to Tikrit. Debbie had been at work on an overnight shift when she saw an alert bulletin that a Blackhawk had been shot down near Tikrit and that all JAG personnel aboard were confirmed dead. Aware that no names would be released until the families had been notified, she spent an anxious six hours checking her e-mail and praying that her cell phone didn't ring.

Hitting reply, I assured her that Kolb and I were okay and then poured out my frustration and anger over the tragedy, the senselessness of the visit, and how too few people seemed to grasp the danger out here. It was a private "I told you so" of sorts, but the kind that brought no satisfaction. Scanning the e-mail for typos, I was bothered by its tone. Why was I always complaining? Hadn't I just witnessed how short life could be? What if this was my final e-mail home?

Behind me a soldier cracked his gum loudly, a reminder that he was still waiting and that I had exceeded my time limit. I pushed the morbid thoughts aside and hit send, still wishing I'd said something positive.

Several hours later, when we finally saw General Romig, it looked as though a gray shadow had settled on his otherwise genial face. Addressing the group, he confirmed in a steady, somber voice that Sgt. Maj. Cornell W. Gilmore, Chief Warrant Officer Sharon T. Swartworth, and four crew members from the 101st Airborne Division had been killed that morning when their Blackhawk helicopter crashed. He offered no other information about the nature of the crash but did add, "I will be accompanying their bodies back to the states."

Embracing his more comfortable role as our leader, he thanked us profusely for our work and dedication. He praised us for our courage. "Sergeant Major

Gilmore and Chief Swartworth were so proud of you. They wanted to be here to tell you that," he said, his voice trailing off, his bald, raw eyes fixed on something in the distance. A long moment passed before he declared plaintively, "They were my friends."

Stepping out from under his stars, he then recounted how many years he had known both Gilmore and Swartworth and described how they had become a team.

"They were my team," he repeated. "They were my family."

I wondered if there was an appropriate way to comfort a general.

Romig offered a final thanks to all of us and stayed to shake the hand of each officer, NCO, and enlisted soldier in the room.

Afterward, Kolb and I hurried to find a convoy leaving for Anaconda before sunset. Romig's morale visit had been anything but. The November 7, 2003, deaths of Gilmore, Swartworth, and the four soldiers from the 101st Airborne Division kicked off what would become the deadliest month for U.S. forces since the start of the war.

Nearly ten days later, I felt anxious as I prepared to leave for four days of R&R at U.S. Central Command headquarters in Qatar. For the second time that morning, I checked the chamber on my 9mm pistol before returning it to its holster. My armored vest was safely tucked away beneath the bed mat on my cot, with a sleeping bag laid neatly on top. After one last look around my cubby, ensuring I'd left nothing valuable in plain view, I grabbed my backpack and gun and headed to the JAG workspace to answer any last-minute inquiries from division.

It was just before 0700 and Philibert was already busy helping a soldier when I stopped by.

"Need help with something, captain?" he asked, as I moved a crate of dusty files off our trunk.

"No, I'm fine," I said and motioned for him to continue helping the soldier.

Opening the trunk, I looked for the best place to store my Kevlar and gun, now wrapped in a black garbage bag, while I was away. Under the constant, watchful eyes of Carter and Kolb, our trunk felt like a safer storage option than signing them over to some soldier in headquarters company with extra space in his footlocker.

"Hey, Captain G, they're already forming up outside," Kolb said as he arrived.

Taking the hint, I pulled books over the trash bag and closed the trunk.

"Alright guys, I'll see you in a few days," I said, not wanting to belabor the goodbye.

"See you," they replied in unison.

Philibert added, "Have a good time, ma'am!" to cover their obvious relief at the impending four days without their officer.

Outside the brigade headquarters building, I joined a group of nearly twenty soldiers near the entrance. The majority were quiet, dozing against their backpacks, or cut off from the world by their headphones. Sensing my confusion, one of them explained, "We're just waiting on one replacement, ma'am. They're just getting some of their stuff together."

I nodded, feigning relief. No need to trouble a helpful corporal with my own concerns about leaving. After six months without a day off, it was almost easier to stay. My fear was that my job might be like a gym habit: tolerable when you're used to slogging through it, but difficult to kick-start if you spent the weekend eating pizza and carrot cake. *JAG work? I'll start on Monday. Definitely, Monday.*

I found Tom sitting with his back against the building, elbows resting on his knees, forehead resting on his forearms.

"Hey," I said throwing my backpack down next to him.

"Hey, yourself," he said lazily as he lifted his head up to squint at me. Tom and Jay Arthurs had found last-minute slots to Qatar a week earlier.

"We're waiting on a replacement," he explained.

"Yeah, I heard."

The wait for the replacement soldier fed my anxiety. Beneath the concrete overhang outside the brigade's glass front doors, I paced back and forth like a nervous new parent searching for any excuse to pester the babysitter. Being without my Kevlar and weapon for the first time in months only heightened the feeling. I contemplated popping in to check for messages one last time. The prospect of seeing the disappointed looks on Kolb's and Philibert's faces, however, kept me in check, especially after they had so graciously ensured my timely arrival at the pick-up point. In the days leading up to my trip, they had gone out of their way to assure me that they could handle everything. It seemed we all needed a break.

When the replacement guy finally arrived, I glanced one last time through the front doors before grabbing my backpack to join Tom and Jay in line. Jay nodded hello but was otherwise entranced by the music screaming from his headphones.

It took nearly a day to get to Doha, Qatar, where the military had erected a small compound for soldiers stationed throughout the Middle East to unwind for four-day stints. From the window of the airplane, the endless sea of lights illuminating the dark landscape made Qatar seem like an enchanted world. Before we could explore that world, we were taken to a hangar to check in and learn the rules of R&R. Officers were directed to sit on one side and NCOs and enlisted on the other side, even though we were hearing the same briefing.

"Makes months in the desert feel almost worth it for this, doesn't it?" Tom said, leaning back in his chair from the row ahead of me. We both turned to see if we could spot Jay in the crowd across the aisle. We had planned to meet up with Jay after the briefing.

"There he is," Tom said. "He looks thrilled, as usual."

I followed Tom's finger to find Jay, sullen faced, among a group of teen-aged soldiers. A twenty-five-year-old reservist from Manhattan who worked in financial services in his civilian life, Jay had little in common with most of the kids around him.

The guidelines were pretty straightforward: no uniforms, no formations, and for those of us who wanted to leave the compound, there were dozens of activities available, so long as you signed up in advance. As the briefing drew to a close, the crowd across the aisle became increasingly antsy. Not having done any homework about the trip, I had no idea that the growing frenzy was due to our final perk as soldiers on leave: three beers per soldier per day. Real beer. Not the non-alcoholic cider that passed for a celebratory beverage at Anaconda. Having saved the best for last, the briefer's first mention of the beer tickets caused the crowd to erupt in hoots and hooahs. Jumping to their feet, several soldiers began punching the air with their fists.

Expecting that Jay was at his wits' end by now, I searched for his sulking face among the rowdy crowd of enlisted soldiers. In a matter of moments, however, the aloof sergeant had become the private's hero. Jay was pounding his fists on his knees and leading a "beer, beer, beer" chant.

Catching Jay's eye, I smiled and widened my eyes at his sudden change. Grinning, he shrugged his shoulders as if to say: why fight it? Why fight it indeed.

Only those unfortunate few who had been subjected to life in the Iraqi desert would find the concrete-barricaded trailers as inviting as we did. The actual R&R area consisted of a cordoned-off section of a U.S. base in Qatar. A mix of trailers, prefabricated buildings, and several large aviation hangars sat side-by-side in ten parallel rows, each a quarter-mile in length. Our activities revolved around the first four streets, which include a trailer-size PX, well-equipped gym with basketball courts, barber shop and beauty salon, Burger King trailer, computer lab, phone trailer, video game arcade, movie theater, and the main chow hall.

Before releasing us, the briefer reminded us one last time that we had the option of taking field trips outside the area, to shop, tour, or take part in adventure sports. I felt giddy. My time in Qatar felt like a hallucination. By the time I laid down that first night—in my private room equipped with cable TV and an overhead light—my face was sore from smiling.

Meanwhile, the violence back "home" was worsening. I returned from Qatar to learn that 1-8 was responding to a surge in violence in Abu Hishma, a town just south of Balad that had been giving them trouble for some time. On November 17, during a patrol near the town, twenty-six-year-old Staff Sgt. Dale Panchot's Bradley Fighting Vehicle was hit by a rocket-propelled grenade, killing Panchot instantly.

Kolb had actually met Panchot a few times and described him as a tall guy, well-liked by his fellow soldiers. The rocket-propelled grenade that struck Panchot's Bradley, Kolb explained, had directly hit Panchot, nearly slicing him in half. I swallowed, wishing I had been spared that detail. The news that another one of our soldiers was dead was terrible enough.

The early morning attack on Panchot's convoy and the firefight that ensued, as 1-8 pursued the perpetrators, seemed to confirm for 1-8's commanders the high price of failure. Sassaman and his men responded by destroying several homes and buildings, wrapping Abu Hishma in barbed wire, enforcing a strict curfew, and restricting entry and exit to a handful of checkpoints.

Suddenly, I thought 1-8's tactics better resembled Israeli tactics in the Gaza Strip more than they resembled American tactics in the Sunni Triangle.

Initially, I was concerned with the legality of Sassaman's tactics. But when I learned that the division commander, Maj. Gen. Raymond Odierno, had approved Sassaman's methods, my attention turned to answering several media inquiries from journalists visiting Anaconda.

In order to respond to a reporter's claim of excessive and unlawful force, however, I first needed the facts. Namely, how many homes and buildings had we destroyed, and what led to their destruction. General answers would suffice. When the information wasn't forthcoming from 1-8, however, I began to worry about a potential public relations disaster.

The lingering doubt compelled me to double-check with the division JAG office to confirm that there was no legal issue with Sassaman's tactics. Surprisingly, division had no concerns regarding 1-8's response to the insurgent activity in Abu Hishma.

Division's assurances aside, I worried about how a diligent journalist might spin the situation. I felt relieved, however, not to have to second-guess Sassaman. And in the wake of so much recent violence against Coalition forces, playing nice no longer felt like an option.

CHAPTER EIGHT

Samarra

"CARTER, KICK DOWN THE DOOR!"

His eyes huge with disbelief, Carter turned to face the captain who had delivered the order.

Seeing that this was no joke, Carter raised his leg and landed his foot forcefully in the center of the door. Nothing. He kicked it again and it fell open with a thwack.

We were about to find out if the building we were entering was available. Worst case scenario, we were going to have to make it available.

We were in Samarra, and our reconnaissance trip to determine whether the sprawling pharmaceutical factory in the center of the city would be suitable for a new brigade headquarters was quickly turning into on-the-job training in urban combat. On this particular day, Lieutenant Colonel Welsch was forced to do just as Secretary of Defense Donald Rumsfeld had said we would do: Welsch went to war with the army he had, Carter and me. Fortunately, for Welsch, at least four other soldiers in our group had some legitimate door-kicking experience. They led the way. Splitting up in pairs, and taking different parts of the complex, we put our boots to work.

Drowning In The Desert

That was the end of our first week in Iraq, May 2003, and the beginning of a long and complicated relationship with Samarra. For starters, nothing in Samarra happened as it should. That first day, with our hearts in our throats, we had expected to find some resistance, maybe booby traps, behind the doors we kicked open. There were none. The Iraqis who ran the pharmaceutical company had simply boarded up the building complex to deter looting.

It wasn't until our two-Humvee convoy was navigating its way back through Samarra's tight streets that we heard gunfire. Unfamiliar with the city, Welsch radioed for assistance from the brigade reconnaissance troop, and we exited our vehicles to form a loose circle of security.

As the gunfire faded, we began speculating whether it had even been directed at us. Uncertain, we kept our weapons in plain view. We waited, and waited, and waited some more, at which point, a dozen happy, spirited children began crowding around us. Several more spilled out from a nearby ally. They took turns yelling, "We love you! We love you!" as they surrounded us, their hands thrust forward with thumbs up. Observing my rank, several of the older boys adopted a new chant. "Cap Tin! Cap Tin!" To the side, a young girl who had watched everything with big curious eyes, summoned her courage and ran up to me, screeching to a stop when she was about a foot away. Smiling shyly, she produced a rose from behind her back and handed it to me.

Sweet, frightening, unexpected. That's Samarra. It is like no other place.

The turbulent city on the east bank of the Tigris River was our first home in Iraq. After days spent in a convoy, followed by more days of uncertainty over our ultimate destination, we were excited to get off Iraq's dusty roads and get to work.

Following our recon trip that day, the grounds of the pharmaceutical factory became the brigade headquarters' makeshift home. We met the neighbors and started establishing working relationships with local leaders. This bonny period lasted forty-six days before orders arrived directing us east, to the city of Tuz. The division's growing area of responsibility meant that a single battalion would have to take over Samarra from our brigade, killing all hope that many of our local efforts would be continued.

Still, we set our sights on Tuz, hopeful it would be our final stop. Little did we know that moving, or "jumping," locations would become our brigade's specialty. While other brigades enjoyed the comfort and stability of a fixed location and known threats, we were nomads on a city-by-city tour of Iraq. Every few weeks we were hanging our hats in a new town, learning new threats, and making new contacts whom we would soon abandon.

First, Samarra, then Tuz. After that, we were somewhere along the border with Iran. Next, we moved north to the outskirts of Kirkuk, near Daquq. By late June, we finally landed at Camp Anaconda in Balad, just forty miles north of Baghdad. This final move included a massive area of responsibility, which spanned from Samarra, east across the Tigris to Ad Duluyiah, and south to Tarmiya. The good news was that we also acquired some help. First Brigade's 1-66 Armor Battalion, the unit currently securing the city of Samarra, came under 3rd Brigade's control. Lieutenant Colonel Ryan Gonsalves, commander of 1-66, had the awesome task of securing the restive city with a battalion and the periodic support of a lone infantry company.

There were signs of trouble immediately. For starters, Gonsalves's soldiers had difficulty patrolling Samarra's narrow streets in their cumbersome Abrams tanks. To aid their efforts, Colonel Rudesheim made sure 1-66 received top priority when a coveted shipment of armored Humvees arrived in Iraq. The Humvees made little difference.

By late November, Samarra was teeming with insurgents. Operation Ivy Blizzard was conceived as the antidote, a division-level operation to quash Samarra's growing violence. The Blizzard concept was presented as a sort of one-two punch. Phase I: get the bad guys out. Phase II: infuse the city with civil affairs projects, and money.

Phase I required working with local sources to identify Saddam loyalists and anti-Coalition cells. Intelligence sources were used to identify the probable locations of these target individuals, thereby avoiding the time-consuming effort of random house-to-house searches. The most important component was an agile, effective force to get the job done, and the lead role would not go to 1-66.

The answer was obvious: the division would move Sassaman's 1-8 Infantry Battalion from Balad to Samarra on a temporary basis. Equipped with Bradley Fighting Vehicles and armored Humvees, 1-8 would be the lighter and faster muscle of the operation, killing and capturing key insurgents. 1-66 Armor would supplement 1-8 Infantry by providing stationary security throughout the city, in addition to manning a temporary detention center.

With the bad guys dead or detained, the operation would move into Phase II, flooding the city with cash and rebuilding projects. Civil affairs teams would descend on Samarra and initiate a boom in high-profile construction projects that would hopefully convince the locals that the Americans were there to help and that Samarra's glory days were still ahead. Timing was critical. There couldn't be any lag after Phase I. We needed to be on the ground making sure Samarra was building and booming even before Phase I was over.

By November we had spent enough time working with local sheiks to know it took forever for them to agree on anything. With that in mind, Rudesheim had civil affairs personnel in Samarra weeks before the operation to work with the locals and lay the groundwork for the Phase II projects.

I moved up to Samarra in early December to oversee the JAG component of the operation. I spent a lot of time meeting with judges downtown, finding a contractor to repair Samarra's courthouse, and lining up a somewhat reputable vendor to deliver requested supplies. I spent the rest of the time at Forward Operating Base Brassfield-Mora, 1-66's home on the northern edge of Samarra, where they occupied a partially built industrial warehouse park.

There, I shared a tent with six soldiers, mostly fellow staff officers. To my surprise, our small tent, with its potbelly stove in the corner, proved to be a curiously happy place to live, albeit temporarily. Perhaps it was the cold and rainy weather outside that resolved the tension between some of the staff officers. I'm not sure why, but the flare-ups I envisioned never surfaced. For whatever reason, our cozy little enclave was thriving with the combined talents of its inhabitants.

Captain Sandra Chavez, the resourceful brigade public affairs officer, was known for her stinginess when it came to her "personal" Internet connection, even going so far as to unplug her cable when she wasn't around so that no one could get online. This time, however, she shocked all of us by bringing a television and DVD player for everyone to enjoy. Captain Matt Provost, our acting S6, communications officer, pilfered electricity from a neighboring generator and set up the entertainment center. And finally, the brigade's chemical officer, Capt. Emma Toops's diligent, borderline-compulsive hoarding ensured a cornucopia of snacks.

So what did I bring to this smorgasbord? My sunny disposition! That is, at least when the potbelly stove was running. Actually, nothing, except my gratitude. I relished the camaraderie the little enclave offered during this particularly lonely stretch of my deployment.

Tonight the group was climbing into their sleeping bags when I returned from the tactical command post (TAC). They had stayed up late watching the most recent season of the television series *24* on DVD. After missing episodes three to five, I was hopelessly lost and didn't mind having to work late that night. Still, I appreciated Sandra's drowsy whisper that they'd missed me.

Although Ivy Blizzard was a division-level operation, the division JAG was allowing me, a brigade-level JAG, to monitor detention procedures, offer ROE guidance, and ensure that civilian claims were handled properly. I had spent the evening at the TAC taking care of loose ends and sending updates to Tikrit, going out of my way to keep everyone at division informed. I had also been waiting for a phone call that never came.

I was ready to end my night, but an hour after lying down, warm and snug in my sleeping bag, I was still awake, pondering Dave. Captain David Croswell was Datray's lead defense attorney. Back at Anaconda, we had discussed a possible plea agreement for Datray. Since I had arrived in Samarra two days ago, however, Dave had not returned any of my phone calls. A plea agreement made so much sense for *all* interested parties. For Datray, the more culpable of the two carjackers, a plea meant a limited punishment. For 1-8 Infantry, now operating in Samarra, it would spare them the hassle of sending soldiers down to Balad to testify. A plea agreement also would spare me the trouble of having to recreate the most challenging trial of my career.

It was daunting: flying in Datray, Cobb, their security escorts, the judge, and the court reporter; prepping the testifying Iraqis and soldiers; and coordinating convoys for everyone involved, not to mention the actual legal work. The silver lining was that, if we did go to trial, at least we wouldn't have to build a new courthouse.

Our last conversation had been heated, but my conversations with Dave usually were. He was pugnacious and vocal, ready to lord even the slightest perceived advantage over me. And Dave had a lot of material to work with because both he and his co-counsel had attended the Cobb trial. Even then, Dave had aimed to irritate me. After Cobb's trial, Dave's first words to me were, "Look, I know you don't have much of a case." He was argumentative, obstinate, and a contrarian. He was many things. One thing Dave was not, however, was silent. The silence worried me.

As the fire in the stove petered out, the sleeping bags around me began to shift into positions to better trap the remaining heat. Tugging on my sleeping bag's hood strings, I rolled onto my right side, feeling very much like a 7-Eleven hot dog rotating beneath heat lamps. In the distance, I heard a droning sound. It was the Muslim call to prayer, a haunting, rhythmic chanting broadcast five times a day from the local mosques. Was it that early already? My watch confirmed that it was indeed 0400. I couldn't afford to lose another minute of sleep. I had spent the entire night worrying about the case. With only two hours before my watch alarm went off, I shut my eyes and tried concentrating on sleep. Dave's just playing hard-ball, I told myself. He'll call soon. He will.

Three straight days of rain in Samarra turned Camp Brassfield-Mora into a mud pit. Humvees were packed with shovels and wood planks to negotiate some of the more treacherous areas. The rain had turned the narrow grid of dirt roads that surrounded the TAC command tent and our living quarters into alleys of thick, glue-like mud.

At Anaconda, the path leading up to brigade headquarters, nicknamed "Welsch's kingdom" by several smart-aleck soldiers, was covered in rocks, truckloads of rocks, which kept the mud at bay. A heavy October rain had Welsch on the phone ordering rocks weeks earlier. His foresight, however, resulted in a shortage of rocks at many of the battalions. Welsch was unapologetic. He'd acted early; it wasn't his fault other executive officers hadn't thought to do the same.

At first, I had agreed with Welsch. By my third rainy day at Brassfield-Mora, however, I was cursing Welsch's selfishness as my ankles disappeared in mud. That is, when I wasn't climbing a mud-slick ladder to reach the porta-potties. No time for fist shaking there. You had to hold on.

Somewhere early on in Iraq, I had tempted the gods by saying, "I can't imagine a worse bathroom situation anywhere!" With each new location, I received their laughing response. Brassfield-Mora was not the nightmare of our location outside Kirkuk, but it proved again that the gods had a sense of humor. Twelve-foot-high brick walls separated the porta-potties from our living/working area near the TAC. For reasons that still elude me, someone had decided not to blast a hole in that wall. Instead, two ladders had been set up, one on either side of the wall, turning each bathroom trip into an adventure. Every so often, when it was windy, a ladder would fall over, and you would find a soldier peering over the top of the wall, like a gargoyle, waiting for someone to come by and replace the ladder.

Pouring rain, muddy boots, and slick ladder rungs added a touch of whimsy to our mission. The climb was annoying, nothing more. It was the descent that I worried about. Because one of the ladders was significantly shorter than the wall, there was always an uneasy moment when you rested your chest on the wall and blindly felt around with your leg for the top rung of the other ladder. After a while, it wasn't funny, but downright cartoonish. Like some animated villain, I slid clear down the ladder on two occasions. On one particularly magical evening, I not only slid down the ladder but also managed to pull it down on top of me. And where did I land? In the mud, where else?

Unfortunately, unlike in the cartoons, no coyote ever grabbed TNT and blasted a hole in that damn wall.

The only people who didn't gripe about the weather, or the crude conditions, were the fresh-faced soldiers from the Stryker Battalion (1-23 Infantry Battalion). Shortly before the start of Ivy Blizzard, this newly equipped and untested battalion, which was part of 2nd Infantry Division's 3rd Brigade from Fort Lewis, Washington, arrived in our part of Iraq with the army's latest eight-wheeled "Stryker" vehicles. They were the first in a wave of replacements expected to relieve units that were nearing the end of their one-year tours.

Because the Stryker battalion was new to Iraq, not to mention war in general, the 4th Infantry Division decided that these green soldiers would first train alongside 1-8 in Balad. There, the Strykers would learn the area of operations before having to assume total control of Balad when 1-8 decamped to Samarra to lead Ivy Blizzard. Then, when 1-8 returned to Balad, the Stryker battalion would move north to Mosul. Although the majority of the Stryker Battalion remained in Balad during Ivy Blizzard, one Stryker company did travel to Samarra to assist 1-8. In the days preceding Ivy Blizzard's kick-off on December 17, several soldiers from the Stryker battalion also found time to stop by the TAC, where I worked.

"Excuse me, ma'am, we're here to get our wills done. Can you help us?"

I looked up to discover two soldiers from the Stryker battalion standing in front of me.

"Sure, guys, but one question: why did you guys wait so long?" Prior to deploying, soldiers are repeatedly hounded to get their wills and personal affairs in order.

The taller of the two soldiers replied, "Well, ma'am, I was pretty busy before I deployed, and I got here and, well, I realized that anything can happen."

I nodded, fully aware of the incident that had spooked him. Earlier that week, three soldiers from their brigade had died when one of their Stryker vehicles overturned in an irrigation canal near Ad Duluyiah, just outside Balad. They probably were not comforted to learn that Camp Brassfield-Mora had been renamed after two 1-66 soldiers, Specialists Artimus Brassfield and Jose Mora, who were killed in separate mortar attacks just two months earlier. When the second soldier asked what Samarra was like, I did my best to lighten the mood.

Within weeks, another base in our area would also be renamed.

Lying on my cot later that evening, I overheard someone say that we might catch Saddam tonight. I didn't think much of it until the rumor surfaced again the following morning. Hours later, I joined dozens of soldiers in a hangar to watch the televised press conference announcing that Saddam had been captured.

Operation Ivy Blizzard began on the evening of December 17, 2003, four days after a special operations team, backed up by the division's 1st Brigade soldiers, pulled a shaggy-headed, unshaven Saddam from his "spider hole." By day two of the operation, dozens of insurgents had been captured or killed, and Ivy Blizzard was being hailed as a success.

Although the operation was criticized for lacking any element of surprise, it was a bona fide victory from a JAG perspective. It was the first time we had a detention plan in place *before* an operation began. Not only was 1-66 assigned to oversee a detention facility at Brassfield-Mora, but trained soldiers were assigned, and equipped, to run the facility. This may sound like small potatoes, but it reflected a major shift in the commanders' understanding of the role legal issues play in combat operations.

Prior to Ivy Blizzard, detainment procedures were almost never discussed at the operations briefings. During our first few months, operations orders always ended with "capture high-value targets." In the days leading up to our first "snatch and grab" mission in Samarra, commanders and their planning staffs had maintained a "we'll cross that bridge when we come to it" approach to what happened *after* we successfully captured someone. As the brigade JAG, it was my job to remind them that we would reach that point much faster than they realized.

So just hours before we captured our first insurgent, I was still scrambling for a place to put him. Geneva Convention guidelines call for adequate shelter. That evening, back in April, my best option had been some arctic tents we had brought from Fort Carson. Without an order from Rudesheim, no soldier was going to give up any extra tent, poncho, or spare anything else under which we could house the detainees.

That's the thing about legal landmines: they aren't always obvious, and their implications are cleverly concealed. A commander may agree that the spirit of the Geneva Conventions applies, but enforcing, or even explaining, that order is another matter. Harping on these issues at the start of an operation does little good, often labeling yourself as a busybody. *Captain, we haven't even caught these guys yet and you want me to worry about where we are going to put them?* But the dilemma remains that if you wait until it's on your commander's radar, you'll have twenty Iraqis corralled in a dirt pit, surrounded with barb wire, in the blazing sun, a plain violation of the Geneva Convention guidelines.

In my effort to avoid such a nightmare, early on in our deployment I strove to make things as straightforward as possible by establishing detainment standard operating procedures, so that there would be no confusion about how to treat detainees. Give soldiers clear guidelines and you give them a chance to do the right thing. Detainees must have a place to lie down. Detainees must have a place where they can wash their hands. Detainees must have appropriate shelter. Detainees must be allowed to worship.

Some of these sound obvious, but it was our job to have them on the record. As the JAG, I was protecting the detainees, but, equally important, I also was trying to protect my commanders from allegations of human-rights abuses and other things that could impair our rebuilding efforts in Iraq. Getting these

119

detainment procedures out to the battalions in those early days was one of our efforts to deactivate a legal landmine.

In Samarra, the natives were restless. Lieutenant Colonel Gonsalves alerted me to the fact that his soldiers had been so busy trying to control the city that civilian claims had fallen by the wayside. Gonsalves was acutely aware of the importance of claims, and I was impressed by his diligent reminders that claims help was desperately needed. As bad as the backlog of claims was, it was the locals' anger and resentment, built up over months of neglect, that we dreaded most.

On a previous trip to Samarra, an elderly Iraqi man claiming damage to his front door and driveway shook with rage as he told us how American soldiers had treated his house like garbage. It was the old man's entourage, however, that had really concerned me. Two younger, well-dressed men, presumably relatives, flanked the old man, and a contingent of four more men stepped forward from the rear of the crowded room. Whom had we offended now?

My nineteen-year-old translator turned to me and said, very seriously, "Captain, this is an important family, they're not lying. You should pay him." The translator's tone suggested I would be making a big mistake to anger this man further. I'm no fool, so I paid him instantly, but I'm not sure it made much difference, as versions of that same angry scene repeated themselves throughout that claims day. Would his anger infect his family? His neighbors? How deep did his anger run? Was he so angry that he wanted revenge, or would support killing us?

Shortly after the eager Sergeant Philibert had arrived in Iraq, Kolb, Carter, and I persuaded Phil that claims day was hands-down his best opportunity to meet the locals. When Phil cheerfully informed us that he had a great time on his first claims day, we were highly suspicious. *You enjoyed doing claims? In Samarra?*

Sergeant Phil was nothing short of a claims savant. He had just the right personality for claims. Always easy and breezy, never in a hurry, he rarely tired of the back and forth with Iraqis. Phil's short attention span also came in handy, enabling him to move from person to person at a nice clip. He didn't feel too guilty about the old lady with a limp, nor did he waste too much time on the family with young children. When he suspected a claim was fraudulent, Phil sparred confidently and cheerfully. No hard feelings. I just think you're lying. Next.

Philibert, we discovered, also never forgot a face. When he noticed several guys turning up at claims days in different cities, he just waved them off. Nice try, guys.

So, while Carter still processed the claims at the JAG workspace at Anaconda, Phil would handle the frontlines.

As Operation Blizzard wore on, soldiers from 1-8 were increasingly interested in their departure date from Samarra. With no clear answer, it fueled 1-8's growing resentment of 1-66, whose soldiers largely remained at Brassfield-Mora running the detention operation while 1-8 handled the bulk of combat patrols. This situation revived earlier perceptions that division commanders routinely dealt the Fort Carson-based 3rd Brigade the short hand and favored with plum assignments the units that division had brought with them from Fort Hood. Although many 3rd Brigade soldiers felt stung by the real or imagined inequity of the operation's division of labor, this sense of injustice was felt most deeply by 1-8's soldiers. In conversations with 1-8's company commanders, staff, and soldiers, many of whom I knew from the Cobb trial, some were quick to share their poor opinion of 1-66, characterizing 1-66 as a bunch of "pansies," or cowards waiting for 1-8 to do the dangerous work.

Just when we had reached the point when the operation was winding down, we learned that 1-8 would remain in Samarra for several more weeks. Even I began to wonder whether there was truth to the rumor that 1-66 was incapable of securing the city.

I returned to Anaconda on December 21. Brigade headquarters was eerily quiet and empty, with a large number of soldiers home on two-week leave and the remainder still at Brassfield-Mora for Ivy Blizzard. Carter had already left for his two-week leave. Over the next four days I bid farewell to Brian Gebhardt, Jay Arthurs, and Sergeant Kolb, each of whom was giddy about being able to enjoy the holidays at home.

Carter's absence was particularly demoralizing. After nine months of living and working together, I had come to depend on him both at work and as a friend. Mendoza sang Carter's praises as a mentor while Mendoza brought me up to speed at the JAG workspace.

Drowning In The Desert

On Christmas Eve, the skeletal headquarters staff and I mourned the death of three civil affairs soldiers who were killed when an IED detonated beneath their Humvee as they traveled south on Highway One near Samarra. Tragedies like this, combined with the separation from Mike and my family and the burnout from eight months' work without a real day off, had me down. I couldn't bear to listen to Christmas music in the chow hall or the ALOC.

Christmas Day was quiet, with little foot traffic through brigade headquarters. Mendoza and I manned the desk and shared a late dinner at the chow hall where he entertained me with stories about his favorite pastime: racing modified Hondas along deserted stretches of California highway.

That night I fell asleep to the depressing sound of Christmas carols playing on someone's stereo in the distance.

Several days later, Dave finally called to give me the bad news: Datray had rejected my plea offer and wanted to go to trial. It was my twenty-eighth birthday, and the end of my eighth month in Iraq. This was the start of what I had hoped would be the quiet homestretch. It took all of the restraint in the world not to explode when Dave said, "That shouldn't be a problem, right?"

Datray's rejection of the plea offer unleashed a tidal wave of logistical problems. Where were Amar and Murtdadah these days? Previously, I had relied on Tina, 1-8's translator, to call Amar's uncle, his only relative who owned a phone. With 1-8 still in Samarra, I wouldn't be so lucky this time. November's violence also heightened my concerns about security. Already depressed, the logistical nightmare reduced me to the lowest point of my tour.

The next day, December 29, Philibert called from Samarra to apologize for missing my birthday. "I know how hard you've been working," he said.

Touched, I shared the bad news about the plea agreement falling through. The conversation marked the beginning of a smoother working relationship between us.

I ushered in 2004 with a plastic cup of sparkling, nonalcoholic apple cider at the JAG workspace, resigned to the fact that the next month would be consumed by trial preparations. With this enormous task before me, I paid scant attention to the latter phases of Operation Ivy Blizzard, which was poised to unleash a chain of events that would cost lives and take down several careers in the process.

CHAPTER NINE

Soft Spot

A BOOM JOLTED ME FROM MY sleep.

Everything shook. My cot, the ground, the walls. In the dark, I reached for my Kevlar, which was vibrating under my cot, and grabbed my vest from the hook it was shaking on. Throwing my Kevlar on my head, I started to secure my vest when: BOOM.

The sound of the second mortar round exploding thundered in my ears. Damn. This one was close. And loud. So damned loud. But strangely I felt as though I were in a silent movie. I couldn't hear the scratch of the Velcro as I secured my vest. The dull hum penetrated the earth and filled my ears with ringing.

Somewhere on Anaconda, field artillery folks were scrambling to determine the mortars' point of origin so that we could prepare a counterattack. My body, every nerve ending, was in a state of high alert, primed for action. There is, however, little you can do when you're being shelled. If it had happened while I was outside, as it had in the past, I would just run for cover. Now, all I could do was wait. Another one might be coming. Or not. Just sit in the dark and wait.

When we first arrived at Anaconda, many of us were still living in tents. I, of course, lived in my deluxe trailer-hooch with the canvas top. When the mortars would impact, we'd see dozens of soldiers scrambling out of tents to hurl themselves against the large, empty storage trailer that had carried much of the brigade's supplies. I guess they figured they'd be shielded on at least one side.

The moments afterwards are actually the worst. Nothing to do but wait some more, and speculate. Will the enemy reload? How long will it take them? Hopefully, their aim hasn't improved. There was nothing like a mortar attack to remind you that you weren't safe anywhere in this country.

A stack of Christmas and birthday gifts sat unopened near my cot. I'd lied and said there had been delays when my friends and family e-mailed to ask whether I had received their packages. I was in no mood for the rollercoaster of emotions that a loved one's thoughtfulness would provoke. I had reached the point, I realized, where I missed Mike and my family so much that it was just easier not to call. They would only worry more if I lost it on the phone.

The Christmas Eve deaths of the three civil affairs soldiers and the previous month's record number of U.S. fatalities had me more concerned than ever about the logistics of a second trial. As painful as the first trial had been, the steps I'd taken to minimize the risk to my guys and others had paid off. The mortars made me doubt we would be so lucky the second time around.

New Year's Day, with all its promise and hope, felt ripe for an attack. It seemed only polite not to travel on New Year's Day. If something happened to me, I didn't want the start of each year to be tainted for my family. So I waited until January 2 to head to the division JAG office in Tikrit where I spent the day getting a large chunk of Datray's court-martial paperwork reviewed, signed, and copied. I also dropped off a bunch of legal papers that needed to be hand-delivered.

Because I planned to have Cobb testify at Datray's trial, I needed to get an immunity order and get in touch with Captain Campion, Cobb's lawyer, who had returned to Kuwait. Taking advantage of division's ample resources, including a scanner and Xerox machine, I was able to knock out a bunch of administrative work that would have taken me days at Anaconda. With the Datray trial now scheduled for January 21, I wanted to get ahead of the curve.

I hitched a ride back to Anaconda in an armored Humvee. The fact that the three civil affairs officers had been killed on this same route only a week earlier dominated my thoughts. Technically, my chances of surviving were probably just as good in my own hajji-armored Humvee, but traveling Highway One in a real armored convoy also meant one less thing in common with the Christmas Eve casualties. I didn't know the soldiers personally, but I did know that their unit, the 5th Engineer Battalion, had a multifaceted mission and a reputation for getting things done, despite limited resources and personnel. I also knew their names: Maj. Christopher Splinter, Capt. Christopher Soelzer, and Sgt. Benjamin Biskie. They were just out doing their jobs that morning, likely traveling from one meeting to another, working out another rebuilding project.

Twenty minutes outside of Tikrit, we encountered a line of vehicles at a near-standstill. Our Humvee inched forward in short spurts. The sergeant in the passenger seat in front of me shifted nervously in his seat, checking his side mirror repeatedly. The sergeant's unease fueled the driver's unease.

When traffic started moving again, the driver kept both hands on the wheel until Balad's water tower finally came into view. Approaching the exit for Anaconda, the traffic began to clear and the radio crackled with activity. The driver turned up the volume, though it was impossible for me, in the backseat, to decipher what was being said. I was distracted by a group of peddlers running toward our convoy. They had appeared out of nowhere.

"Wait, what?" the driver asked excitedly, as he tried to follow the radio chatter and negotiate the unruly intersection. Waving an assortment of bayonets for sale, the Iraqi peddlers had nearly reached our convoy when we pulled off.

"Sounds like they said mortars impacting," replied the sergeant in front of me. The driver turned up the volume again. I could finally make out the frantic chatter for myself. It did not sound good.

"They're calling for medevac," the driver exclaimed, confirming what we already heard. The transmissions were brief, and the information minimal, but the anxiety-ridden voices and halted manner of the soldiers' speech, as they struggled to put words together, suggested serious trouble on the ground, somewhere.

Pulling through the gates at Anaconda, the radio chatter spiked again, but static interference from the airfield radar systems made it harder to follow. Still unclear where the mortars were impacting, I leaned forward hoping to catch the name of a base or landmark.

Drowning In The Desert

The sergeant caught it first. "It's at FOB Eagle," he said sternly before turning the volume down to a low murmur.

"Wait, how many hurt?" I asked, now leaning forward between their two seats, ignoring his attempt to return our focus to the road.

"I don't know, ma'am," the young driver said, his voice echoing my own desire to turn the volume back up.

"Sounds like one man down and some injured," replied the sergeant curtly. Deflated by the news, I sat back and tried to focus my attention on the road. Seconds later, I started praying for 1-23 Infantry. *God, please help them fire back.*

Outside brigade headquarters, small groups of workers from Nepal, India, and the Philippines were gathering for an end-of-the-day briefing. They shuffled slowly to the sides of the gravel road as our convoy approached, exhausted after a long day assembling aluminum trailers. The aluminum trailers were the latest improvement to soldiers' living conditions across Iraq. Welsch oversaw the foreign workers and the construction of our trailer village, neat rows of trailers about 100 yards away from brigade headquarters. He also oversaw the pool of foreign workers who had been brought in. Increased concerns about security meant we were relying less on Iraqis for work within Anaconda's perimeter.

Those of us living inside the brigade headquarters building were scheduled to move immediately. Go figure. After being evicted from my wagon trailer just two months earlier, I was again being forced to move. Back into a trailer. Only Welsch, Rudesheim, and our brigade command sergeant major would remain inside the headquarters building.

At this point in our deployment, soldiers' desire for more space had drowned out many of their initial concerns about the flimsy construction of the trailers. Most units surrounded the trailers with sandbags and concrete barricades to fortify them. At Camp Eagle, there had been significant resistance to the "tin coffins," which sat unopened for weeks. Eventually, 1-8 gave soldiers permission to move into the trailers, but not before Captain Paliwoda's engineers had created berms around the entire trailer enclave. Although these efforts were significant, there was little that could be done about the trailer's roofs. Too weak to sustain the weight of sandbags, the roofs were particularly vulnerable.

Had I not been so distracted by the prospect of having to move before Datray's trial, I probably would have noticed how quiet the headquarters building was when I returned. There were no soldiers mingling in the lobby, and the JAG workspace was conspicuously vacant. It wasn't until I saw Carter standing with a crowd that had gathered in the TOC that my heart started racing.

"Hey, ma'am," Carter said when he saw me. Ushering me to the side, he leaned in close and whispered, "Did you hear? Eagle was hit by mortars."

I nodded, ashamed that I had forgotten about the attack so quickly.

"They called for medevac, ma'am. Captain Paliwoda was hit by a mortar." Carter paused before adding, "He died, ma'am."

"No, that's wrong. 1-23 Infantry is at Camp Eagle now," I said. "The engineers are with 1-8 in Samarra."

"No, ma'am, the engineers were at Eagle," Carter said, shaking his head.

While 1-8 had moved to Samarra to kick off Ivy Blizzard, Paliwoda's company of engineers had relocated to Camp Eagle to help 1-23 Infantry until 1-8 returned.

Despite this realization, I still could not wrap my mind around the news. I had just seen Eric the day before at a change-of-command ceremony for another captain. I stood right next to him as a bunch of us chit-chatted afterwards.

Captain Eric Paliwoda, commander of Bravo Company, 4th Engineer Battalion, was dead. Eric, the gentle giant who had joked that wearing his armored vest constantly was a great way to lose weight. I could still see him slapping his stomach and saying he didn't want to go home fat.

The balmy morning I'd spent with him and Sassaman came to my mind. As dark and as cynical as I could sometimes be about the army, I felt nothing but pride and hope for its future that day. As I left, I felt strangely satisfied that a leader of Eric's caliber had chosen to make the army a career, that someone good was staying in. Every life is valuable, but it was especially hard to lose someone who was so alive, so good at what he did.

A combat engineer and West Pointer, Eric was a bona fide member of the huddle, who went out of his way to be approachable. Operations briefings could be intimidating, filled with jargon and acronyms, and mired in protocol. One foolish question or misstep could forever mark you as the village idiot. The briefings could be so intimidating that many attendees were content to simply understand their own tiny piece of the puzzle and forgo the hassle of trying to understand the big picture. Eric had made copies of the maps and slides used during these briefings available to me so that I could decipher them in private. All of my guys thought Eric was a great guy, and that spoke volumes.

Eric and his fiancé had planned to marry shortly after we redeployed to the states. Their wedding was scheduled for May 28, exactly one month before the original date of my own wedding.

Eric, the sort of leader the army could never have enough of, was dead. It felt like the world had just punched me in the gut.

The irony of Eric's death was thick. After all of his efforts to secure Camp Eagle, Eric had been killed standing outside one of the trailers he had built berms around. It was one of the few times he was seen without his vest. Shrapnel struck him in the back the moment he had stepped out of his trailer. Medics pronounced him dead on arrival at the field hospital fifteen minutes later.

Eric's memorial service was held five days later in a hangar on Anaconda. For reasons I couldn't fully articulate at the time, it felt like no other memorial service I'd ever attended. Beyond the layers of immense sadness, loss, and regret, there was something strangely charged about the air in that hangar.

The turnout was massive and included the division and 3rd Brigade's top brass, large contingents of soldiers from the three battalions Eric had worked with, friends from the brigade headquarters company, and his fellow West Pointers. Tucking myself into a seat next to Capt. Emma Toops, I listened to the speakers struggle to articulate the uncommon decency that made Eric one of the best of the best.

I cried openly, as did many of the soldiers around me. I tried to push from my mind thoughts of Eric's grieving parents and his fiancée. Our own loss was so great, I couldn't begin to comprehend the magnitude of their grief.

The memorial service program had been carefully thought out, with the requisite speakers scheduled in order of descending rank. Scanning the program, I saw that two of Eric's lieutenants were scheduled to sing.

The typically unflappable Sassaman looked dazed as he delivered his remarks. He spoke to us through a fog of stunned disbelief. Watching him speak, my mind drifted back to the day that had felt so filled with promise. The mutual respect and admiration between the two commanders, both former West Point athletes, had been apparent. Eric had walked out to meet us in his usual unassuming manner, and I remembered Sassaman patting Eric on the back several times during our short exchange. That warm, amber morning felt like another lifetime.

Today, with haunted eyes, Sassaman echoed his earlier words about Eric's tremendous contribution to 1-8's mission. Sassaman looked as though he had woken up in his worst nightmare. His voice fell flat at times, and his eyes widened every few minutes, freshly jolted to the reality that he had lost one of his most cherished soldiers.

Lieutenants Tim Hudson and Ryan Larson, both staff officers who served in Paliwoda's company, finally stood near the end of the ceremony. The two young lieutenants had been several feet away from Eric when he was hit. Both had escaped with minor bruises. When they approached the podium, it was impossible to ignore Larson's massive black eye. Unable to tear my eyes from the purplish gradations of the bruise, I felt nervous that the lieutenants might have overpromised with their offer to sing a tribute. After watching their commander die and barely escaping death themselves, I wondered, would they be able to get through this?

I needn't have worried. Hudson and Larson's voices were beautiful and strong. They had decided, at least for this moment, to be strengthened with purpose and not collapse with grief. The two soldiers clung stubbornly to the notes even as their eyes grew moist. It was a tragic and unforgettable image: the emotionally and physically battered lieutenants singing their hearts out for their fallen commander. Their tribute drew tears from an audience that thought it had none left.

It wasn't until afterward that I realized exactly what felt off about the service. In the hangar that day, we were devastated, toppled by the loss of a dear friend and remarkable soldier. We were not, however, united in our grief. The memorial service had a distinct undercurrent of tension. It stemmed from the belief that Eric's death could have been prevented, that had 1-8 returned to Balad before the day of the attack, the insurgents would not have grown so bold. There was talk of hostility between 1-66 and 1-8, specifically over 1-66's failure to secure Samarra. Others said that 1-8 blamed Eric's death on the 1-23's ineptitude in responding to the mortar attacks that preceded the one that killed him.

If anyone was to blame for the tragedy, it wasn't 1-8. And Sassaman was not the type to stand aside while some inept replacement unit responded to the attack. No, Sassaman's boys would restore order to Balad and mete out justice to the enemy.

Change was pervasive throughout the brigade in January. With the trailer village outside the brigade headquarters building complete, everyone began moving. Kolb, just back from leave, Carter, Philibert, and Mendoza wasted no time. Overhead lights, electrical outlets, and air conditioning units were pure luxury after the many months they had spent sharing one room, and one fan, with six other soldiers. With only three soldiers permitted in each trailer, Kolb, Carter, and Phil occupied one, and Mendoza shared a trailer nearby. Nevertheless, I could usually find all four of them together after dinner, watching a bootleg DVD of their favorite movie, *Finding Nemo*.

I also moved into one of the trailers for what I hoped would be my last move. My new roommate was Capt. Hartleigh Caine, an Apache helicopter pilot recently attached to the brigade as our aviation liaison officer. Hartleigh was an easygoing West Point grad with white blonde hair and a passion for flying. She lamented that her new responsibilities with the brigade kept her on the ground more than she liked. Good-natured and considerate, Hartleigh was an ideal roommate.

It wasn't until mid-January that I got around to calling my parents. Poor cell phone reception on their end cut the conversation short. Hanging up, I dialed my sister instead. She would later recall our conversation as the most bizarre one of my deployment, and a clear sign that I was depressed and had been in Iraq too long.

"Viv, you sound irritated. Is everything alright?"

"Oh, I am just so annoyed with the medics."

"The medics?" she asked. "The folks who tend to the injured?"

"Yeah, they just bug," I said stubbornly.

"You mean the doctors, nurses, paramedics? Those folks?" she asked, racking her brain for some alternate definition.

"Yeah."

"Did one of them say something to you? Did you have a disagreement or something?" she asked, bewildered.

"No, just let me talk, okay? I just can't stand them right now," I said. "They're always so emotional, always crying about something," I said. "I can't deal with all of their constant crying and carrying on. For God's sake, I wish they would just be quiet, get on with it."

"You don't like their crying? You think they're too emotional?" she repeated, as though she were speaking another language.

"Yeah, exactly."

She was silent on the other end, clearly unsure how to respond. Finally, tentatively, "Viv, did something happen? You don't sound like yourself."

"Deb, I told you nothing happened. I'm fine," I said grouchily. "Everything's fine."

"So, it's just the medics?"

"Yeah."

"Okay," she said, her voice smaller, and more distant, than ever.

CHAPTER TEN

Surfacing

"YOU'VE GOT TO BE KIDDING me!" I exclaimed.

"I swear, they were lining the streets, waving flags, the whole nine," Carter said, his face glowing like a jack-o-lantern.

I shot him a look of disbelief. Over dinner in the chow hall, Carter was giving me the play-by-play of his two-week leave in the states.

"It's true. It's true," he insisted. "Complete strangers turned up to welcome me home."

"Actually, the whole town turned out to welcome me home," he corrected himself. Recalling the scene, Carter broke into a smile that softened every inch of his angular face.

"They were there for you? How did they know?" I asked, barely able to conceal my glee.

"I guess word got around or something. My mom kept telling me to call when I was close, but I just had no idea," he said, shaking his head.

"How did you know they were there for *you*?" I asked indulgently.

"At first, I wasn't sure they were there for me," Carter said, savoring the nuances. "But then," he paused for effect, "I saw this lady on the side of the road holding a sign with my name on it."

"What? That's crazy!" Even in its second iteration, the details of Carter's triumphant return to Wisconsin still satisfied. Just imagining the bewildered look on Carter's face as he drove by in his meticulously neat, dark green Saturn two-door made my day.

While Carter had been back for two weeks already, things had been so hectic that we were only now catching up. Since Paliwoda's memorial ceremony, I had added about fifteen more issues to my priority task list, so Carter, Mendoza, and I had been working around the clock to stay on top of things. Plus, Carter wanted to tell me about his trip properly, in one long sitting without interruptions from the phone or other soldiers. Now, I understood why. His small town in Wisconsin had given him a hero's welcome home, the kind of patriotic display you read about in World War II books but could never imagine happening today.

"Ma'am, at the airport, when we got in, people just started clapping. They saw our uniforms, just these DCUs [Desert Combat Uniforms]," he said, tapping at the blouse of his uniform, "and broke out." Sitting up straight, Carter began clapping and struggled to imitate the serious faces of the strangers in the airport. Not even knowing, I thought, how brave this twenty-one-year-old really was. If anyone deserved that sort of greeting, it was Carter.

I felt a lump of emotion rise in the back of my throat. "Well then, what did you do?" I asked roughly, coughing to try and clear my voice. I looked down at my lap, pretending to fuss with my napkin, as I waited for the lump to go away. Hell, why was I tearing up?

"I said 'Thank you,' and just kept nodding at everyone." Eager to spare both of us the discomfort of my now welling eyes, Carter deftly steered the conversation toward a topic guaranteed to elicit a fiery response.

"So, ma'am, I stopped by the office at Carson," Carter tossed out enticingly, just before taking a bite of the dinner he had neglected during our two-hour catch-up session.

The mere mention of Fort Carson was enough to suck all of the moisture from my eyes. *Don't worry, there won't be much legal work in Iraq*, they had said. *You won't need a full staff*. I caught myself before I slid too deep into this familiar rant. This was about Carter's trip home.

"Well, how did it go? How were people at the office?" I asked.

Carter pressed his lips into a thin smile.

SOUTHERN IRAQ—The original JAG section of the 3rd Brigade Combat Team (left to right): me, Sgt. Michael Kolb (seated), Spec. Benjamin Carter, and Sgt. Michael Simester next to our soft-skin Humvee en route to Baghdad in April 2003. Unarmored vehicles like ours forced soldiers to be resourceful. The team constructed a plywood roof for the vehicle and added two doors, just days before we began our drive from Kuwait into Iraq. Simester returned to Colorado two months later due to a family medical emergency. He was later replaced by Sgt. Jonathan Philibert.

LSA ANACONDA, IRAQ—The team and I posed for this photo outside of brigade headquarters shortly after adding what was known as "hillbilly" or "hajji" armor to the Humvee. Locals retrofitted the Humvee with pale green armored doors and armor plates for the bottom of the vehicle. (Left to Right: Sgt. Jonathan Philibert, Spec. Benjamin Carter, me, Spec. Kissthopher Mendoza, and Staff Sgt. Michael Kolb.)

Near KIRKUK, IRAQ—The JAG team's "hooch," or living area, in June 2003 was comprised of an arctic tent and my equipment trailer against the wall. Soldiers nicknamed this camp "Andersonville," comparing our squalid living conditions to the infamous Civil War POW camp. Daytime temperatures on Andersonville's blacktop surface often reached the mid-130s degrees Fahrenheit. "Flushing the toilet" involved climbing a ladder to hurl your bag of human waste into a burn pit on the opposite side of the wall.

SAMARRA, IRAQ—Catching up with Captain Noel Pace at the JAG workspace, inside the Tactical Operations Center tent, in early June of 2003. Pace, the brigade's preventative medicine officer, developed one of the more memorable cases of short-timer's syndrome before he left Iraq.

BALAD, IRAQ—Talking with Iraqi judges following a meeting at Balad's courthouse.

Near JALULAH, IRAQ—Making final changes to the disarmament agreement between the U.S. and the Mujahedin-el-Khalq (MEK), outside of the MEK's headquarters. The MEK is an Iranian resistance group that opposes Iran's Islamic regime. The Division JAG, Lt. Col. Flora Darpino, tapped me to assist 4th Infantry Division commander, Maj. Gen. Raymond Odierno, with negotiations after the first day ended in a stalemate.—Getty Images

FORT BRAGG, NORTH CAROLINA—My father, Lt. Col. Andrew Gembara (center), discussing special forces team deployments to Liberia and Lebanon, with Major Mike Simpson
(left) and Col. George McGovern (right), Commander of the 5th Special Forces Group, at Ft.
Bragg, North Carolina, circa 1979. From the flak jackets he suggested we line the bottom of
our vehicle with, to the extra cash he recommended I have available to pay local informants,
my father's sage advice was invaluable during my deployment.

BALAD, IRAQ—Returning with Thanna Azawi and Amar Hussan to the spot where he escaped
Privates Jason Datray and Thomas Cobb by running into the nearby orchard. Iraq's treacherous
environment made securing a crime scene and gathering evidence extremely difficult.

LSA ANACONDA, IRAQ—Judge Colonel Stephen Henley takes notes as I question Amar Hussan during United States v. Thomas Cobb, the first court-martial of a U.S. soldier held in Iraq. With little precedent and no venue, my team helped construct the one-room building shown here just a week earlier. The trial, which took place during Ramadan, had an additional complication: my two Iraqi witnesses were cranky from fasting. (Left to right: author, Henley, Hussan, and Capt. Magda Prystulska.)

TIKRIT, IRAQ—This bridge over the Tigris River was the main route to reach Division Headquarters in Tikrit. It was bombed by the U.S. prior to the March 2003 invasion to impede the movement of Iraqi forces. Sgt. Kolb and I had to travel this route each time we visited division headquarters. U.S. forces repaired the bridge within the next few months.

BAGHDAD, IRAQ—With Capt. Thomas Roughneen at the Coalition Provisional Authority's headquarters after attending a Ministry of Justice meeting. The palatial setting, along with the mandatory weapons check at the compound entrance, confirmed my suspicion that a serious disconnect existed between soldiers in the Sunni Triangle and decision makers in Baghdad.

SAMARRA, IRAQ—Army investigators and I visit the site of Zaidoun Fadhil's drowning in Samarra. Here, I am indicating the spot where 1-8 soldiers forced Zaidoun into the Tigris River after Zaidoun pleaded for the soldiers to spare him. The dam, just past the platform, was open the night of the incident, creating a strong undertow in the water, an additional obstacle for a non-swimmer like Zaidoun.

BALAD, IRAQ—Spec. Carter (left) and Sgt. Philibert (center) meet with Balad's Chief of Police after paying claims to locals whose property was inadvertently damaged by U.S. forces.

BALAD, IRAQ—The first of several meetings between 1-8 commanders, the Christian Peacemakers Team, and local Iraqi lawyers. The Peacemakers arranged the meetings in hopes of facilitating more dialogue between 1-8 and local lawyers hired by Iraqi families seeking to end aggressive tactics by U.S. soldiers and to obtain information regarding detained family members. (Left to right: Capt. Matthew Cunningham (A Company commander); Lt. Col. Nathan Sassaman (1-8 Battalion commander); Sassaman's translator, Thanna Azawi; me; two Iraqi lawyers; and Stewart Vriesinga (Peacemakers).)

IRAQ—Lt. Col. Paul Welsch, 3rd Brigade's executive officer, shaking hands with Staff Sgt. Michael Kolb at Kolb's promotion ceremony during the first weeks of our deployment.

IRAQ—This seven feet by four feet canvas-covered equipment trailer was my home for several months of our deployment. Too low for me to stand up in, I grew accustomed to squatting. When I later moved into a cubby in the "female space" added to the brigade headquarters building, I relished being able to stand upright.

Remembering back, even the farewell party the office arranged before we left had been a debacle. Arriving late from a mandatory briefing, I found only the judge recounting her courtroom adventures for several eager captains. "Where are my guys?" I asked. *You know, the people you were supposedly throwing this party for.* Blank stares all around. No one even knew whether Carter or Kolb had shown up. I later learned from the guys that they had, in fact, shown up but felt so uncomfortable that they ate a slice of pizza and split. Not a single goodbye from any of the senior JAGs, to either of them.

"So, how were they?" I demanded, tiring of the suspense.

"All of them came out to say hello," Carter said, his surprise apparent even weeks later. Even the Staff Judge Advocate, Fort Carson's highest ranking JAG, made a point of coming over and slapping Carter on the back.

"Ma'am, I told them how hard we're working, what a great job we're doing out here. They kept saying they had heard good stuff. It was pretty cool," he said excitedly. "I wasn't planning on stopping in, especially after they didn't send us a new battery for the camera."

Unsure what to say, I simply nodded and waited for him to continue.

"Oh, and one another thing, I asked if they had switched over to a four-day work week, like you said."

"Wait. You what? What do you mean? Carter, I was just joking, I didn't mean they had *really* gone to a four-day week," I sputtered, envisioning the scathing fallout. Things were bad enough as it was. How the hell would I mend this fence?

Across the table, Carter finished up the last of his water.

"Gotcha," he exclaimed, slamming his glass down on the table as he exploded into laughter. "You should see your face! I totally had you!" Carter continued, slapping the table with his hands.

"Funny, Carter, really funny," I said, smiling. I felt foolish for doubting his judgment.

Carter had returned from his leave buoyant and purposeful. The adolescent neediness was gone. And so were the self-doubt and uncertainty. Around the JAG workspace, he was a coiled spring, eager to tackle my growing task list. Shoulders erect and jaw set firmly, he never flinched when I rattled off at least a dozen high-priority items. He had responded to each one with a confident nod that said, "Consider it done."

Drowning In The Desert

Looking up from my list one day, I saw an expression on Carter's face that I had never seen before. He was looking at me with concern. The boy-soldier, who had once wilted without my effusive praise, was now worried about how *I* was holding up, assessing my sallow complexion and the bags beneath my eyes. Even when I'd reached "claims" on the list and paused, reluctant to douse Carter's enthusiasm, he had surprised me. He reached over and picked up the tally sheet. Looking it over he said, "Forty-eight claims, eh?"

"Yeah," I confirmed.

"No problem, ma'am," he replied confidently, flashing a bright and reassuring smile.

Kolb had returned from his two-week break similarly revitalized.

"Ma'am, I'm planning on going to 4th Engineers and 3-29 next week, if that's okay with you," he stated. These were two of our outlying battalions.

"Sure, no problem," I replied, tempering my enthusiasm. The unit visits, which I had been reluctant to ask Kolb to handle, had turned into a project he really embraced. Intended as a way to give soldiers a chance to address unresolved personal legal issues (wills, power-of-attorney forms, family law), these unit visits were ideal for Kolb. He was a natural with soldiers. They felt comfortable enough to be candid with him and felt confident that he knew how to help them. I had received such great feedback after his first few unit visits, that I began tentatively suggesting a few more.

When Kolb said, "No problem," I was speechless. It grew from there. For me, this was an important lesson: sometimes the best way to motivate your soldiers is to just get out of their way and give them room to flourish. Soon, Kolb was coordinating with all of the units in the brigade. By the end of the week, the project had even earned a nickname: JAG-a-palooza. Our take on the famous traveling music festival.

Around the time of those initial house calls, Kolb had embarked on a fitness kick. Now, several months into it, he was at least thirty pounds lighter. His two-week leave and the positive responses he received on his new physique only affirmed his commitment to continue. As we worked beside him every day, however, we had not noticed his massive weight loss until he returned from leave. Months of hard work and discipline had transformed Kolb from a Pringles-hoarding softie into a hard-bodied health nut. Kolb not only wore the uniform better, he seemed more at ease with his role as the senior noncommissioned officer.

136

Somewhere, somehow, we had turned a corner. Carter and Kolb's renewed vigor flooded the days with a golden ease. Even my stubborn melancholy yielded to my team's buoyed spirits. We glided like old hands familiar with each other and the work.

I headed into my second trial with none of the tug or resistance of the first trial. The bitter, jagged months of discord were over. We forgot the outrage of the undermanned and under-equipped and embraced the abundance of survivors. We were pros now. No longer scolding and micromanaging, I smiled to myself often and enjoyed the contentment of being a part of something good. Make no mistake, the road was no smoother, we were just easier on it.

If anything, we were still putting out fires left and right. A slew of bizarre scenarios made me wonder if there was a full moon over Anaconda. There were several soldiers inquiring about the legal requirements for bringing home a dog. And there were the spooning soldiers: two men, one of whom was a senior NCO, who were now sharing a cot on a regular basis, to the chagrin of their third roommate. Then, there were the lieutenants. One bought alcohol for his entire platoon while the other embraced Islam, and announced that he could no longer participate in actions that could potentially harm his fellow Muslims. We would resolve one issue only to find two more waiting.

Then there was the matter of Pfc. Paul Lightfoot.* Lightfoot's problems began early in our deployment. As his squad finished searching a house one evening, an elderly Iraqi woman burst from the house and accused the soldiers of stealing from her. The soldiers denied the charge, but when the woman insisted, the squad leader had his soldiers empty their pockets to prove the point. It was then that cash in the exact amount the woman claimed was discovered on Lightfoot. The squad leader returned the money immediately, apologized profusely, and reported the matter to his chain of command.

Aware that he could soon be facing criminal charges, and desperate to leave Iraq, Lightfoot shot himself in the foot several days later. He claimed it was an accident. Lightfoot was immediately taken to a combat hospital outside of Baghdad to be treated. When I called to check on his status several days later, I learned that doctors had sent him home to the U.S. to heal. Up

* The soldier's name has been changed to protect his privacy. Unlike the other subjects of investigations identified in this book, the identity of this soldier has not been publicly disclosed by the army.

to my ears with other equally bizarre legal work and the trial, I notified the Carson JAG office about this turn of events and asked for their assistance.

After a bit of back and forth, the Carson JAG office begrudgingly agreed to handle Lightfoot stateside. Relieved to have at least one legal situation off my hands, I mailed them his case file and every scrap of paper and piece of evidence they would need to go forward. Like I said, there must have been a full moon over Anaconda.

Returning to our workspace one afternoon about a week before the Datray trial, I found a yellow Post-it note with the message, "Call division JAG ASAP!" waiting for me on my laptop. A second note attached to the computer screen warned, "Call them or they will call you!" Below that, Kolb had drawn a smiley face. Kolb did not leave me notes unless he was directed to, so I took this as a pretty bad sign.

Division's urgent matter concerned a group called the Christian Peace-makers Team, a peculiar group of human rights activists who traveled Iraq's deadly terrain in an unarmored civilian minibus. The Chicago-based group opposed the war, and all violence, and had the expressed goal of "reducing violence by getting in the way." Great.

According to the captain I reached at the division JAG office, the group was now in Balad and had some concerns about 1-8's detainee and arrest procedures.

"What are their concerns based on? Didn't they just get here?" I asked.

"They say they've been speaking to locals."

"Wonderful. What does this mean to me?" I asked bluntly.

He went on to inform me that I was required to attend a meeting that the group had scheduled with 1-8 and some local leaders in Balad. Naturally, the scheduled meeting was just two days away.

The second urgent issue involved a civilian claim from Samarra. A local family, the Hassouns, had alleged that soldiers from 1-8 drowned their son. CID investigators had been at Brassfield-Mora when the claims were made, so they handled the initial inquiry.

"So, the file is headed your way, though it looks like it may be a false claim."

"Alright," I said, putting a star by my notes as a reminder to be on the lookout for the file.

* * *

Several days later, Capt. John Taylor, a JAG from division, handed me the file.

"It's the drowning claim file," he explained, "from Samarra."

"Oh, okay." I perused the folder's contents. It was thicker than I had expected. Eager to return to the more pressing matter of Datray's trial, I set the claim file aside to read during the Battle Update Briefing that evening.

Captain Taylor and Specialist Weatherspoon had just arrived at Anaconda to help out with the trial, scheduled to begin the following morning. Weatherspoon would reprise his role as the court reporter, and Taylor would be taking Captain Prystulska's place as my assistant trial counsel. For Taylor, who was just transitioning into a trial counsel position, Datray's trial was a good chance to get his feet wet in the courtroom. When we discussed some of the differences between this trial and the Cobb trial, it was clear he had read the transcript closely.

At the BUB that evening, I collapsed into a seat near the back, wishing I could just take a nap. Welsch's didactic droning about redeployment procedures wasn't making things any easier. While Welsch detailed each unit's responsibilities, I thumbed through the drowning file.

In a written statement, an Iraqi mother claimed that U.S. soldiers had drowned her son, Zaidoun Fadel Hassoun, when they pushed him and his cousin, Marwan Fadel Hassoun, off a bridge into the Tigris River. She also claimed that the soldiers had destroyed the white truck her son was driving that night. Okay. Drowned son and destroyed vehicle.

The soldiers' statements about the night were short. They acknowledged stopping two Iraqi men who were out past curfew. After checking their identification cards and searching their truck, the soldiers decided that the two men didn't pose a threat. The men were released with a warning to stay off the roads after curfew. There were a few small discrepancies between the soldiers' statements, but nothing major.

The soldiers' accounts and the locals' accounts, however, were so dramatically different that I wondered if the Iraqis really were trying to make money with a fraudulent claim. We had seen a number of false claims, including one where an Iraqi family claimed soldiers stole $2 million during a routine raid. And I hadn't forgotten the old man who claimed Cobb and Datray had shot him in the arm, either.

Seeing no immediate red flags, I closed the file and replaced it on my lap with the trial checklist for tomorrow. Post-BUB, Taylor and I were meeting for dinner to discuss which witnesses he would handle. Looking at the list, I briefly considered giving him Murtdadah. *He did say that he wanted to jump right in.* I smiled and resisted the urge.

Yet another urgent message from division was waiting for me when I returned from dinner. "Call CID." I bid Taylor goodnight and picked up the phone, already dreading a long-winded discussion about the drowning claim. Instead, the problem was logistical. The agent from CID told me they were having trouble getting 1-8 commanders to make the soldiers involved in the alleged drowning available for additional interviews at division headquarters in Tikrit. Familiar with the struggle of logistical problems in an investigation, I assured her that I would give Major Gwinner a call myself. We had already navigated these rough waters for the Cobb and Datray investigation.

When I reached Gwinner, I was surprised by his resistance to the idea.

"They've already talked to them," he said. "Now I have to send another convoy of guys up there for another day?"

I acknowledged this was a hassle and murmured some sympathetic words about how annoying these investigations could be. I appealed to Gwinner's sense of expediency.

"Sir, this investigation will be closed a lot faster if you just send them up there, but it's up to you. You may want to just call them and coordinate," I said, using the gentlest, most "same team" tone I could muster. Beyond that, however, it was his call. Tikrit wasn't an easy trip, so I ultimately left it in their hands.

"They've already given their statements," Gwinner replied, his irritation crisp and clear even through the fuzz on the TAC phone.

CHAPTER ELEVEN

Odd Man Out

I SHOULD HAVE KNOWN THAT THE renaissance the JAG team was experiencing was all in preparation for something. I just assumed it was the trial. I could not have been more wrong.

The following day, I represented the army in *United States v. Datray*. In keeping with the newer, more streamlined course my life had taken, the trial went off without incident. I made a compelling case for loyalty and duty, and the "band of brothers" theme settled easily over the chapel. Lieutenant Colonel Sassaman reprised his role as my star witness, only this time the considerable threats facing 1-8 were underscored by an updated map featuring the freshly renamed Camp Paliwoda, formerly known as Eagle. Murtdadah and Amar testified confidently, buoyed by their experiences in the first trial.

Cobb also returned and testified, under immunity, against Datray. Cobb must have rued the day he had met the troublemaker Datray. Datray was just as smug and unrepentant at his own trial as he had been at Cobb's.

In stark contrast to Colonel Henley, the judge, Col. James Pohl, listened attentively to both the American and Iraqi witnesses, accepting the translation delay as the unavoidable reality of a trial in theater.

Several hours later, the verdict silenced the courtroom. Private Jason Datray was found guilty of AWOL, making a false official statement, stealing by force and with a firearm, and two counts of assault with a loaded firearm. Two hours after that, the court sentenced Datray to ten years' confinement and a dishonorable discharge.

Captain David Croswell did not extend his hand for the customary post-trial handshake.

The following morning, I was up much earlier than I had planned. Instead of sleeping in, I was watching the early morning light illuminate the edges of the trailer's window.

I did it.

This singular, rewarding thought had all but yanked me from deep sleep. *I did it.* Even in my head it sounded odd. My usual post-trial, self-critical dialogue was a weary, mildly relieved, "It's over." Today, however, was different.

I wasn't tired. I wasn't relieved. I felt the stirrings of something far more elusive. I felt proud of myself. Proud that I had delivered justice for the brigade, and especially for 1-8. Trying a case out here took monumental effort and careful strategy; nothing just "fell into place." There were a million points at which you could surrender to the extenuating circumstances.

The outcome was icing. Just knowing that I had done everything I could was the greatest satisfaction. It felt wonderful to do right by my fellow soldiers.

An hour later, Carter was banging on the door. "Captain G, sorry to bother you but CID just called," he shouted through the trailer door.

"Okay, Carter. Thanks. I'll be there in about twenty minutes." So much for luxuriating.

"Ma'am, she's on the phone," Kolb relayed as soon as he saw me. Seated behind the laptop, Kolb stretched the TAC phone line across the table and handed me the receiver.

"Hello, this is Captain Gembara." On the other end, CID Special Agent Irene Cintron introduced herself.

"Sorry to wake you, ma'am, but we've made some progress in the drowning investigation that I think you'll want to hear."

"Oh, no problem, really," I said, prying my vest open as quietly as I could. "Sorry to keep you waiting. What happened?" After a nine-month CID-drought, I welcomed any call from CID, even if it was 0700 the day after a trial. It took me a minute to recall the drowning claim.

"Well, ma'am, last night we questioned one of the soldiers again about what happened that night, and his story changed. Actually, it changed a lot. He told us that they did push the two Iraqis into the river."

A shiver went through me. This was no longer some off-the-wall claim.

Pulling the cord even further, I used my shoulder to pin the receiver against my ear as I flipped open my notebook. If our soldiers pushed people into a river . . .

"Did he say if the Iraqis were handcuffed when they pushed them in? Were their hands tied?" It was a sickening thought. What would make them do such a thing?

"No, ma'am. He said that they weren't handcuffed or anything. They just pushed them in. He also said that they saw the two Iraqis standing by the road when they pulled away."

"Wait, the two guys that they pushed in?" I interrupted. Slowly, the details of the file I had reviewed were starting to sound more familiar. The cousin— was it Marwan?—had described how they were pushed into the river and how he had heard his cousin struggling to stay afloat.

"Yeah," she snorted, "see, it's still confusing, but the soldier that broke, Spec. Ralph Logan, he actually wasn't there when the other soldiers pushed them in. He was by the Bradley." Anticipating my reaction, she added, "I know, it sounds really suspect, but I think he's telling the truth. He was really bothered by the whole thing, seemed uncomfortable even the first time we spoke to him."

Logan claimed that they were ordered to push the Iraqis into the river and, after refusing to take part, he had stayed by the Bradley. The other soldiers walked the two detainees toward the river and Logan couldn't see anything. He only heard the splashes. The confusing part was that Logan also claimed he saw the two Iraqis standing on the road as the Bradley pulled away. None of it made sense.

"I'm going to be re-interviewing some of the soldiers, but I will call you as soon as I'm done," she said. "Depending on your schedule, we'll also need to make arrangements to meet with the family."

"Okay, I'll see what I have here and we can figure it out the next time we talk," I acknowledged.

"Hey, everything all right?" Captain Taylor asked as I hung up. Taylor and Weatherspoon were meeting Philibert for a ride to the airfield to catch their return flight to Tikrit.

"Yeah, though it feels like people are losing it out here sometimes," I said, still stunned by the soldiers' actions. He nodded understandingly and, thankfully, didn't push me to elaborate.

Instead, he turned and pointed to the autographed photo of the cast from the television series *JAG*, above our desk. "Hey, at least you've got Hollywood behind you." Taylor smiled, and we both laughed.

I started to explain, but Taylor cut me off, "Hey, don't worry, really. Whatever motivates you guys out here is fine by me." He picked up his bags to leave, and I thanked him and Weatherspoon again for their help with the trial.

The photo was actually a gift from Capt. Sandra Chavez, the brigade public affairs officer, a product of her celebrity letter-writing campaign. Sandra had written to the *JAG* producers on our behalf, albeit without our knowledge. For weeks, we had endured her gasps of delight as she opened letters and boxes full of signed memorabilia and autographed pictures. All for the troops, of course. Offering Sandra anything more than a polite smile and you risked a beseeching "Don't encourage her!" from any one of the soldiers who worked in the ALOC.

Philibert was the exception, providing Sandra just the audience she was seeking. Phil "oohhed" and "aahhed" with each delivery. When the *JAG* photo arrived, Phil had gone right to work hanging it up above our workspace. Positioned prominently over the laptop, it invited comment from everyone who came within a one-hundred-foot radius. Even the most neutral observation prompted Philibert to extol Captain Chavez's generosity. Moving the photo wasn't an option. That would only antagonize Phil and Sandra.

Today, the smiling faces of Catherine Bell and David James Elliott, the show's stars, dressed in pristine Class A uniforms, seemed to mock me. Hmmm. I peered closer to see if Bell wore regulation earrings. Only 1/4-inch-diameter gold, silver, pearl, or diamond balls were allowed. Prior to deployment, most of the situations the show's stars found themselves in seemed farfetched. After several months in Iraq, however, I was learning that not only could anything happen in the field, it often did.

With the second trial now safely behind me, I was convinced I'd already had what you might call my Excalibur moment in Iraq. Truth be told, I'd had the same feeling some months earlier. At the time, we were only several weeks into our deployment, stationed outside the city of Jallulah, located in the northeastern part of Iraq, close to the Iranian border.

I'd managed to snag a satellite phone and called my sister, waiting for her to reflexively ask the one question I could never answer.

"So, Viv, where are you?"

"Near home," I responded cheerfully.

"Huh?"

"Near home," I repeated. Security concerns prevented us from disclosing our specific location, but today I'd found a loophole.

"Near home," she repeated, searching for meaning in the two words.

"Near Colorado? Near the U.S.? What's that mean?" she asked.

"No, near home," I said with emphasis.

"Near home, near home," she parroted back.

"My home, near where I'm from, place of my birth," I offered.

"You're near . . ."

"Don't say it," I warned.

"Oh my God, you're near home, near where you were born," she said with understanding. "Near the border?"

Atta girl. Finally.

"Yeah, near there," I explained, pleased with my own cleverness.

"What the hell? You were just in . . ."

"I know, we're all over the place."

"Near home," she chuckled, "you're such a smart ass."

I was born in Tehran, Iran, just before the revolution. My father's assignment in Iran was to collect intelligence on the Iranian military and also find out what the Russians were doing there. Until I served my time in Iraq, it didn't strike me as odd that the army had allowed my mother, sister, and great aunt to accompany him to Tehran. I guess it was part of his civilian cover, and everything is relative after you've survived the fall of Saigon. How bad could Tehran be in comparison?

My parents settled into an apartment with the most jarring wallpaper in existence and busied themselves with life as a young family. Our family vacation consisted of a two-week road trip into Afghanistan, with stops at its major cities. You know, just to check things out. Of course, this was three years before the Soviet invasion of December 1979.

Having Tehran listed as my place of birth on my passport always made for interesting foreign travel. I've come to anticipate at least a forty-five-minute delay with U.S. customs officials. First, there's the inevitable chuckle over my middle name. *Her middle name's "Happy." Wow.* Then the smile disappears and the customs officer blinks to make sure he read the next part correctly. *Isn't that interesting. Born in Iran, along the axis of evil.* "Miss, we're going to need you to step over here to the side please."

After September 11, nobody wanted to be the weakest link.

Returning from Costa Rica a few years ago, my sister and I were waiting in the holding area for my inevitable meeting with the supervising customs agent at Miami International Airport. Checking her watch, Debbie asked, "Do you have my ticket for my connecting flight?"

I shot her a look.

"No, no, I just wanted to make sure I didn't lose it," she said. A minute later she added, "I do have to work tomorrow."

It wasn't until those early weeks in Iraq that my being born in Iran actually came in handy. Our mission in the region was to negotiate the surrender and disarmament of an armed Iranian resistance group operating in Iraq. The Mujahedin-el-Khalq (MEK) or People's Mujahedin are Iranian Shiites who sought to topple Iran's Islamic regime.

I only knew this because I'd been diligently eavesdropping around the TOC tent, trying to glean what our mission was. It was early on in our deployment and information was at a premium. Those "in the know" weren't eager to hand it over for nothing. Never mind that I was the brigade's legal officer. Every inquiry to the planning folks elicited a "It's nothing big, Captain." Or "It's not your lane, Captain." Don't worry about it, they assured me.

Making no headway there, I turned to the division JAG office in Tikrit where I learned that my then-boss was listed as one of the people scheduled to attend the negotiations with the MEK. Lt. Col. Flora Darpino was Lieutenant Colonel Barnes's predecessor. When I reached Darpino on the tactical phone, she told me they planned to meet with the MEK the next day. She also said that neither she, Colonel Rudesheim, or General Odierno knew what to expect from the group.

Odierno is involved, I noted. This must be big.

"It's pretty crazy. We're all going in unarmed, so if you don't hear from me tomorrow evening . . ." Darpino said.

"What? You're going in unarmed?"

She explained that it was one of the terms of the meeting. Our division's leadership was heading into negotiations with a group I'd learned was on the U.S. terrorist list and they wouldn't even have as much as a 9mm on them. This was getting more interesting by the second. I wished Darpino luck with the mission and thanked her for keeping me in the loop.

The next day, I resumed my lingering routine around the TOC, waiting for an update on the negotiations. Morning passed into afternoon with no word and the afternoon was quickly giving way to evening. It was well past dusk before we heard Colonel Rudesheim's voice on the radio.

"Get Captain Gembara immediately," he ordered the battle captain.

Looking up to see if anyone else had heard the same thing, I found everyone in the TOC turned in my direction. They'd heard it all right and were as baffled as I was as to why the JAG was needed so urgently.

Instructions followed. I was to report to an outlying unit's location and told to be "prepared to chopper out with Colonel Rudesheim first thing in the morning." I learned the negotiations with the MEK that were supposed to have taken a day had ended without an agreement. Heading into day two, General Odierno was in overtime and the pressure to deliver was even more intense. The MEK had proven tougher negotiators than anyone expected and weren't going to go easily. Darpino was particularly determined not to let her boss walk away empty-handed a second time. She surmised she would need to be able to respond to any of the MEK's issues in as rapid a fashion as possible. Basically, she needed back-up legal help and decided the pesky JAG who seemed interested in the mission and also happened to be born in Iran, would do.

Affecting my most nonchalant expression, I listened as further instructions came in as though it were every day that I was summoned to assist General Odierno. Nodding, I took a quick inventory of who was witnessing this. In those early days with folks still asking what we needed JAGs for and me still having to use a crowbar to get details from our planning folks, I wanted this little moment on the record.

That evening, Kolb and I scrambled to get the Humvee to the staging area where we spent the night beneath the stars. Kolb had wisely opted to bed down on the Humvee's roof while I slept beside the Humvee and woke up to find a stray dog licking at my face. That morning, Rudesheim and I flew out on a Blackhawk to meet up with the rest of the American team.

The plan was to rendezvous at a hangar not too far from the MEK compound. When we arrived, Odierno was seated on a collapsible camping chair just inside the hangar. I'd seen him before but only at a distance. He was a rugged and formidable presence, easily over six feet two inches, and bald with high, prominent cheekbones. Gathering all eight of us for a pregame huddle, Odierno outlined his strategy for the second day of negotiations. He reminded us we were to leave our weapons and body armor outside the MEK compound. He also reminded us we could not leave without an agreement and a final point, one he was adamant about: we were not to eat any meals with the MEK today.

"No meals, no eating," he repeated. I fought the urge to laugh at the general's almost comical insistence on this point. Not only were the MEK fierce negotiators, they were apparently very insistent hosts. I resisted the urge to sidle up to Lieutenant Colonel Darpino and ask, "What the hell did you guys eat yesterday?"

Our mission for the day was clear: negotiate the "voluntary" disarmament and surrender of the MEK to U.S. forces. The alternatives were forcible disarmament or all-out war. We weren't, it turned out, the first U.S. soldiers to deal with the MEK. Special forces soldiers who had arrived in northeastern Iraq shortly before the U.S. invasion had become well acquainted with the MEK. Experts at training foreign armies and locals, the SF soldiers urged Washington to look beyond the group's 1997 "terrorist organization" designation and consider working with them. They pointed to the MEK's value as human intelligence sources. They also noted the group's considerable assets. Supported by Saddam, the MEK had bases throughout northern and central

Iraq. They had tanks and weapons. They also had radio stations and members who were fluent in English, Farsi, and Arabic. Most importantly, they had the desire to work with the United States to secure northern and central Iraq. The State Department summarily rejected this idea, pointing to the group's violent activities and unsavory tactics against Iran in the early 1980s. The decision to ignore the recommendations of some of the army's most experienced soldiers was, unfortunately, a harbinger of things to come.

Leaving our body armor and weapons in the Blackhawks, the eight of us walked unarmed into a compound so lush, it resembled nothing we'd seen in Iraq. Large palm trees lined the compound's perimeter wall. Plants of all varieties appeared to thrive within the compound's confines. The array of greens and browns with the occasional touch of pink, was in striking contrast to the country's otherwise monochromatic landscape.

The MEK negotiating team was as advertised: fluent in English, Arabic, and Farsi; familiar with the terrain and the local communities; and eager to work with us. They were also nearly all women, widows whose husbands had been assassinated by the Iranian government. I noticed their posture immediately. It was the sort of ramrod straight posture that would make a drill sergeant proud. They watched us carefully, evaluating our words as well as our expressions. I understood instantly why the previous day's negotiations had gone so poorly. As outmanned and as overpowered as they were, they refused to be humiliated by the process.

Nonetheless, we duly informed the MEK's leaders that they had no choice but to agree to our terms. Being a good soldier, I played my legal role and also trumped up my personal connection to Tehran and the Iranian people's struggle for democracy. I didn't mention that my father had been working as an intelligence operative as the U.S. government tried in vain to prop up the Shah.

While the bulk of my contribution to the negotiations wasn't particularly glamorous, the opportunity to witness a first-rate JAG like Lieutenant Colonel Darpino in action was well worth the price of admission. Darpino's decision to tackle each of the MEK's objections with an immediate response on paper systematically removed the obstacles standing between Odierno and an agreement. The MEK eventually agreed to our terms, though they remained insistent on one point: we stay and eat with them. We did.

Drowning In The Desert

While we were relieved to have completed our mission, we left the compound that day with mixed feelings, the dominant one being a sense of missed opportunity. The wisdom of disarming and ultimately detaining such a valuable potential ally seemed shortsighted even then. Here we had a group with an intimate understanding of the terrain and Iraq's volatile neighbor to the north. Under our direction, the MEK could have secured buildings and provided us with valuable eyes and ears in the region. Instead, 4th Infantry Division soldiers began dismantling the MEK compound the next morning and delivering the group's members to an internment camp known as Camp Ashraf where they remain to this day.

I was grateful to have played a role in this important mission, especially because it was the first recognition I had received from the brigade leadership. The JAG team had demonstrated its value added.

Now, three-fourths of the way through our deployment, my JAG team had just the opposite problem. We were in the loop all right, but the more we knew, the more we wished we didn't.

Division's guidance on how to handle the drowning victim's family was to leave the final payment decision up to me. With that question answered, I told Cintron to pick a day.

Later that night, after the BUB, Lieutenant Colonel Gonsalves, commander of 1-66 Armor Battalion, handed me another file.

"Sir, what is this?" I asked.

"I'm only the messenger," he said as he backed up, arms raised in the surrender position.

Inside the file, I found two additional statements regarding a video provided by the alleged drowning victim's family. The file also contained a CD case.

CHAPTER TWELVE

Following Orders

FIRST, YOU ARE BLINDFOLDED. NEXT, *you are walked to the edge of a platform high above the ground. Before you know it, you've been pushed and your body is in free fall. The shock of hurling through the air is cut short by the realization that your body is about to make contact. You scramble to brace yourself but nothing prepares you for the cold, hard smack of hitting a wall of water.*

The brutal collision is followed by silence as your body plunges deeper beneath the surface. It isn't long before an alarm sounds in your head. You're drowning. Move! Move! Kick! You recognize it as your survival instinct and you try to reclaim control of your foot and leg. Eventually, your limbs comply. Yanking off the blindfold, you begin thrashing around, trying to simultaneously shed your clothing and boots while keeping that damn M16 above the water. Let it get wet and you've lost the best friend you've got. Keep it dry. And keep treading until you pass the test.

Marwan's account reminded me of one of the more anxious moments of my army basic training: the water survival course. My experience was only an exercise, but Marwan's description of the terror and helplessness he felt as he fought to keep his head above the water resonated with me.

Now imagine it if you couldn't swim.

I went for a long run around Anaconda that evening, the details from both Marwan's and Logan's accounts still on my mind. With each footfall, my brain demanded an answer to the question that had plagued me all day. Why? Why would soldiers do something so cruel? This wasn't bombing the wrong house or panicking and shooting a child. Both terrible things, but I could understand how they might happen in the heat of battle. I could even understand how Cobb and Datray arrived at their predicament. The drowning, however, was incomprehensible, so needless. For kicks? They forced a man to jump to his death for kicks? And it wasn't just one or two soldiers either. At least four of them had walked Marwan and his cousin Zaidoun to the river's edge.

As I plodded along, the velvety night sky offered companionship but no answers. My legs settled into a rhythm but my neck and shoulders still felt tight. Surely, Logan wasn't the only one with a conscience. Some of those soldiers had to know that what they were doing was wrong.

Chasing the stars along Anaconda's uneven pavement, a more disturbing thought came to me. What did it matter if the others knew it was wrong? They still did it. What was conscience without courage? And, finally, what would I have done?

I grabbed a quick shower and returned to the workspace, eager to take advantage of the quiet. With most soldiers living in the trailers now, the headquarters building was nearly deserted after dark, a welcome change from groups of bored soldiers loitering around our area hoping to hear the latest reports of their misbehaving brethren. I didn't get much done before the phone rang. It was already 2200. It was Cintron.

"I'm sorry to be calling back so late," she said.

"That's okay. What's the latest?" I asked. CID agents didn't call back this late in the evening if things were going well.

She sighed deeply. Then, "One of the pushers confessed."

"Really?"

"Yeah, Bowman. Specialist Terry Bowman confessed that he forced one of the two Iraqis they detained into the water."

Flipping through my notepad, I searched for Bowman's name. I hurried to confirm that Bowman was the guy fingered by Logan as one of the pushers. Bingo.

"So, he confessed?" I asked.

"Yeah, he confessed to everything. That's why it took so long."

"Sure, sure," I said, eager for her to continue. I flipped to a fresh page in my notebook.

When Bowman finally cracked, he said that he and Sgt. Reggie Martinez had cut the zip ties off both Marwan and Zaidoun and walked them to the water. They ordered the Iraqi men to jump. Bowman insisted they did.

"He said he did not push him in?" I asked.

"Yes, that's what he said. He said that he just ordered him to jump."

Not sure what to make of that detail, I asked what Bowman had to say about Logan. "Is Logan legit?"

"He confirmed that Logan stayed back by the vehicles and did not have anything to do with the incident."

"Okay," I said, relieved that Logan was credible.

Like Logan, Bowman blamed his superiors for the incident. Bowman claimed that his lieutenant, 1st Lt. Jack Saville, and the platoon sergeant, Sgt. 1st Class Tracy Perkins, had ordered Bowman and Martinez to lead the guys down to the water. According to Bowman, he was simply "following orders."

"So what's your impression of Bowman?" I asked, finally setting my pen down.

"I think he's telling the truth. He knows it's over," replied Cintron. "Bowman basically named everyone: Saville, Perkins, his CO, Cunningham, even Gwinner."

She said this so casually, like what Bowman had said meant nothing.

"What? Oh, come on, you think he's telling the truth?" I asked, incredulous that he would attempt to implicate Gwinner.

A good investigator, Cintron didn't commit herself. She agreed that Bowman lost credibility points by blaming everyone for his decision to force the men into the river and for his decision to lie about the incident afterward. Cintron also stated that CID definitely had not forgotten that Bowman pushed a detainee into the river and seemed intent on bringing everyone down with him.

Satisfied, I asked whether Bowman had also seen the two Iraqis on the side of the side of the road before the platoon drove away. Cintron sighed audibly before continuing.

Bowman's statement corroborated Logan's on nearly everything except this one issue. Were the Iraqis standing on the side of the road when the soldiers left or were they not? Good-guy Logan claimed that he was "fairly certain" that he saw the Iraqis again before the unit left. He didn't stand to gain anything by lying. And yet, Bowman adamantly denied ever seeing the Iraqis again after forcing them into the river. If anyone had reason to lie, it was Bowman. So, who was lying now? And why? Wasn't the jig up at this point?

Cintron didn't bother trying to conceal her frustration. So much for two neat and tidy confessions. While seemingly minor, because both soldiers had initially lied, this latest inconsistency was a red flag signaling that something was still wrong. For Cintron, this meant a lot more questioning.

CID would need to re-interview Martinez, the soldier identified as the other pusher. I agreed to notify Gwinner that the soldiers would be staying overnight in Tikrit for further questioning. After my last tense conversation with Gwinner, calling 1-8 tonight would be a good opportunity to clear the air. With Bowman's and Logan's confessions now on the record, Gwinner and I would return to our previously cordial rapport. The soldiers had lied, so he wouldn't continue to argue the futility of the investigation.

Gwinner couldn't have disagreed more. I had barely finished talking, explaining that the soldiers would have to stay at division headquarters in Tikrit for further questioning, when he interrupted, unable to conceal his frustration.

"What now? Why is this taking so long? How long does it take to question them? I need them back here!" His heated reaction took me by surprise; perhaps he still hadn't heard?

"Sir, CID may not have told you, but Specialist Bowman . . ."

Gwinner had heard all right.

I changed course then. "Sir, it's just so they can finish the interviews; it's taking longer than they thought because the soldiers weren't honest the first time." The word "liars" had come to mind, but I refrained. Gwinner was in a foul mood this evening.

My reserve hardly mattered. Gwinner was steaming. Turning, I checked the ALOC to see if anyone else was around. I didn't want to start pleading if I had an audience.

"Sir, your guys should be headed back to Balad tomorrow. Please, just let CID finish the investigation. If you pull them back now, it will just drag it out longer and be more of a hassle in the long run." I was unsure what else I could say.

The amity between Gwinner and me now felt like a distant memory. Gwinner lamented the lost manpower, the wasted time, the protracted nature of the investigation. He was rightfully frustrated. During 1-8's absence from Balad, the city *had* become more violent, the insurgents more brazen. Now, as 1-8 worked to regain lost footing in the area, they did so with fewer men.

My attempts to explain only stoked his anger and combativeness. When I again reminded him that the soldiers had lied, he replied that their omission was irrelevant, that the Iraqis were alive and had found an ideal way to extract retribution: by telling lies that CID was buying into.

He repeatedly asked, "Where's the body? Where's the body?"

I was dumbstruck.

The conversation ended with Gwinner dismissing the Iraqis' claim and calling them "lying opportunists." Gwinner's hostility baffled me but also caused me to second-guess my own judgment. Had I been too quick to believe the Iraqis' story?

Where was the body? It was a valid question. The two drowning files I'd received were already stowed in my backpack for my trip to Samarra tomorrow. Cintron and I were going to meet with Zaidoun's family. Throwing on my vest and grabbing my Kevlar, I was suddenly anxious to look at that second file again, kicking myself for not checking it sooner. Why else would Gonsalves have made such a big deal about "only being the messenger"? The tension between the units was high, so he didn't want to seem like he was implicating 1-8.

Outside headquarters, where the rocky gravel had been laid so thick to deter mud, I slowed to a walk, finding it impossible to run through the shifting, slippery surface. Once I reached the wooden walkway around the trailers, I ran the remaining distance to mine. The lights were off inside. I opened the door slowly, careful not to disturb Hartleigh, and crept towards my bed, feeling for where I had left my backpack. As soon as I felt the rayon surface lined with zippers, I retraced my path towards the door and returned to my workspace.

Was this the video showing Zaidoun's body? Once seated, I took a closer look at the white CD jewel case, searching for any marking that might indicate

155

it was a DVD, or Iraqi for that matter. Seeing nothing, I wondered if I'd just overreacted. I'd assumed it came from division because technology was hardly the norm among Iraqis. While cell phones were more common now, the evidence most Iraqis submitted with their claims usually consisted of Polaroid photos and handwritten accounts. None of the courthouses had computers, or even typewriters. Everything was handwritten: all the files, records, even licenses. When I'd asked for a copy of a document once, the judge had snapped his fingers and a female assistant took the document and delicately placed it between sheets of carbon paper to begin tracing the original.

I placed the disk in the tray and pushed it firmly into the laptop. Then, I waited. When the screen icon stopped scrolling, nothing happened. I tried two more times before I gave up and opened the DVD manually. According to my computer, the material was unreadable. As it turned out, my crappy laptop couldn't read DVDs.

I would have to wait until the next day to have my answer.

CHAPTER THIRTEEN

Only for Flowers

AGENT CINTRON HANDED ME THE envelope containing $2,500. The crisp stack of fifty-dollar bills was all there, along with a receipt booklet. Smiling, she seemed relieved to be free of the money, and the decision. That would be my call. I would handle the decision and the money, also known as a solatia payment. I would decide how much, if any, we gave Zaidoun's family. My only requirement was that we meet the family first.

Solatia payments are "expressions of condolence" to the family of an Iraqi who may have been unintentionally killed or maimed as a result of our soldiers' actions. These payments are not, let me repeat, NOT an admission of guilt. That's the official definition, anyway. But you feel guilty, regardless.

For the first half of our deployment, solatia payments were explicitly banned by the Coalition Provisional Authority. While policymakers in Washington were arguing about the vulgarity of putting a price on a human life, those of us on the ground struggled with how to handle the discordant policies. We had a system in place to compensate a family for damage to their fence but nothing to offer them for accidentally killing their daughter.

This was in keeping with the disconnect I saw on my trips to Baghdad to meet with representatives of the CPA. I would arrive with a list of questions that required immediate answers—detainees, solatia payments, payroll problems—and the majority of our meeting would be spent discussing the de-Baathification policy or the ill-advised weapons turn-in program. The further removed the policymakers were from the action, the easier it was for them to say "no."

Meanwhile, other soldiers and I kept pushing for the policy to change, and it finally did in September 2003. The solatia limit per incident was set at $2,500, precisely the amount that Cintron had picked up from division today.

As soon as Logan confessed, we immediately started talking about solatia, quietly wondering whether the family would accept the payment and fade away. Today's situation was different. There was an ongoing investigation. If these people were lying, as Gwinner claimed, why the hell was I going to pay them?

Before meeting with the family, Cintron and I were meeting to discuss the drill. When I arrived at Brassfield-Mora, Cintron and the translator were waiting for me in the shade outside the small concrete buildings that comprised 1-66's command center. A tall brunette in her mid-twenties, Cintron was, to my surprise, wearing a uniform. CID agents in garrison typically wear civilian clothing, usually a suit or some other professional dress. Instinctively, I checked her Kevlar to identify her rank. Not surprisingly, there was no sign of it on her Kevlar or her collar, which was tucked under her body armor. That was done deliberately, a point that drove some higher-ups insane.

Periodically, back at Fort Carson, I would get a call from a first sergeant or major asking me what Agent Jim Bob Joe's rank was. First, they would ask discreetly, and when that didn't work, they would try to be chummy, as though it would be our little secret. They were inevitably disappointed because I made a point of not knowing or caring about an agent's rank. This further irritated the inquiring higher-up, having to deal with some half-wit agent who wasn't gauging his or her next move based on the higher-up's seniority. How to explain that it's precisely people like them that make rank a hindrance to CID agents? Rank equals power, and meddling power is anathema to an independent investigation.

Agent Cintron informed me that the family had just arrived. Zaidoun's mother, however, did not come. Too distraught, Cintron said, repeating what the family had told her. Mother's a no-show? Red flag. Cintron gave no indication she thought the family was lying. *Give it a second, Viv. She'll make some*

facial expression, or say something, to indicate whether the family's legitimate or not.
Cintron said nothing else. She'd be a good poker player. She went on to tell me that I would be meeting with three men: Marwan, the cousin that was with Zaidoun that night; Zaidoun's father; and the family's lawyer, recently hired to help them deal with us. Great. They've lawyered up. Cintron said I'd spot the lawyer right away but didn't elaborate.

The drill was to have Marwan tell me what happened again; let the lawyer and father say anything they wanted to; watch the DVD of Zaidoun's body; and then, on my signal, I could either pay them the money or say that we needed to take a break. Taking one last peek at the envelope, I stuffed it into my backpack and motioned for the translator to finish his cigarette.

"Let's go." I wanted to get this over with.

Cintron was right about the lawyer. I spotted him the second we entered the room. An older man, probably in his fifties, he had a full head of silvery hair and wore a three-piece suit. My guess was that it was custom-made considering how well it hugged his lean frame. Everything about him was immaculate, polished, and well considered. Not a scuff mark or loose thread on this one. Even the suit's odd light-grey color seemed perfectly coordinated to match his silver hair and mustache. He approached me immediately with a handshake.

Zaidoun's cousin, Marwan, placed a hand on his uncle's forearm before turning to greet me. He smiled at me nervously, the corners of his mouth rising and pressing at his full, cherubic cheeks. It was clear he wanted to be gracious, despite the unfortunate circumstances. He was dressed like a European university student in tight jeans, a button-down oxford, and a sweater vest beneath his windbreaker. At five feet ten inches, Marwan was chubby, with a round face and clear, luminescent skin. His close-cropped beard and glasses made him appear at least a decade older than his twenty-one years.

Even if I saw Zaidoun's father in silhouette, I could have told you who he was. His shoulders were slumped, a sloping shelf atop a mound of unimaginable grief. His head was pitched forward, heavy with the weight of his eyes. He watched my interaction with the lawyer dispassionately. He wore a deep orange robe with gold trim over a brown tunic. Every few minutes he would adjust the robe, pulling one side flat and tight across his chest and then the other. He was resigned to be the father of a dead son; forced in his time of grief to be the strong one.

Drowning In The Desert

Seeing him, I forced myself to remember that anything was possible. It could be an act. Marwan could be lying. Maybe he killed his cousin? I reminded myself to tread lightly as I leaned forward to begin.

"I'd like to start with you, Marwan. If you could, please tell me what exactly happened that night."

Marwan's eyes widened as the translator repeated my request and he responded in anxious tones to the family lawyer. Before he could finish, the translator turned to me.

"Marwan does not want his uncle to have to hear the story again. Is it possible for him to wait in another room?" he asked.

Their expectant, fearful eyes awaiting my response filled me with shame, that they should even have to ask for that miniscule amount of mercy.

"No problem," I said, in a thin, unfamiliar voice. "Of course, he can leave." Cintron stepped forward to escort Zaidoun's father to a waiting area. In my clumsy request, I discovered it was possible to inflict more pain on a man enduring the worst pain.

Marwan and Zaidoun had begun the evening of January 3, 2004, in Baghdad, where they were borrowing a friend's truck to haul toilets and plumbing parts back to Samarra. Because of the late hour, they debated staying overnight, fearful that they wouldn't make it home before curfew. In the end, they had decided to leave Baghdad, heading north for Samarra. The truck stalled several times. The first time, Zaidoun was able to fix it, but the truck was sluggish, and only reached a maximum speed of 20 mph the rest of the way to Balad. They had considered staying in Balad overnight, Marwan recalled wistfully, after the truck had broken down a second time. That time, however, the truck was more responsive to Zaidoun's tinkering, so they continued on.

As Marwan described being stopped by the soldiers in Samarra, the lawyer passed me a picture of Zaidoun. Taken in a studio, it resembled a senior year portrait of a high school student in the states. Zaidoun smiled uneasily at the camera, his eyes not quite as relaxed as his mouth. He wore acid-washed jeans and a sweater with a bold geometric design and posed awkwardly with his elbow on his knee. Taller and leaner that his cousin, Zaidoun was handsome despite his blotchy complexion. He looked like his father.

I forced myself to pay attention to Marwan and stopped looking for similarities between Zaidoun and his father. Adjusting, I sat back in the metal folding chair to concentrate on Marwan. I studied his full, round cheeks and listened for changes in his pitch. Cintron sat to my left as impassive as ever. How many times had she heard this already?

Marwan described the soldiers checking Marwan's and Zaidoun's identification cards, then searching the truck. "They found nothing," he repeated, "and let us go."

I was familiar with the story. I had reread Marwan's statement this morning during my convoy ride to Samarra. Hearing it told by Marwan, via the translator, heightened the tension as I waited for the bad part. Why was this taking so long?

Fifteen minutes after releasing them, the soldiers returned and stopped the curfew breakers again. This time, the soldiers zip-tied Marwan's and Zaidoun's hands behind their backs and led them to a Bradley, where the two men were directed to sit on the floor. Marwan arched his back to show me how the handcuffs pitched him forward, throwing his balance off.

"No English," he cried out plaintively. Waving his hands, he searched for words to explain the confusion and fear he felt as the Bradley began to move.

Here it comes, I thought.

The soldiers drove for about fifteen minutes before stopping. A group of five soldiers led them down to the river, near the side of a bridge. When they were standing at the edge, the soldiers cut off the handcuffs and began yelling at Marwan and Zaidoun in English. Marwan said it took several seconds before they realized that the soldiers wanted them to jump. Zaidoun, who could not swim, began pleading with the soldiers. Fearing his cousin was only encouraging the soldiers, Marwan implored Zaidoun to be quiet. It hardly mattered.

The soldiers pushed Zaidoun into the river first. His screams filled the air.

Marwan heard his cousin hit the water, then splashing frantically, calling out for help the entire time. The next thing Marwan knew, he too was hurling toward the water. Even as he fell, Marwan scanned the river, trying to locate his cousin. The January water was cold, heavy, and weighed him down. Marwan thought he would die. He struggled to surface. When he did, he thought he heard his cousin scream, so he called out to Zaidoun.

Looking up, Marwan saw the soldiers still watching him. A wave of terror shot through him. Would they do to something else to him? Still struggling to keep his head above the surface, he grew frantic. Spotting some low hanging branches, he struggled toward them, but felt himself sinking. Desperate, he lunged for the concrete wall from which he had fallen and clung to it shakily, his fingers unable to find their grip on the smooth surface. He moved along the wall to get closer to the branches. It took several attempts, he said, before he felt the thin tip of some branches in his palm. Gripping them firmly, he slowly pulled himself forward, willing his body to follow. When he was close enough, he grabbed a thicker branch and continued his tentative climb.

"I was so scared," Marwan told me. "I heard them laughing. I was afraid they were still there and would come get me again. It was so steep," Marwan explained, holding out his forearm to demonstrate the grade of the river's bank. "I kept falling in and I was so tired."

Eventually, he pulled himself onto the shore where he laid drenched and gasping for air for several minutes. Fearful that the soldiers might see him, he moved toward a tree, crouching there for several minutes before returning to the edge of the river.

"'Zaidoun!' 'Zaidoun!' I kept calling out to him," Marwan said.

Hearing no response, Marwan felt his heart race and he ran to the road. He didn't stop running until he reached a checkpoint run by Iraqi security forces. With his matted hair and sputtering claims, the police thought he was crazy. It wasn't until they saw him under the light that they realized he was completely drenched.

Two members of the security force walked back to the river with him. Standing at the river's edge, they yelled for Zaidoun repeatedly and looked for any sign of him.

"We couldn't see anything in the water because it was so dark," Marwan explained. It was no use.

Marwan's last memory of his cousin: Zaidoun's desperate clawing at the air as he plunged into the river. Marwan found their truck the next day, smashed like a pancake, Bradley tracks all over the top of it.

I felt exhausted just listening to him, and sat up to release the tension in my shoulders and neck.

"We should take a break," I said.

Standing outside with Cintron, I was talkative and adamant.

"It's like your worst nightmare come true. They laughed? They stood there and watched!"

She simply shook her in head in dismay. Did Cintron have any thoughts on this?

"Well, did anything change from what he initially told you?" I demanded, irritated by her silence.

"Well, no, not really. But he was calmer this time. Oh, and we had him describe the soldiers more and he did a pretty good job. Oh, and he said he saw them pointing at the water when they were standing there, but the rest was the same as you heard. Terrible."

At last, some sort of reaction. "Hey, have you seen the bridge where it happened?" I asked.

"No, I haven't, but I'm supposed to set that up with you and the family, to visit the bridge, have Marwan show us how it happened."

When we returned to the room, Cintron pulled out her laptop and set it on the table. The first bit of video showed the smashed truck, porcelain toilet bits all around it. It was parked obscenely on a median in the middle of a busy street. The distinctive tread marks of a Bradley were visible and overlapping. The soldiers had run over the truck more than once. For good measure.

Cintron moved to forward the DVD to Zaidoun's funeral, and our half circle held its breath. The image on the screen was difficult to discern as the camera panned back and forth erratically before zooming in and out. It finally settled on Zaidoun's head. His shockingly dark hair was a stark contrast to his pale, bloated face. Small, round, coin-like objects covered his eyes. There were several gashes on his face. His body was wrapped in cloth and visibly bloated.

The camera panned up and down the bloated body before landing on a tight shot of his face, at which point Zaidoun's father stood up, gripped the back of my chair to steady himself, and walked over the window. Marwan leapt to his uncle's side.

"He's not sure if the father can watch it. Perhaps he should leave again," the lawyer said.

At the window, Zaidoun's father turned to face us, his eyes brimming with tears. Placing a hand on his chest, he bowed slightly as if to apologize, and motioned for us to continue.

"I've seen enough. Let's take a break," I said.

* * *

"I just want to express my deepest sympathy to your family for the loss of Zaidoun," I began after we reconvened. "We truly appreciate your cooperation with this investigation and for meeting with us again today."

"The family asks for justice. They want justice for their dead son," the lawyer jumped in. "They want the soldiers held accountable for their actions."

"We will continue to investigate this incident. I have to tell you, however, it's difficult because Zaidoun's body has been buried," I paused hoping something more appropriate or encouraging would come to me. "Some people don't believe that the body in the video is Zaidoun," I said. "Because of that, they will always say that he, Zaidoun, is out there trying to trick us."

Zaidoun's father just nodded.

"The body proves that he is dead," I said flatly. What value was there to sugarcoating this reality? I would never be able to prove anything if we didn't have a body.

The father leaned forward and said something to the lawyer.

"These soldiers have confessed. They admit to pushing Marwan and Zaidoun into the river," the lawyer said. "We want justice, we ask only for justice. They know they cannot bring him back."

"Yes, yes, of course," I said unsure where to go next. "That is my job, to help bring justice. But to get justice," I continued cautiously, "I must prove that it is Zaidoun. The body."

I looked over at Cintron. She already knew what was coming.

"I am asking for your cooperation so I can prove that Zaidoun is buried, that he died. With all due respect, I am asking you if we can exhume Zaidoun's body." I waited anxiously for the translator to finish. I had prepped him for this conversation during the break, making certain he understood the word "exhume."

There was some back and forth, a lot of gesturing, and a few clarifying questions between the lawyer, the father, and the translator while I forced myself not to look away, steeling myself for the worst.

"No, absolutely not," the father and Marwan agreed. Both men shook their heads. Zaidoun's father tapped his palm against his chest and shook his head vigorously as if to expel the mere suggestion. They were more resolute than angry, too worn down it seemed for the energy that anger required.

"I understand," I responded, lowering my chin to underscore the point. "But, please, let me assure you that the body would be removed and handled respectfully, under your supervision, and then we will return the body to the grave in the same respectful manner."

"They don't want this under any circumstances," the lawyer said.

The translator's head swiveled back to me.

I just listened, despite a gnawing desire to try to force them understand. It would make me feel better to talk, I realized, but it wasn't about me right now. So I just sat and tried to imagine myself in their position, because, in some sense, I couldn't believe I was here in mine. Asking a family to dig up their dead son whom our soldiers killed?

I watched as the father stood up again and walked to the window, drawing his robe tightly around him. Marwan followed, as the lawyer reiterated how crazy the idea was, and how Zaidoun's mother would never stand for it. She was inconsolable as it was, he said.

Was there anything else to say? So far, I had avoided the issue of guilt, taking special care to express only my sorrow and condolences. I may as well have started singing at that point because that's as inappropriate and inadequate as "I'm sorry" would have sounded.

Grief, mingled with futility, permeated the cold, dreary cinderblock room. I inspected the dirt floor, refusing to react to the thoughts churning inside. How sickened and devastated would I be if this was my child, or brother, or beloved friend?

These soldiers, they killed Zaidoun. He suffered a horrible, frightening death. Then, they deny it, deny everything as my boy's body is missing for weeks. What nightmare am I living when I find myself *thanking* a farmer and his wife for recovering Zaidoun's body, grateful that they saw that large object washed up on the river bank and decided to take a closer look. Grateful that, instead of leaving him there to rot, they had called neighbors to help carry my boy's body to their home. Grateful that despite not knowing who he was, that they still tried to clean his battered and bloated body, covered him, cared for him. Now, after I've finally buried him and these soldiers have confessed, you want me to let soldiers dig him up? Will this nightmare ever end?

It was lunacy and yet my gut still told me to push, to make them understand, at least, that this was, in fact, the justice they craved. Otherwise, I'd explain, these soldiers would claim Zaidoun was out there forever.

Clearing my throat, I nodded and began, "I understand your concerns and accept your decision. But please, let me explain again. As the prosecutor, seeking justice, the truth, in your son's death, there can be no doubt that the body you recovered is your son, Zaidoun. And because we did not see the body, how can I do that?" I waited for the translator but continued before they could react. "So please, I ask you to first take some time and consider this matter, discuss it with your wife. And," my voice grew stronger, "let me also assure you that the body would be removed and handled respectfully, under your supervision, and with both an American and an Iraqi doctor present. We would return the body to the grave in the same respectful manner." I maintained eye contact as the translator repeated my words in Arabic.

Before the lawyer could speak, I abruptly called another break. I wanted to make it clear that I didn't want a response right now. Plus, I needed a break, too, before tackling the next ugly issue of the day.

God, what had I signed up for? Stepping outside with Cintron, I reminded her that the money matter was next. Solatia. Was there ever an appropriate moment to hand it over? Not in my experience. The very notion that money could be a salve for such dense and impenetrable loss was offensive. Still, it was one of the few things we could offer.

"What are you thinking?" Cintron asked, referring to the amount.

"That it's going to be awkward," I replied.

When we reconvened, I let the lawyer speak first, and listened blankly, trying to figure out the best way to begin. After acknowledging the lawyer's repeated list of concerns, I discussed our next meeting. I wanted to visit the bridge at our next meeting, and asked them if they would accompany me, allow Marwan to show us what happened. They agreed and we discussed a few dates.

I turned to Marwan next and discussed the destroyed bongo truck that belonged to his friend. I would process the cost of the truck and its destroyed cargo before our next meeting. I took the envelope out of my backpack then.

"The final matter I have today concerns an expression of sympathy I offer to your family on behalf of the United States Army."

The lawyer stepped forward to take the envelope, which he promptly opened. The sight of cash triggered the refusals all over again.

"We don't want your money. We have our own money. We don't need your money," the father exclaimed, on his feet now. "We don't want money, we want justice!"

Marwan and the lawyer appeared equally disappointed by this turn of events.

I was tired of explaining. "No, no," I insisted, "this is not a trade. The investigation continues no matter what. Please, this is just for your suffering, for your grief."

It was the most angry I'd seen them. The father paced back and forth shaking his head and holding out his arm in a gesture of refusal. The lawyer closed the envelope and handed it back to me.

Back and forth we went for maybe fifteen or twenty minutes, during which I conferred with Cintron to see if she had any ideas on how to get them to accept. She had none. Eventually, I began focusing my efforts on the lawyer, imploring him to understand and explain to his clients that this wasn't a "buy-off," as they'd called it, but simply an expression of sympathy, a token offering. That's all.

Another ten minutes passed as we argued over the meaning. Fed up that I wasn't backing down, the lawyer finally asked, "So, what do you want from them if they accept this money?"

His question confused me. "Just their signature," I replied, producing the receipt booklet that division had included with the money. Flipping it open to a blank page, I explained that their signature would simply show that they had accepted it.

Wrong answer, Viv. We continued to argue, now over the meaning of the signature. This was a trick, they said, a trick so the army could wipe its hands clean, and then point to the signature.

"No, no," I desperately refuted this understandable assumption. "That's not it. It's just so my bosses don't think I stole it. It's just accounting . . . accountability." It was all I could come up with on the spot. I didn't dare look at Cintron or the translator. It was partially true, I mean, I could pocket it, right? I prayed the lawyer would sense my sincerity, that it really was just an expression of sympathy. I placed the money in front of him again. "Please," I pleaded, "I know the family doesn't need it, and doesn't want it, but it's a token offering, nothing more. Use it for anything, the cost of traveling here, the funeral cost, anything. I can assure you that we are investigating this case no matter what."

Drowning In The Desert

The lawyer hesitated, and I forced the money into his hand and pushed forward the receipt booklet. Tiring of the argument, he turned to address Zaidoun's father and me.

To the father, he said, "Look, accept the money and use it for flowers for Zaidoun. As sympathy, the army has given money to buy flowers in Zaidoun's memory." Turning to me, he said, "Captain, he will sign, but only if that condition is written on the receipt."

At first the translator had a hard time explaining this, but I eventually understood the condition. It was genius. Thank God for lawyers. I was impressed by the lawyer's quick thinking and relieved, at last, to relinquish the money. I could have taken it home, returned it to division, but for some reason, I didn't want to wait. If they never spoke to us again, at least they had the money. As crass as that seemed, that's how I felt.

As soon as Zaidoun's father finished signing, the lawyer pulled the booklet towards him and wrote in Arabic, pressing firmly with each stroke to ensure its duplication on the contact paper, "Only for Flowers for Zaidoun." At his instruction, the translator asked me to write the same in English.

Above the Arabic translation, I neatly printed, "Only for Flowers, for Zaidoun."

CHAPTER FOURTEEN

Sergeant Phil

KOLB AND CARTER hurried into the JAG workspace.

"What's wrong? What's going on?" I asked impatiently, looking up from the stack of Article 15 papers I was reviewing.

The lack of color in Kolb's usually rosy cheeks and the anxious expression on his face stopped me cold.

Kolb spoke first: "Ma'am, a report just came in. A car bomb just went off in Samarra."

"A car bomb?" Car bombs were highly unusual for Samarra, where RPG and rocket attacks were the norm. Baghdad had car bombs, not Samarra.

"Yeah, they said it exploded at the CMOC [Civilian Military Operations Command]," Carter injected.

"Shit. Sergeant Phil's there."

They nodded.

"There's no word yet on any casualties. They can't get through to anyone up there," Kolb added.

The CMOC didn't have a TAC phone, but the small contingent of military police and the civil affairs team that lived there usually could be reached by radio.

We spent the rest of that morning waiting, constrained by what we didn't know and silenced by what we feared.

Carter stared blankly at the papers in front of him before setting them down, irritated.

"Hey, ma'am, is it okay if me and Mendo go pick up our water?" he asked.

Mendo? Carter's question caught me off guard. I'd completely forgotten about Mendoza, who was sitting just feet from me, sorting through war-trophy applications on one of the trunks.

"Yeah, go ahead." I waved them off distractedly.

After organizing the weapons card applications in front of him by city, Kolb set them beside the laptop to begin inputting them into the computer. Momentarily transfixed, I watched as he pulled up the PowerPoint slide containing the master weapons card template. I created it for use in our brigade's area of operations. Seeing it reminded me of my earlier promise to arm the judges before we left. I scribbled "Guns for Judges" in my notebook. Meanwhile, Carter and Mendo returned with the first stack of water bottles, our section's weekly allotment.

Returning to the file on my lap, I began reading the same sworn statement I'd read at least a dozen times already. This time, I forced myself to concentrate. The entire matter felt trivial, though, compared to the car bomb in Samarra. I checked the clock. Nearly an hour had passed and Phil's status was still unknown.

I reread the same two sentences again, forcing myself to think of anything but Philibert. He was the only one of us with a child. A little girl. He adored her, too, always showing us her latest photos and reading her letters to us. She was a beautiful little girl who clearly had her father's smile. They were going to go on a cruise together when he came home.

"Hey, excuse me, do you mind if I use your phone?" a tall soldier asked, reaching for the TAC phone.

"Sorry, we're waiting for a call, so use another phone," Kolb said sharply, reaching to pull the phone closer.

Stung, the soldier mumbled something as he walked away.

Kolb watched him for a second before turning back to the laptop screen. The weapons card template had since been replaced with a solitaire game. None of us, it seemed, could concentrate.

I had been at the CMOC in Samarra a month earlier, just ahead of the start of Operation Ivy Blizzard. Even then, I'd been shocked by the building's appearance. The CMOC was located at the center of a tangle of narrow streets in downtown Samarra. A whitish-gray concrete building, it was situated on the back third of a sizeable plot of land, an oddity in the congested area. A small courtyard with a cinderblock wall ringed the building, buffering it from the street and the adjacent parking lot. Evidence of daily rocket and RPG attacks was visible all over the building's exterior walls. They showcased a range of damage, everything from several-inch nicks to six- and seven-foot scars that exposed the wall's inner layers. The ground had been littered with crumbled mortar.

Captain Dave Fujimoto, the 418th Civil Affairs Battalion team chief, had been quick to downplay the attacks that day I arrived, and even noted that the CMOC building no longer held the distinction of being the most frequently attacked location in Iraq. He was eager to show me how fortified the building's walls were.

The interior walls were surprisingly pristine, smooth, and completely untouched by the mayhem that seemed to settle on the building's exterior.

"It's amazing how thick they built them. These layers of concrete keep getting hit but nothing penetrates," Fujimoto had said.

Fujimoto and his team of three civil affairs soldiers had been living in Samarra since we arrived in Iraq, some nine months earlier. They convoyed in with us and immediately established the CMOC downtown during our initial stint in Samarra. When the brigade received orders to move north to the cities of Tuz and Daquq, outside Kirkuk, Fujimoto had insisted that he and his team be allowed to remain in Samarra and assist the unit replacing us. He had grown accustomed to the autonomy living at the CMOC offered and recognized the uniqueness of his situation, the result of insisting early on that his team live and work downtown. If he moved, the chances of having a similar arrangement were slim to none, because commanders were far less inclined to accommodate the civil affairs mission with the rising number of attacks.

A while later, as I was leaving the CMOC, Dave had remembered to show me the CMOC's latest attraction. He led me to the front of the building where a fully intact RPG was sticking out of the concrete exterior wall of the building. With its nose embedded inside the wall, only the tail piece was visible outside. Had it not been for the string and plastic cones cordoning off the ground beneath it, I would have assumed it was fake.

"A dud," he said brightly. "So, do you want to take a picture?"

"No, thanks. I think I'm good," I said, causing Dave's smile to fall a fraction.

It was clear that Dave had been in Samarra too long. Everybody knew how dangerous the city was. Why had I let Phil go by himself?

Done unloading the water bottles, Carter scanned the workspace for something to lift, move, or rearrange. Seeing nothing, he said, "I'm going to see if there's any more news."

I nodded, and Mendo joined him. Kolb and I watched them leave as Sergeant Arthurs arrived, wearing his usual look of resignation. His M16 hung loosely over his shoulder and banged loudly against the table as he settled into the civil affairs workspace across from us.

"Hey, why so serious, JAGs?"

Two sentences into my explanation, he interrupted, "No, I heard about the bomb. I didn't realize Sergeant Phil was up there. The report said no MPs were hurt so . . ."

"What report?" Kolb and I asked in unison.

"I don't know who said it, I just heard it on the way in," he replied. "Hey, they said the MPs were okay and nothing else, so that's good," he said. Leaning forward, he plugged a set of earphones into the back of his laptop before adding, "If Phil was hurt, you would know by now. Trust me."

Neither Kolb nor I said anything in response. We knew Phil.

Phil saw Iraq as a sunny place, filled with people he had yet to meet and roads he had yet to travel. He launched himself at every opportunity that brought him closer to Iraqis and other soldiers. I couldn't count the number of times I had exited the courthouse in Balad, or Dujayl, after a long round of meetings, only to find our Humvee overrun with Iraqis, mainly children. Yards away, Philibert would be in the middle of another crowd of Iraqis, snapping photos or handing out parts of an MRE (Meal, Ready to Eat).

"Oh, come on, ma'am," he'd say, beckoning me over, "come meet . . ." or, he would start gesturing for me to join a photo. Phil's complete lack of concern for our security was exasperating. I could tell him a million times not to leave the Humvee unattended, and not to let anybody near it, but he never really got it. That was the downside of his fearlessness, a certain naiveté that made him incapable of malice, and thus he assumed others were, as well.

Phil drove Iraq's treacherous roads worry-free and spoke to a man on the street in Samarra the same way he would speak to a man on the street in Colorado Springs. Fear and danger never gripped Phil the way they gripped so many of us. Today, I prayed, it would not be his undoing.

Phil could be forgetful and easily distracted. After one particularly long day, I returned to the workspace to find him exuberant, having just booked a father-daughter Disney cruise. These coveted cruises were booked months in advance and he was thrilled to have finally extracted his daughter's summer schedule from his ex-wife and locked in a date. I was happy for him and listened as he described the painstaking process of booking tickets online through the Disney website.

It wasn't until the next day, when I received an admonishing e-mail from the Fort Carson JAG office demanding an update about the Cobb trial, that I realized that Phil had neglected the one task I had assigned him. He had forgotten to inform Carson that we had won the trial. Their admonishing e-mail left me at a loss for how to motivate Phil or simply get him to reorganize his priorities.

Now, as I waited to hear if he was alive or dead, I couldn't help but wonder if it was Phil who had it right all along. Phil had written his daughter just yesterday. If something did happen, he would have no regrets. I could hardly say the same. With the exception of a brief phone call, I suddenly realized that I hadn't been in touch with Mike in almost two weeks. *Terrible, Viv. What's wrong with you?* I had allowed work, my job, and this constant need for approval to distract me from what was really important. *You know better, Viv.*

Sprinting to the computer lab to dash off a quick e-mail wasn't going to do it, either. It was up to me to make the time. Because, in the end, whose opinion really mattered the most? I stared blankly at the paperwork in front me and thought about all of the mail I still hadn't opened. *God, what was wrong with me?*

Intent on making a change now, I pulled my backpack out to check if I'd stashed any mail inside. Seeing none, I tossed it beneath the table and scanned the area hoping to spot some mail I might have accidentally left around. It would have been a miracle if I had. Unlike Philibert, I was concerned with maintaining some privacy. I never left personal letters out.

Spotting Phil's clipboard, I picked it up to examine the chart of his run times. Yeah, Phil definitely didn't care what anyone thought. On the front of his clipboard, where the half-page chart didn't cover, Phil had taped the photo of an attractive woman's smiling face. Beneath it, he had written, in bold black marker, "For this!" His motivation, that is, for staying fit. Yeah, Philibert was a little kooky, a true original.

On one particularly memorable evening, Tom had come by and announced, "I think your guy has lost his mind."

"What are you talking about?" I asked.

"Do you know that Sergeant Philibert is outside running around with a tire chained to him?"

"He's thinks it will improve his run time," Carter volunteered, "you know, resistance." Technically, Philibert ran with the tire dragging behind him.

"Well, was he whistling, Tom?" I'd replied. It had been the end of a particularly bad whistling day for Phil.

When Phil arrived in theater we had been horrified to discover that our new replacement was a whistler, a man who literally whistled while he worked. And when he wasn't working he whistled as he wrote letters, read magazines, even when he cleaned his weapon.

To his credit, when Phil was wrong, he was apologetic, never huffy or defensive. He was a good sport who genuinely felt bad if he let the team down. He apologized to me profusely for forgetting my birthday. A month later, when he returned from R&R in Qatar, he left me a card that popped open to reveal an elaborate mosque. In it, he apologized (again) for missing my birthday. I rarely heard him complain, not about Anaconda or the army, or even Iraq. Six months in Iraq had not added so much as a cloud to his disposition.

By the time Carter and Mendoza returned, I had given up on work completely. From my seat, I watched Kolb play solitaire for a few minutes before deciding to clean my weapon. It was overdue. Just as I was pulling out my cleaning kit, I saw Carter barreling toward the workspace, weaving past several soldiers in his haste to reach us. Mendoza was close behind. Carter's frenzied return did not bode well. Kolb and I stood instinctively, steeling ourselves for the news.

Resting a hand on his hip, Carter took a moment to catch his breath as Kolb and I tried to read his face.

"Phil's okay, he's okay. They found him," he said, his smile growing even as he said it.

Still breathing heavy, he added, "It sounds like he wasn't hurt."

Thank you, God. And, just like that, the world felt right again.

"Whew!" Kolb said, beaming, "I was starting to worry there." He smiled unabashedly at Carter and Mendoza, the bearers of great news. After the longest morning, and afternoon, we all just stood there, surrendering to our big, dopey, grateful smiles. I wanted to hug all of them, Carter, Kolb, Mendoza. Just pull them in for a cheesy group hug. We had been through so much together, so much that we could never really explain to anybody else. We knew each other with an intimacy that some people never even knew their own family.

Our tremendous relief that Philibert was safe slowly turned heavy, as the gravity of what we had been spared filled the workspace.

What no one ever explains is that, even if you go to war wanting to be a hero, your day-to-day hope is that you just get to go home. To survive, you have to believe that the war is just a phase. You have to believe that, in a few months, you will be back to your real life, maybe a little tanner, and a little more confident, but all in all, the same person you were when you left.

When a friend dies, it kills a great part of that hope. When someone you spent nearly every waking hour with dies, it shatters that hope. You not only lose a dear friend, but the person you were before also dies. You can never go home again, at least not the way you were. If Phil had been killed or seriously injured, it would have ruined the war for all of us, and changed us forever.

Phil's daughter had been on my mind all day. A new wave of emotion washed over me thinking about the endless grief she had been spared. Unlike the children of so many soldiers, she would be able to make new memories with her dad. They were going to take that cruise. She would never have to rely on strangers to tell her how much her father loved her and how she was the most important person in the world to him. I studied the ground, hoping this feeling would pass quickly.

Carter was the first to speak. "You know Phil's going to be talking about this for months, don't you?"

Drowning In The Desert

"Talking? You mean writing postcards about it," Kolb said, following Carter's lead.

"It's funny, but even before we heard about the bomb, I missed having him around today. I think I've grown used to the whistling," I said, joining in.

"The whistling is okay, but if he starts with those keys," Carter said, doing a perfect impression of Phil swinging the cord that held his keys in large circles, winding and unwinding it around his fingers.

Kolb, Mendoza, and I dissolved into laughter. Philibert was fine, and we would be, too. Our slightly dysfunctional and frequently off-kilter JAG family was intact, and we could not be more grateful.

Sergeant Philibert not only survived the Samarra car bomb, he saved a man's life. While others stood by, Philibert had acted quickly and fearlessly, dragging a man away from the burning wreckage. He was recommended to receive a medal for his bravery.

CHAPTER FIFTEEN

Conduct Unbecoming

THE STAFF SERGEANT APPROACHED THE desk with a look of consternation. It was clear he needed to talk to someone.

Although it was probably a matter I could have given him a quick answer to, I gestured for him to sit down. I knew how these things went.

Settling heavily into the chair across from me, the sergeant sighed deeply before beginning. He was still having problems with a particularly belligerent private.

"Last night, ma'am, he started picking a fight because someone moved his magazine," the sergeant said, rolling his eyes. "When I counseled him afterwards, he told me that he was depressed, that he was thinking about killing himself."

I nodded, encouraging him to continue.

"His girlfriend broke up with him. He wants to go home," he tossed out flatly.

"Is that what he said, that he wants to go home?" I asked, already aware of the answer.

"No, ma'am, he didn't say it," the sergeant replied with a smirk, "but I know him. He thinks that if he can see her, he can work things out, or something."

"So, how serious do you think it is, the whole suicide thing?"

The sergeant rested his elbows on the table, already weary of the subject. "I don't know, ma'am," he said with resignation.

Staring off into the distance, he shrugged. "Well, what can I do? I can't have him carrying around a weapon if he's going to kill himself." His voice trailed off.

"Definitely not," I answered, hoping that he would continue. When he didn't, I added, "From what I've heard, a depressed soldier with a weapon is about the last thing you need right now. Things still aren't slowing down over there, eh?"

He snorted. "No ma'am, they sure aren't."

He needed a soldier threatening to take his or her own life like he needed a wool sweater in Iraq's 130-degree heat. It wasn't that he didn't care. He simply had his hands full preparing for the considerable external threats facing his soldiers, namely IEDs, RPGs, and mortars.

The burden of leadership in theater had few acceptable outlets. The staff sergeant's commanding officer had his own worries and, as a senior NCO, the staff sergeant couldn't burden his soldiers with these concerns. If his soldiers knew that he was struggling, how could he inspire their confidence?

His eyes met mine briefly before he pushed away from the table where he'd been leaning. "Combat Stress, right?" he said, referring to the mental health facility for soldiers on Anaconda.

I nodded. "Yeah, you know the drill. Let him talk to some of the counselors. Maybe that's all he needs. At a minimum, he should be gone for about two days."

"Yeah, I know, ma'am," the sergeant replied, nodding his head glumly. Since arriving in Iraq, at least three soldiers in the sergeant's company had reported that they were contemplating suicide.

"Hey sergeant, we've got less than ten weeks left in Iraq." Lowering my voice, I added, "Hang in there. I know you've had a tough ride, but you've done a great job pulling everyone through."

"You're telling me, ma'am," he said emphatically, slapping the table.

I was glad to see it nonetheless. "Hey, better safe than sorry with this kid," I added lightly, as the sergeant picked up his Kevlar, preparing to leave. "You know where Combat Stress is located, right?"

His head popped up in response.

Seeing my smile, he offered a small one of his own. "Yeah, ma'am, I think I should be able to find them."

It was acknowledgement, served with a side of legal advice, increasingly the most popular item on the menu. A very important thing I'd learned while working with soldiers in Iraq was that it could be lonely and challenging for soldiers at all levels, especially midlevel leaders. While Combat Stress counselors were available to everyone, midlevel leaders were often disinclined to use them, as they rightfully feared the negative repercussions to their careers. So, while it could be time-consuming to listen to soldiers vent, it was a worthwhile duty that also had the advantage of giving me a window into the environs at different units.

With the staff sergeant taken care of and the morning's panic regarding Sergeant Phil behind us, I settled down to get some work done. First order of business was the latest statement from the drowning investigation, a confession from Sgt. Reggie Martinez, the soldier identified as the other pusher. I was hoping Martinez's statement would serve as the tie-breaker regarding some of the inconsistencies between good-guy Logan's statement and pusher Bowman's statement.

According to Martinez, the platoon had been on a regular patrol when they stopped the two Iraqis for being out after curfew. Zaidoun, "the skinny guy," and Marwan, "the chunky guy," were both handcuffed and loaded into Lieutenant Saville's Bradley, one of four comprising the convoy. The Iraqis sat on the floor at Martinez's feet. Instead of heading toward the detention and processing facility at Brassfield-Mora, the convoy drove to Samarra's outskirts, stopping when they reached a bridge along the Tigris. From the Bradley's turret, Saville ordered the group of soldiers, led by Martinez, to throw the two detainees into the river.

"The LT said if you don't feel good throwing them off of the bridge just throw him by the shore," Martinez recalled.

He opted for the shore. With his weapon trained on a handcuffed Zaidoun, Martinez led the group, which included Bowman, platoon medic Sgt. Alexis Rincon, and the gunner, Specialist Hardin, down a path toward a concrete platform that comprised part of the dam's side wall along the shoreline. When they reached the platform, Martinez told investigators, "I told one guy, the skinny guy to jump, and he didn't, so I kicked him in the butt."

Drowning In The Desert

Martinez's explanation for why he participated echoed Bowman's. "I did this because I was following orders."

The words stuck like a shard in my mind: "Following orders."

As the squad leader, Martinez said that he was worried about setting a bad example. "I felt that if my team saw me not obey orders from my chain of command then they would think that it is okay to not obey me." Martinez also admitted to yelling at Logan for refusing to participate. "I told him when I tell him to do something he has to do it."

For Martinez, throwing the Iraqis into the river was an order, not a matter of right or wrong. There were consequences for not following orders. Only later did I fully understand that Martinez's automaton allegiance to rank was a matter of survival.

As it turned out, this wasn't the first time that the platoon had thrown an Iraqi into the Tigris River. Months earlier, they had thrown an Iraqi off a bridge in Balad. That time, Martinez explained, their platoon sergeant, Sergeant First Class Perkins, had only one criteria for their victim. He wanted someone "big." At a market in Balad, Perkins pointed to a large Iraqi man and ordered Martinez and another soldier to pick him up.

"We took him, threw him in the Bradley and stopped by a bridge somewhere. We uncuffed him and threw him off of the bridge," Martinez said.

In a story that should have been his undoing, Martinez echoed something that had disturbed me about Logan's and Bowman's accounts. This indisputable fact asserted itself continually: all of the soldiers lived in fear of their platoon sergeant, Sgt. 1st Class Tracy Perkins. With well over a decade of service under his belt, Perkins was a swaggering force to be reckoned with. Soldiers in his charge learned quickly that unquestioning obedience and a low profile were key to their survival. Any misstep could trigger the platoon sergeant's legendary temper.

In Balad, when Martinez and the other soldier failed to push the big man off the bridge properly, Perkins became enraged.

"Sergeant First Class Perkins started screaming at us and called us stupid fucks, because we did not do it the way he wanted us to."

The whole bridge-throwing thing began as a competition between their platoon and another platoon in Alpha Company, Bowman explained to investigators. The challenge was to see who could throw an Iraqi off a bridge first.

Regarding the Balad incident, Bowman added, "The guy had done nothing wrong that I am aware of, Sergeant First Class Perkins just wanted to be the first to do it."

A sense of desperation reverberated through all of the soldiers' accounts. Asked why he didn't come forward and report the incident earlier, Martinez replied, "I was scared."

Describing the night of January 2, Bowman said, "I felt I had to follow the orders, Sergeant First Class Perkins would not have any problems putting his hands on me."

After he confessed to investigators, Martinez asked to be removed from 1-8 Infantry Battalion. It wasn't an unusual request considering the nature of the investigation. Bowman and Logan had done the same. Kept apart throughout the questioning process, the soldiers' similar, unprompted explanations for their requests were chilling.

"I am afraid of personal injury and physical harm if I return after telling the truth here tonight," Bowman said.

Martinez went a step further, requesting a permanent change of station. He explained that he could not go back to Fort Carson because he needed "to get away from everybody and to protect my family."

Following their confessions in Tikrit, Martinez, Bowman, and Logan never returned to 1-8, or 3rd Brigade.

All three accounts of the drowning highlighted one thing: there was a dangerous and highly explosive element deeply entrenched at 1-8. Whether Perkins's sadistic streak was evident back at Fort Carson was not clear. It was clear, however, that it had flourished in Iraq.

Straightening up from the table, my eyes felt crispy and itchy. It was definitely operator error; I'd been wearing my contacts for at least seven hours too many. I had also spent several of those hours hunched over the soldiers' statements, my left index finger leading the search for common threads as I scribbled notes on a legal pad. Pressing the heels of my hands against my eyelids helped relieve some of the strain. I should have worn my glasses. Here, I'd thought Martinez's confession was going to wrap everything up. Instead, it was like tossing a live grenade into a crowd.

As far as my eyes were concerned, Perkins's role was the easiest to discern. Details about the sadistic sergeant leaped off the page. He loomed large in the soldiers' lives, and their fear was palpable. There was no straining to form an impression of Perkins, just flinching as his frightening presence had materialized. He was simple and straightforward, your standard bully.

The soldier I was more interested in was 1st Lt. Jack Saville, probably because he was a fellow officer. Like Saville, I had also spent four years training to lead a platoon, studying everything from strategic planning to military ethics. I searched the soldiers' statements for clues about Saville, his temperament, his leadership style. Was he responsible for creating the climate of fear and violence within the platoon. Did it extend to the company? Saville was the highest-ranking person there that night; if anyone could have prevented the drowning, it was him. I figured that if I understood Saville, I might understand how everything went wrong.

The soldiers' statements, however, offered few clues about Saville. While he was their platoon leader, he seemed to be more of a secondary, peripheral figure, especially in contrast to their vivid descriptions of Perkins. Saville had taken over the platoon in September while Perkins had been a member of the platoon from the start. As the new platoon leader, I suspected that Saville had his work cut out for him.

Even under the best circumstances, it's tough for freshly minted officers to give orders to soldiers who are nearly a decade older, and considerably more experienced, than they were. By the time Saville took over, Perkins was already a well-established member of the tribe, trusted by the leadership, and feared by his fellow soldiers. Perkins probably took one look at Saville, the baby-faced West Pointer, and knew that things would continue, business as usual. It didn't matter that Saville was supposed to be his commanding officer. Guys like Perkins could smell weakness. Saville may have given Martinez the order in Samarra but I couldn't help but think that it was Perkins who really called the shots that night

For the soldiers who carried out the deadly order that night at the river, things were about to go from bad to worse. No longer would their biggest concern be surviving the day without triggering Perkins' wrath, the Hassoun family's drowning claim now meant they were possible suspects in a murder case.

They weren't the only ones concerned about the drowning investigation. While the pushers agonized over the frightening predicament their own fear had led them to, Saville and Perkins knew it wouldn't take long for investigators to trace the incident back to their unlawful order.

Martinez described an anxious Saville approaching him just after the lieutenant learned about the drowning allegation: "He said it's gotten big and that we must not tell nobody about this," Martinez recounted to investigators.

That afternoon, Martinez, Bowman, and Logan found themselves sitting down with Perkins, Saville, and their company commander, Capt. Matthew Cunningham, to discuss what they would say to investigators. According to Martinez, the senior leaders in the group wanted the soldiers to lie. They instructed the soldiers to tell investigators that they'd stopped Zaidoun and Marwan for violating curfew, checked their IDs, and released the men on the side of the road.

"Tell them about everything except the water," Martinez recalled them saying.

"I really wanted to tell the truth but I felt a lot of pressure from my chain-of-command to go with the lies," Bowman said.

A lot of pressure? Cunningham was Bowman's company commander, one of the most important officers in the battalion. If Bowman and Martinez were already so scared of Perkins that they pushed two innocent men into a river, lying for a senior officer would be easy by comparison.

What bothered me was the extent to which their leaders had gone to ensure compliance. I could only imagine how gentle Cunningham's "encouragement" had been. A West Point grad, Captain Cunningham had a sense of entitlement that matched his patrician features. Dark-haired, with a long slim face and elegant nose, he wore an ever-present scowl. He was an angry fusion of ambition and arrogance. Lacking Sassaman's charisma and Paliwoda's quiet confidence, Cunningham endeavored to compensate with methodical efficiency.

Months earlier, while presiding over a meeting with Balad's police chief and community leaders, I recalled that Cunningham had been poised and courteous. He welcomed everyone at the start of the meeting, and thanked everyone when it was over. However, he didn't smile once during the entire meeting, which is a necessary practice when working with locals, especially when communicating through a translator. With Cunningham, the flaw was always execution. No amount of preparation could compensate for what boiled down to a jarring absence of ease.

Bowman recalled Cunningham telling him that if he stuck to the story, "it would be over with faster." Cunningham, Saville, and Perkins were impressively thorough. They drilled the soldiers daily about their interviews and sometimes as often as three or four times a day.

"They would ask us individually, 'Okay what are you going to say?' and we would answer them. They even had us practice in the Bradley where we would sit and rehearse how and who got out," Martinez said. Saville and Perkins even stated that they would take a polygraph, on the condition, of course, that the three junior soldiers went first.

"They told us the results of the test did not matter and they [CID] could not use them against us," Bowman said.

Cunningham, Saville, and Perkins remained incredibly on point, telling the soldiers repeatedly, "CID is out to get us." "CID is bad." "CID is trying to destroy 1-8."

Their efforts to control the junior soldiers' testimonies didn't end there. They even brought them back to the concrete slab on the side of the Tigris River. Martinez told investigators he was asked to the show the group, which included squad members and several of their leaders, the precise spot where they forced the Iraqis into the river. At one point, Saville jumped into the murky water to check the depth. Saville had come prepared, bringing a set of clothes to change into. The group spoke candidly about the night in question, Martinez said, discussing everything from the strength of the river's current to the answers they would give CID in their upcoming interviews.

I was so busy shaking my head at the lengths Cunningham and company went to ensure the soldiers' compliance that I almost breezed over the bombshell nestled in Martinez's statement.

"While we were standing there, we told Major Gwinner how we forced them into the river," Martinez recalled.

I read the line again. "While we were standing there, we told Major Gwinner how we forced them into the river."

There it was. Gwinner had returned with the soldiers to the bridge. He had directed the cover-up.

"He [Gwinner] told us we would say we just dropped them off on the road side and not to tell anyone about the water. Then he gave us a big speech about how CID is bad," Martinez told investigators.

I dropped Martinez's statement as though I'd been singed. It all made sense: Gwinner's defensiveness, his refusal to cooperate. My brain went into overdrive, recalling all of the clues I'd missed. Just as one memory materialized, another cascaded from it.

Here I'd thought Martinez would clear up the discrepancy about whether the soldiers ever saw the two Iraqis again and instead he confirmed the one allegation I was certain was a lie. Gwinner involved with the coverup? At the time, Bowman's claim about Gwinner had seemed inconceivable. In the context of 1-8 against the world, it now made sense. Cobb and Datray were traitors and as such, the unit had supported my efforts to go after them. You were either with them or against them. Resist 1-8 in any way and you were on the team to beat. In Gwinner's eyes, the moment I started looking into the drowning, I'd joined the team to beat.

By the time the junior soldiers met with investigators, they'd had the "correct answers" drummed into them by everyone from Perkins to Gwinner. I suspect the officers feared one inquiry would spawn others.

For a few days, at least, the leadership's plan had appeared to work. I recalled how the soldiers' initial accounts had differed so dramatically from the Iraqis that the drowning claim seemed implausible, another off-the-wall claim by the locals. Had Logan kept quiet, they probably would have gotten away with it.

Shuffling through the investigation file, I pulled out Cunningham's statement, dated January 18, two days after the soldiers' initial interviews. Confident they were in the clear, the commander got cocky. Cunningham, who wasn't even present that evening, was so determined to discount the Iraqi's claim, he had offered investigators his own sworn statement, completely unsolicited.

He used this voluntary statement as a platform to discount every one of the Hassoun family's claims as well as the video they had submitted to substantiate their claim. Cunningham offered observations on everything from the damaged truck to Zaidoun's corpse. He didn't let the fact that he wasn't a crime scene investigator, or that he'd never even seen Zaidoun, stop him from describing the corpse in the video as "body unrecognizable."

"Soldiers remember [the] individual in question as wearing dark slacks, black jacket over non-button-up T-shirt during night in question. Individual on tape is wearing button-up dress shirt," Cunningham said.

Drowning In The Desert

A regular Perry Mason, Cunningham also parsed the details about the positioning of the white truck on the median, saying it was inconsistent with the soldiers' accounts. As for the Bradley track marks seen surrounding the destroyed truck, Cunningham concluded that they were present on the median prior to the truck being there. "Similar tracks are evident on roads throughout city due to heavy Bradley traffic." In other words, they were preexisting, mere happenstance.

As to the impact a Bradley could have on a vehicle, Cunningham dug deep. "Based on experience, a vehicle run over by a Bradley is almost unrecognizable. All wheels blow out and vehicle is totally crushed under 70,000 lb weight forced upon it. Only one of four sets of tires is deflated and contents of vehicle [are] intact even though bed of truck [is] destroyed. The vehicle appears to have been run over but looks more consistent with being run over by a high centered vehicle with smaller wheel base causing the side rails to collapse. . . ."

I wondered if it had ever occurred to Cunningham that it might be incriminating to offer himself up as an expert on how Bradleys damage civilian vehicles. I could just imagine cross-examination:

Captain Cunningham, you've been with 1-8 since the start of the deployment?

And, you've been the commander of alpha company for the majority of the deployment?

Based on your experience, you've witnessed several vehicles crushed by Bradleys?

So, this is not an unusual practice for your company?

Cunningham's galling statement was consistent with every encounter I'd ever had with the company commander. Each time we'd worked together, I walked away shell-shocked by his inexplicable surliness. At one meeting with some local officials, Cunningham had made a point of interrupting me almost every time I spoke. Concerned that I may have stepped on his toes, I kept a decidedly lower profile at our next meeting. It hardly mattered. Nor did it matter that I tried a bunch of different approaches—everything from businesslike to chummy—Cunningham was consistently prickly.

* * *

Later that evening, Cintron called to touch base about the investigation. "Did you have any luck with Saville?" I asked, still unsure what to think of the elusive platoon leader.

"He agreed to talk, ma'am, no problem there," Cintron said.

After struggling to form an impression of him from the other soldiers' statements, I was more than ready to hear from the lieutenant himself. My delight was short-lived, however, as Saville's responses to sensitive questions were devastatingly consistent:

> CINTRON: Did you discuss with your soldiers how they were going to be released into the river?
> SAVILLE: I prefer not to answer that question.
> CINTRON: After the detainees were released, did you have knowledge that the two detainees were pushed or forced to jump into the river?
> SAVILLE: I prefer not to answer that question.
> CINTRON: Did you know that these two detainees were in the river that night in Samarra?
> SAVILLE: I prefer not to answer that question.
>
> There were, of course, the occasional deviations.
>
> CINTRON: What was your order when you told Sergeant Martinez to release the detainees?
> SAVILLE: I don't remember exactly and I don't want to guess.

When Saville did deign to answer a question, his answers bordered on the absurd. Asked why he returned to the bridge a week after the incident, Saville said, "I went back there to determine if maybe there could have been a third individual there."

He speculated that what he mistook for the two original detainees standing on the side of the road may have in fact been one of the original detainees and a third Iraqi who conveniently happened to be in the area. This, Saville explained, led him to conclude that the detainees were not in a life-threatening situation.

His responses went from bad to worse. Asked if he was aware of any previous incidents where Iraqis were thrown into the river, Saville said, "I have seen at least one detainee in a body of water in Balad somewhere. I don't know if members of my unit got him in the water or if it was special forces."

His evasiveness coupled with his flashes of creativity, were enough to provoke even Cintron.

"I don't know why he agreed to talk to us if he wasn't going to say anything," she said, her voice bristling with irritation.

"Yeah," I agreed, "he didn't do himself any favors by not coming clean at this point."

Had Saville given me something—the truth would have been a good start—we might have been able to avoid some of the ugliness that was slowly becoming his future. If he had just taken some responsibility for the situation, admitted that he hadn't been up to the challenge, I could have worked with him. When it came to my recommending an appropriate course of action to a commander, I always factored in mitigating circumstances: a soldier's remorse, a soldier's conduct after-the-fact, a soldier's motives. I also took into account a soldier's past performance. There wasn't a commander, jury, or judge on Earth who wouldn't have some sympathy for a twenty-four-year-old soldier who admitted to being overwhelmed by his duties in a war zone, simply admitted said he was in over his head. Saville's behavior in the aftermath suggested he had little interest in mititgating his actions. Instead of taking some responsibility, he chose to compound one bad decision with another.

Lieutenant Saville was a cautionary tale, an example of the high cost a young officer could pay if he or she failed to be a leader. It was exactly the sort of parable you might imagine professors at his alma mater telling the next generation of cadets. It was his responsibility to keep the cocksure Perkins in line and set the tone for the group. As tempting as the lure of camaraderie was, Saville's first job was to look out for his men.

Saville had failed his men not once, but twice. He ordered his troops to commit a crime and then pressured them to lie about it afterward. Even worse, the chain of command helped amplify the message.

The leaders not only used their rank to influence the soldiers, they had seized on the soldiers' sense of loyalty to 1-8. While they preached to the soldiers that it was "1-8 versus CID," Saville's evasiveness, along with Cunningham's and Perkins's refusal to meet with investigators, suggested otherwise: It wasn't 1-8 versus CID, as they told their soldiers, it was every man for himself.

CHAPTER SIXTEEN

Coming Unglued

HARTLEIGH WAS UP BEFORE HER alarm clock sounded. Today there was no struggle, none of the sleepy fumbling for the snooze button that sometimes drove me crazy. Gathering her things quietly in the dark, she slipped outside to brush her teeth.

When I opened my eyes again twenty minutes later, she had already returned and was dressed in her flight suit. Her shoulder-length white-blond hair fell forward as she checked, and double-checked, her kit bag. Satisfied, she set it by the door and reluctantly turned her attention to her hair, smoothing it back into a low, unfussy ponytail. After a quick check for stray hairs around her face, she grabbed her kit bag and was out the door.

Hartleigh's flying time had been limited by her managerial responsibilities of late. Today, however, she was scheduled to fly a mission, and the morning could not have come sooner.

I lingered on my cot a few extra minutes before getting dressed and dragging myself to the chow hall. I figured a few cups of coffee might ease my mounting sense of dread. CID was scheduled to interview Major Gwinner this afternoon. The investigation was rolling forward.

Drowning In The Desert

Planting myself in the corner of the chow hall, it occurred to me that this was one of the few mornings that I hadn't longed for my traditional stateside breakfast of a toasted "everything" bagel with a thin coat of butter. I settled for some coffee.

My disbelief over Gwinner's involvement in the cover-up had given way to a melancholy that seemed to cloud what I had been told was a perfect morning for flying. Up until this point, the drowning had been about a bunch of soldiers whom, with the exception of Cunningham, I was only vaguely familiar. Gwinner, however, was a man who had helped me, who had been instrumental to my success here.

I'd spent every moment of my time in Iraq trying to earn the respect and trust of guys like Gwinner. For me, every interaction had been "make or break," a chance to prove myself valuable to 1-8. Winning the first trial had made me fearful I'd let them down with the second one. And even winning the second one hadn't truly satisfied me. Strangely, it had only made me hungrier to do more, to be more . . . for 1-8, and for Gwinner.

Of course, it had been foolish and arrogant for Gwinner to tell soldiers to lie. After a year of making many good decisions, he'd made a bad one. There would be consequences. I knew that in the context of the army and our mission, there was little room for these kind of mistakes, especially for officers. As well as I understood all of these things, it didn't change the fact that I didn't want it to be this way.

Nursing my now-lukewarm coffee, I couldn't shake the profound sense of failure that now seemed to taint Iraq. After everything, the evidence I'd risked my life to gather, the trials we'd pulled off against the odds, and Operation Ivy Blizzard, we'd arrived at the one place I'd been so desperate to avoid: 1-8 and Gwinner did not consider me an asset or even an ally. At best, I was a hindrance. This outcome had always been a possibility. I'd just assumed that if we found ourselves here, it would be due to some shortcoming on my part, some nuance I'd failed to grasp, or some tactical point I'd overlooked. I never imagined we'd find ourselves here because they would choose the wrong path.

Kolb, Carter, Philibert, and Mendoza were already at the workspace when I arrived. Coffee in hand, I ran through the list of things we needed to tackle as the guys gathered around. Welsch's order for everyone to start winding down in preparation for redeployment had only intensified our workload. The battalions and companies were bombarding us with requests for weapons cards, rewards payments, civilian claims, and now, applications for war trophies. Everything required some sort of legal review.

"Hey Carter, what's the word over at the FSB about confiscated weapons. Do they have any?" I asked. The brigade's Forward Support Battalion was the designated receptacle for all confiscated weapons. I'd asked Carter to check in with them periodically as part of my effort to arm the local judges.

"Nope. Nothing. All they have are a few spare parts, pieces of guns." Seeing my confusion, he added, "Don't ask."

That sounded hopeful. Despite countless raids after which soldiers had reported seizing all sorts of weapons and ammunition, the Forward Support Battalion had received only about five weapons over the course of eight months. An earlier directive had allowed soldiers to keep one confiscated weapon in addition to their army-issued weapon. A good number of the seized weapons were likely destroyed along with the explosives that were found with them. As for the remaining weapons, it was hard to say.

At this late hour in our tour, it was pointless to berate the units. I just didn't want to see anybody mess up a good year of service by doing something foolish like trying to secretly ship the weapons home. If I were going to keep my promise to arm the judges before we left Iraq, it looked like I would have to find the weapons elsewhere.

Over Carter's left shoulder, I saw Welsch pass by in the main hallway.

"Okay, guys, I think that's it," I said, scanning my notebook to see if I'd missed anything.

"Oh, wait. Carter, what's the latest on your promotion packet? How is it?" I asked, one eye still fixed on Welsch.

"Oh, fine, ma'am," Carter replied, waving his hand dismissively to indicate that we shouldn't hold up the meeting. As the senior NCO, it was Kolb's responsibility to help manage Carter's career. Because Kolb's face didn't reflect Carter's dismissive attitude, I sensed something was wrong.

"Hold up. You did finish the correspondence courses, right?" I asked. Being in theater, with limited Internet and phone access, presented obstacles to completing the requisite courses he needed for promotion.

Carter nodded. "Ma'am, I'm just working on getting the packet together now, that's all," he said. Aware of how guarded he sounded, he quickly added, "I got it. Don't worry."

I studied his face. "Okay, but . . . you're certain that you don't need me to do anything?"

He offered a weak smile, "No, ma'am, I got it."

Over Carter's head, I watched Welsch turn toward the ALOC. When I looked up a moment later, he was gone.

"Well, that's all I have," I said distractedly before hurrying to try to catch up with Welsch.

With my task list growing by the minute, I intended to persuade Welsch to help me cross off at least two items. I found him outside, admiring his masterpiece: the brigade's newly built Tactical Operations Center. While our sister brigades had moved their TOCs inside buildings and palaces months earlier, our hellacious city-by-city tour of Iraq had forced us to pack and unpack our TOC tent more than a half-dozen times. By the time we arrived at Anaconda, Welsch was eager to create something more permanent.

A stand-alone structure, constructed entirely of wood, the new TOC was something to behold. As the brigade's nerve center, Welsch's TOC was the product of dozens of observations about traffic flow and information sharing. He designed it to reflect the new war with its new realities. It was also the first TOC to incorporate a section for civil affairs.

Nothing had been overlooked. It was well-considered and well-appointed, complete with built-in desks, plasma television screens, and tiered seating to facilitate the BUB's nightly crowd. As TOCs went, this was the gold standard.

Wearing his Kevlar but no vest, Welsch walked with his hands clasped loosely behind him, quietly surveying the TOC's exterior. In addition to conducting the day-to-day business of the war, the TOC was where we received visiting brass. The sauna-like conditions of our previous TOC, along with the stench, had always made us a quick stop for generals who were eager to visit troops in the field. Visiting brass were more inclined to linger at a comfortable venue. A consummate executive officer, Welsch understood that it didn't bode well for Colonel Rudesheim, or 3rd Brigade, if they didn't get face time with the military's key players.

More than anything, Welsch realized the TOC would be his legacy in Iraq.

It also was his consolation prize for being stuck in the same job for nearly two years. Rudesheim had wisely kept Welsch on for longer: Rudesheim knew that executive officers as effective as Welsch were rare. By this point in his command, Welsch should have moved on to command a battalion, or at least a different job.

As the brigade executive officer, his position was short on glory and long on headaches. This crucial position also offered no protection from soldiers' snide comments. There were always the digs that Welsch didn't get outside the wire enough, or a favorite, if only for its convenient vagueness, that Welsch simply didn't "get it." While no one would ever utter those sentiments to his face, I noticed that even the lowest-ranking soldiers felt comfortable discounting Welsch. If they had directed their comments to soldiers whose fear kept them tethered to Anaconda, that might have been a fair criticism. For Welsch, whose job was to run things at the brigade headquarters, it was a cheap shot. Still, the soldier-authenticity test wasn't about the many different jobs that needed to get done; it was about discounting anyone who wasn't kicking down a door like an infantryman.

Later that afternoon, I managed to get Welsch to help me keep my promise to the Iraqi judges. He signed off on just over a half dozen brand new 9mm handguns to be purchased using Commander's Emergency Response Program funds, which basically provided money to commanders for use on anything from infrastructure to schools.

It wasn't until I looked up and saw Sassaman's uneasy face among the soldiers lined up at the workspace that I felt my own disquiet reflected back at me. While a mandatory commanders' huddle had brought him to Anaconda that day, he'd clearly made the JAG workspace his first stop afterward. Today, the handsome colonel's face was sharpened with concern and there was no sign of the confident walk that had captivated a courtroom. Certain he was looking for an update on the drowning investigation, I ushered him towards the library where we could talk privately. If I felt as though I'd woken up in a different Iraq, I imagined Sassaman felt the same way. With Gwinner, his second-in-command due to be questioned by investigators this afternoon, he looked as though his world were imploding.

Later that day, a soldier dropped off a manila folder containing Gwinner's statement. As much as I wanted to devour it, I resisted, setting it aside carefully.

Turning back to the computer screen, I forced myself to refocus on the message that I was writing to Lieutenant Colonel Barnes. It was a last-minute plea for any additional guidance regarding my upcoming meeting with the Christian Peacemakers Team in Balad. With the meeting now just two days away, I felt increasingly anxious that I'd have little or no response to the group's concerns. I knew these westerners would never accept the noncommittal answers that I routinely proffered in response to Iraqis' concerns regarding our arrest and detention procedures. For instance, publicly announcing the names of Iraqis that we had in custody was a recurring request. It also was a reasonable request. In September, I'd traveled to the Coalition Provisional Authority headquarters in Baghdad, hoping to persuade the folks running the Ministry of Justice that they should change the no-publication policy.

I scanned my e-mail one last time to ensure that I'd maintained a reverent tone. I clicked send and reached for the manila folder containing Gwinner's statement.

That evening, I read Gwinner's statement twice. I suspect my incredulousness had spread to my face. No less than three people stopped in front of the workspace table to ask me if everything was all right.

Gwinner professed to be innocent, claiming that Alpha Company's soldiers never told him that they had forced the two detainees into the river. He disavowed knowledge of any foul play and painted himself a trusting fool.

"I believed what the platoon leader and platoon sergeant told me . . . that neither of the male detainees drowned during that incident," he told investigators.

Gwinner had tried to craft a compelling story, intending to absolve himself of any culpability. When the drowning allegations had first surfaced, Sassaman was in Balad, so he directed Gwinner, who was still in Samarra, to conduct an informal commander's inquiry on Sassaman's behalf. An inquiry, or informal investigation, usually has a single investigating officer who conducts interviews and collects evidence.

Gwinner built his claim of innocence on this shaky foundation: the soldiers' contention that they saw the two Iraqis standing on the side of the road as the unit drove away. Gwinner's statement showcased all manner of weasel-like behavior. Asked if he believed the detainees were released safely on the side of the road, Gwinner offered this cagey answer: "Based upon the statements of

Sergeant First Class Perkins and Lieutenant Saville, who saw them talking to each other in the dirt parking area on the side of the road," tacitly denying any knowledge beyond this regarding the fate of the two Iraqi detainees.

There were blatant lies, too.

CID: Why would soldiers within the unit state they were instructed to withhold information regarding this incident?

GWINNER: No idea.

And there were sins of omission: Not until investigators had directly raised the issue did Gwinner mention that he had asked Lieutenant Saville to jump into the river when they visited the bridge after the incident. Asked to explain his actions, Gwinner said that he wanted to test the water.

Gwinner also made a clumsy attempt to discredit the victim's family: "The reason I had [Lieutenant Saville] jump in the water was based upon a printed copy of an e-mail that the family of one of the detainees had forwarded as far as I know to the President of the U.S. and Tony Blair [British Prime Minister] relating that the 1st Platoon soldiers were intoxicated and that they had thrown the detainees into the swift current and one of them had drowned as a result."

He distanced himself from the incident at every opportunity, repeatedly lobbing responsibility back at the soldiers. "It is difficult when you are not even present and I was not . . . told about it [until] a week later and I am only getting information from the soldiers."

Gwinner played the innocent. Asked whether he knew that the soldiers pushed the detainees into the river, Gwinner replied, "Only off what they were accused of, they were accused of pushing them into the water and that is the only thing I was aware of." And yet there was no indication that Gwinner felt duped or angry that these soldiers lied to him.

For me, Gwinner's most damning statement concerned his claim that he had discussed the incident with the soldiers as part of a commander's inquiry requested by Sassaman. Had there been a commander's inquiry, as he alleged, I should have known about it. It is a well-understood practice, per Army Regulation 15-6, that investigating officers in informal and formal investigations seek legal guidance as soon as possible after they are notified of their duty.

As 1-8's executive officer, Gwinner knew the protocol. He routinely oversaw the investigating officers that Sassaman appointed. Gwinner and I spoke frequently during the month of January, and he never once mentioned that he was an investigating officer.

Any sympathy or sadness I had regarding Gwinner's predicament evaporated the second time I read his calculated answers. At a minimum, I'd expected Gwinner to take responsibility for his role in the cover-up. But he still didn't get it. He seemed to believe he was above the law. Worse still, after using his rank to encourage the soldiers to lie, Gwinner abandoned them the moment the plan fell apart.

Gwinner's statement begged the question: Why? Why would Gwinner risk his career for the sake of these maverick, junior-level soldiers? What did he have to gain from the cover-up? I could see why the cover-up might have made sense to Alpha Company's commander, Captain Cunningham, given his track record of arrogant behavior and his close proximity to Lieutenant Saville in the chain of command. But I couldn't understand what would cause Gwinner to behave so recklessly.

That evening, I learned from CID that they planned to interview Sassaman the following day.

CHAPTER SEVENTEEN

The Peacemakers

"I ASSUME YOU'VE ALREADY HEARD," Rudesheim said. Removing his reading glasses, he turned slightly in his chair, his face somber.

"Yes, sir. I spoke to Lieutenant Colonel Barnes this morning, just briefly though." Did Rudesheim have more news? I was afraid to ask.

Standing in Rudesheim's office with the door closed behind me and the colonel unsure how to proceed, the enormity of it all was beginning to sink in. Today's news appeared to have silenced the typically chatty colonel.

Upbeat and agreeable in nature, Rudesheim had unblemished olive skin and a head full of dark hair that gave him a particularly youthful appearance. His default expression and demeanor were not the stock grimness appropriated by many of the army's most ambitious. If anything, his tidy inviting features managed to always seem suggestive of good news. Tethered to today's dark circumstances, however, the colonel was only vaguely recognizable.

Returning his glasses to the bridge of his nose, he turned back to his computer. A look of concentration settled across the colonel's face as he studied the screen. While he typed, I took the opportunity to do a casual inventory of the room. A twin-sized bed, with a wool blanket folded neatly on top, dominated one corner. A mixture of adventure and mystery novels, along with a few biographies, comprised most of the dozen or so books stacked haphazardly on a trunk nearby. On the wall opposite the bed, and above his desk, was a large bulletin board covered in papers, maps, and a few photos. Rudesheim's office was decidedly neat and orderly. I wondered if his wife, Peggy, would say he was the same way at home.

Peering through his reading glasses at the computer screen, the colonel stopped typing. I looked away instantly, worried that he might think I'd been trying to read the screen. Pretending to investigate a loose thread on my uniform, I didn't raise my head until I heard the click-clack of his typing resume.

Turning my attention back to the bulletin board, I saw something I hadn't noticed the first time. Nestled between the brigade phone list and some recent division orders, was the black and white image of a handsome West Point cadet in his plebe uniform: Rudesheim's son. The image looked as though it had been printed on an office printer. While the top of a PowerPoint chart obscured the lower third of the image, the younger Rudesheim's shoulders and face were prominent. His positioning was strategic. The colonel needed only look up from his computer screen to see his son's face.

The younger Rudesheim had begun his military career while we were in Iraq. The colonel had missed his son's high school graduation, as well as most of his first year at West Point. Cadets, unlike most college students, do not enjoy an extended summer break at home.

Colonel Rudesheim's own military career had begun as a cadet in the University of Texas' ROTC program. Though Rudesheim spoke fondly of his college days and was an ardent fan of his alma mater, he was clearly delighted to have his own connection to West Point. I wondered what role he had played in his son's choosing West Point. Did the colonel encourage it above other schools? Surrounded by West Point grads his entire career, had he ever felt at a disadvantage? Either way, I thought, shifting uncomfortably on my feet, he had every reason to be proud. There were few more promising ways to begin a military career than to go to the Military Academy. While the beauty of the army is that a poor kid with talent and ambition can ascend to the highest ranks, the sense of destiny associated with West Pointers is undeniable.

Minutes passed before Rudesheim removed his glasses a second time and handed me a sheaf of papers stapled together. In the name block at the top of the first page was "Nathan Sassaman." It was Sassaman's confession.

Instead of meeting with CID investigators today as scheduled, Sassaman proffered his own sworn statement.

Holding Sassaman's several-page statement in my hand, I was surprised by the document's lack of heft. I don't know what I expected. Dragging my dry, cracked thumb across the first page, I rubbed the sheets together. Even as I did this, the bold print of his name on the top page continued to scream at me. It was all there, all on three flimsy sheets of paper. Satisfied he'd let me forestall the inevitable long enough, Rudesheim pretended to clear his throat.

In his statement, Lt. Col. Nathan Sassaman, commander of 1-8 Infantry Battalion, admitted to ordering his soldiers to lie to investigators about throwing two unarmed Iraqis into the river. For Sassaman, the confession would mean the end of his career, if not criminal prosecution for obstruction of justice.

Sassaman said he only vaguely recalled giving the order at all. He'd been in Balad when Gwinner alerted him that CID planned to interview Saville's platoon in connection with a drowning in Samarra. Sassaman admitted to instructing Gwinner to tell the soldiers to lie about pushing the Iraqis into the water. He characterized his response as a split-second decision to which he gave little thought, even afterwards.

A good portion of his statement focused on the circumstances surrounding his decision. He made frequent references to his mindset at the time, particularly his anguish over Eric Paliwoda's death and the stress he felt about his growing responsibilities. Eric's death seemed to confirm his suspicions that the responsibility of securing the region rested squarely on his shoulders. Sassaman also inadvertently raised a question about his own fitness to command. While Sassaman contended his despair only impaired his judgment briefly, the reality was that there were few resources available to combat battalion commanders, for whom the expectations were tremendous.

Who could Sassaman or Lieutenant Colonel Gonsalves, or any of the other battalion commanders talk to when they were feeling stressed or anxious? It wasn't unlike the sergeant who came to discuss the suicidal soldier—he didn't want to bother his commanders with his frustrations and risk raising doubts about his ability to handle stress and he couldn't discuss these issues with his soldiers.

While Sassaman admitted giving the order, he also pulled his punch. He maintained that his decision hinged on his belief that the Iraqis had survived their fall into the Tigris. He insisted that the soldiers had given him and Gwinner no reason to believe otherwise. The distinction was significant: instructing soldiers to lie was one thing, but instructing soldiers to cover up a murder was another thing entirely. Sassaman also said he never intended for things to turn out as they did.

The papers in my hand raised more questions than they answered. Had Sassaman sacrificed his career in an ill-conceived attempt to save some of his men from criminal prosecution? Why would he do something so stupid? Did he somehow feel responsible for the platoon's actions? Where was that inherent sense of self-preservation that most senior officers seemed to have? He was one of the army's brightest stars. Was it possible he somehow felt he had no choice?

I stood in front of Rudesheim's desk for nearly an hour that morning, both of us shaking our heads in dismal disbelief. We took turns being stunned, baffled and disappointed. Minutes passed during which we said nothing at all.

Sassaman's decision to discuss his confession with General Odierno before speaking to Rudesheim only added another sour note to the sordid affair. Whether Sassaman intended it as a slap at Rudesheim, his decision to ignore the chain of command was a sign of disrespect. Rudesheim, to his credit, did not appear to be ruminating over the slight. He seemed more concerned with the impact Sassaman's confession would have on the battalion and the brigade. Perhaps, it was the type of slight he'd become accustomed to. A non-West Pointer, I wondered if Rudesheim had accepted that even at the highest levels, the brotherhood still dominated. Either way, it seemed more than coincidence that the younger Rudesheim would join Odierno, Sassaman, Cunningham, and Saville as part of West Point's legendary long, gray line.

After a particularly long stretch of silence, Rudesheim looked up and said, "That's everything, Vivian. Thank you."

"No problem, sir." There was nothing left for either of us to say. Today, we were reluctant witnesses to the end of what should have been a legendary career.

Leaving Rudesheim's office, I passed by Welsch's door. Judging by the quickness with which he waved me into his office, he appeared to have been waiting for me. To my surprise, Welsch simply asked whether my meeting concerned the drowning investigation. When I confirmed that it did, he merely nodded, mouth pursed, and returned to his own computer screen.

* * *

While Sassaman's fate was being decided in Tikrit, I still had an investigation to coordinate. I'd also be doing it with one less man. Division notified me that week that they had arranged for Mendoza's transportation back to Tikrit. We were still two months away from returning home, but division wanted him back to begin redeployment preparations. It was an unwelcome order. We'd grown attached to Mendo. In three months, he'd become a valued member of the team. His transition into our team has been so seamless; I never gave it a second thought. Mendo would also be sorely missed by the Iraqi merchants who assured him a fellow could never have enough gold chains. A fast learner, with people skills to boot, I suspected division was feeling seller's remorse over lending him to us in the first place. It was a lesson to me: I should have complained to division about Mendo, painted him as a slacker. They would have left him with us for good.

Within days, my team of five dwindled to three. Sergeant Philibert accompanied our Humvee on its return trip to Kuwait, where it would be loaded on a ship headed home. The convoy, led by Capt. Brian Gebhardt, was a dangerous trip that snaked through Baghdad on its route south. Loathe to put Phil back on the road, or relinquish our Humvee when I was still traveling to our outlying units, I'd postponed his trip several times in the hope that we could just leave the piece of junk in Iraq for use by a follow-on unit. The cost, risk, and time spent ensuring that our run-down Humvee returned to the states would forever confound me. We should have left it in Iraq.

As loathe as I was to see Mendoza go, I was dreading the other big event of the week even more: the Christian Peacemakers meeting with Sassaman and Cunningham in Balad. The topic for this meeting was 1-8's treatment of Iraqis.

To add to the fun, shortly before the meeting rumors circulated that CNN's Nic Robertson was back to visit 1-8. Robertson had spent a good deal of time shadowing Sassaman several weeks earlier and was eager to capture him in his element. I could just see it: newly tainted Sassaman would be in no mood to listen to Iraqi complaints; Cunningham, brooding as usual; outraged Iraqi lawyers; and to moderate the meeting we would have members of a self-described pacifist group that promoted peace by "getting in the way." It certainly had the makings of good TV, if not good diplomacy.

The citizens of Balad were angry. They wanted to know where their arrested family members had been taken and why they were being held. Still trying to wrap their minds around their new reality and their new American neighbors, they did what they heard Americans did in challenging times: they hired lawyers. Insisting they wanted justice "the American way," the Iraqi lawyers, in dark suits and crisp white shirts, filled the too-small meeting room. A few of their clients were also in attendance.

When I arrived, Sassaman was just taking a seat in front of a set of empty bookshelves at the far end of the room.

"Hi, sir," I said hurrying across the carpeted floor to take the open seat next to Thanna, who was translating that day.

Sassaman looked up, offered the slightest nod, and motioned to the Peacemakers that we were all here. Cunningham sat to Sassaman's right, his face a mask of haughty indifference. Settling in my seat, I pulled out my notebook and reviewed my talking points. Or rather, my non-talking points. I couldn't disclose the locations of detainees whom the United States was holding. I couldn't promise that we would give locals any information on the status of particular detainees. I couldn't admit, or outright deny, any allegations of abuse or mistreatment of detainees. I couldn't guarantee that those held for security reasons had the right to a lawyer. It was going to be a long afternoon. Mercifully, CNN had decided not to cover the meeting.

Stewart Vriesinga, the head of the Peacemakers delegation, was the first to speak. A thoughtful man in his early sixties, Vriesinga, with his salt-and-pepper hair and his white beard, looked like the mythical figure "Father Time," his patterned wool sweater and twill pants notwithstanding. More of a big-picture guy, he began by sharing his "vision for the future of Iraq." As he spoke, he endeavored to make eye contact with every person in the room.

"I want to build a bridge of friendship and harmony between the children of Iraq and the children of the United States," Vriesinga said, clasping his hands together.

A noble enough goal, Vriesinga repeated this sentiment several more times throughout the meeting, with the requisite hand gestures. He said his purpose here today was to help ensure that the Iraqis' concerns were heard.

When it sounded like Vriesinga was yet again heading for the metaphorical bridge, I was convinced there had to be a hidden camera somewhere. *Hey, Father Time, on advice of counsel, it's probably not the best time to be talking about Iraqis and bridges.*

When he was done, he urged the twenty or more of us in the room to likewise share our vision for Iraq's future. Silence followed the translation.

With neither Sassaman nor Cunningham rushing to share, one of the Iraqis motioned to Thanna that he wanted to speak.

"We are representing the families who just want to know where their relatives are," said the man, who appeared to be the lead lawyer. He wore the requisite dark suit and a crisp, white shirt. "They want to know why they have been arrested. It seems like the soldiers just want to arrest everyone."

Neither Sassaman, Cunningham, nor I took the bait.

Finally, Vriesinga said, "The Iraqis would just like to know where their relatives are. They are concerned that they seem to disappear without any information on how to reach them."

Silence. By this point, the sun had moved slightly and I realized the room was not painted brown and aqua as I'd first thought but a slightly more agreeable beige and aqua. Interesting. Cunningham sipped a Coke and I sat there poised to step in if it sounded as if the army's position needed clarification. When it looked like Vriesinga might offer another iteration of the Iraqi's concerns, Sassaman cleared his throat.

"We're trying to bring security to Balad but we can't do it alone. We can't do it if our base is being hit with mortars every day. The security situation is everyone's responsibility," he said, wisely choosing not to address the claim head-on.

That morning, we averaged one response for every three statements made by the Iraqis. Cunningham rested his elbow on the desk next to him and stared off in the distance while Sassaman spent much of the meeting in his own thoughts, looking over when the pitch in someone's voice changed or it sounded like things were getting heated.

Several men down from the main lawyer, another one of the lawyers turned to address us.

"Sometimes you arrest the wrong people based on something that isn't true," he said.

Ugggh. No kidding. I did a quick look around to make sure my groan had remained internal. Intelligence problems had plagued us since the beginning. On our city-by-city tour of Iraq, we frequently found ourselves the unwitting accomplices of one tribe determined to destroy another. For a while, it had seemed as if we worked with whomever made contact with us first. They'd hand us a list with the names and addresses for the "bad guys" and we had few ways to determine whether it was accurate or not.

For me, the meeting was particularly excruciating. The Iraqi's concerns were all issues I'd raised in some form or another back at the brigade. From better accountability at the facilities to evidence gathering. Likewise, I felt Sassaman's frustration. The whole issue of whether the United States should be in Iraq notwithstanding, we'd been in Balad for months, improving the infrastructure, building schools and training police forces. The Goliath in this battle, we were expected to shake off every attack and expect a thrashing by the media if we responded in kind. Today's meeting was the soundtrack of my life, the perpetual dialogue in my head, performed live in English and Arabic.

While we were there to demonstrate good will. I was also there to gauge just how bad things were. How upset are the locals? Exactly how many people are missing or unaccounted for? What exactly do the lawyers want out of this? What do the Christian Peacemakers want out of this? I spent a lot of these meetings searching for some sort of stop-gap measure that would address the local's concerns but would also be in line with the army's current policies.

Sassaman responded to several of these accusations but offered no concrete answers. As unpleasant and undiplomatic as it sounded, we could technically say that the arrested individuals were enemy combatants and therefore had no rights. We could also say that we were under no obligation to tell anyone anything. Of course, doing so wouldn't help us win us any popularity contests.

After one particularly impassioned statement by an Iraqi lawyer, I leaned forward to address the group. "We understand that local citizens are concerned and we are trying to work through these problems. We agree that it is important to hear those concerns and that's why we're here today. But solving these problems will require everyone's cooperation. And that means just as you come to us for help, we need help reducing the number of attacks against our soldiers. The issues are connected. So, local citizens are not helpless; they can help solve these problems and the current situation too."

It was a bizarre answer, likely muddled further by translation, but it beat an answer that might incite them. In situations like this one it was my job to bring the bland.

Cunningham said nothing the entire meeting, his lack of interest apparent. He sat with one leg draped elegantly over the other and his arms crossed in front of his chest for much of the meeting. Every half-hour or so, he'd get restless and start drumming his fingers on the arm of his chair. Sassaman had barely looked at me since the meeting started, and when he did, he seemed to be looking through me, rather than at me. It was the first time I'd seen him since the day he'd stopped by after the commanders' huddle. It was the first time I'd seen him since he confessed.

The meeting continued, with a member from each group taking turns "sharing their thoughts" on the detainee debacle. I was judicious with my limited offerings, doling them out carefully throughout the afternoon. Yes, I can look into the situation, perhaps provide some information on certain individuals if I received the names before our next meeting. Later, I conceded that those families concerned that their missing relative needed medicine would receive first priority if I were able to determine their whereabouts in the detention system. Finally, I agreed to look into the rights afforded those currently detained. The lawyers had produced a recent decree from Baghdad that stated all citizens had a right to a lawyer. I had a feeling that it didn't apply to those detained by Coalition Forces, but I agreed to look into it, nonetheless.

Vriesinga, for all his sincerity, was not the best advocate for the Iraqis. Demanding we respond to specific claims of detainee abuse in an open forum was poor form. I snuck a peek at Sassaman whose mouth was set in a sneer. It was just a matter of time.

Having dissected almost everyone and everything in the room during the morning portion of the meeting, I shifted my focus downward as we headed into the afternoon. Underfoot was a green carpet dominated by endless maroon stripes, the room's other curious color pairing. One stripe would catch my eye and I'd focus on it. It wouldn't take long for the lines to begin to look fuzzy. When it started to look as though the maroon lines appeared to touch, I knew it was time to straighten up and pay closer attention to the meeting. I was set to succumb yet again to the hypnotic maroon stripes when I heard Vriesinga return to the bridge. *Shit.*

This time, Sassaman cut him off. "Look, I have a vision of peace, too, and I agree the best thing about this country are the children," Sassaman said. "Heck, some days they are the only thing that reminds me that everyone in this country is not corrupt or trying to kill us."

It was the least diplomatic I'd ever seen Sassaman. I motioned to Thanna to rephrase parts of his statement before she began. I spent the rest of the afternoon making long, clause-filled declarations about the army's concern for human rights to drown out some of the harsher responses from our side. As I straightened up to offer yet another declaration, someone suggested we save the discussion for a follow-up meeting. *Hallelujah!*

I had little reason to worry about any dialogue I might have with Sassaman afterward. I had just finished writing down the date for the next meeting when I looked up and saw that he and Cunningham were already on their feet with their gear in hand. Despite my efforts to present a united front to the Iraqis, neither said a word as they passed.

As Sassaman and Cunningham exited, a dozen Iraqis spilled into the room, all of them determined to speak with the American *mohami*, lawyer in Arabic. Some handed me scraps of paper with names of relatives. Others pushed claims information at me, for damages U.S. forces allegedly had caused to their property. They wanted money, and despite the fact that they were required to file claims at the police stations, they still hoped to persuade me to approve their claims and pay them on the spot. Still trying to gather my gear, I did my best to fend them off by feigning confusion and pretending to look for Thanna, whom I knew had bolted with Sassaman.

Outside the courthouse, a few of the judges I'd worked with came to my aid. They yelled at the locals to leave me alone. When I saw several people shrink in response, I worried, albeit briefly, about what the judges had said. As always, there were a few Velcro claimants whose arms, hands, and elbows spilled in after me when I opened the door to get into the Humvee. When I had enough room to pull the door closed, I threw a handful of candy out the window. Like Iraqis to an American lawyer, the children swarmed for the candy, creating a buffer between the claimants and the Humvee. Eager to prevent a last minute surge at the vehicle, I threw a few more handfuls of candy. "Go, Go!" I yelled at the driver, whom Welsch had loaned me for the day.

Thus ended another day of bringing democracy to Iraq.

* * *

Several days later, standing on the platform from which Zaidoun was pushed, I felt a shiver of terror. I could only imagine how Marwan must have felt. It was his fourth trip back to the bridge site and probably the hundredth time he had been forced to recount the night his cousin died.

Cintron, the translator, and I had arrived in Samarra around midmorning to visit the site with Marwan, Zaidoun's father, and the family's lawyer. We had followed Marwan to a small pump house near the side of the bridge. The pump house sat on a concrete slab that jutted out slightly over the water. To the left was the dam, a hulking concrete and steel structure situated beneath the bridge. From the cement platform where I stood, we estimated a ten-foot drop to the murky green water below. Slick, amoeba-shaped patches of oil floated across the river's dark surface. The water appeared calm, almost stagnant, except for a small ripple some fifteen feet in the direction of the dam. Beyond that was another ripple, the outer concentric rings of a whirlpool that funneled beneath one of the dam's five gates.

We watched as a plastic water bottle and other pieces of garbage succumbed to the whirlpool, disappearing below the surface, presumably down and through the one dam gate that Samarra's water authorities had left open.

"This is where Zaidoun was," Marwan said, pointing to the part of the platform closest to the dam. Marwan moved nearly ten feet to his right to show me where he had stood just before he was forced into the water. I moved to the spot and tried to imagine being there in the middle of the night with a gun trained on me.

"I was moving my arms and legs so much, but I wasn't getting any closer to the side," Marwan recalled, his eyes fixed on the river. Marwan had struggled with more than just his waterlogged clothing and shoes that night. The entire time he had been working against a powerful undertow. A nonswimmer like Zaidoun didn't stand a chance. He'd been thrown in closer to the whirlpool.

On the other side of the dam, the river rushed forth in a torrent of white rapids. The fast-moving water was significantly lower on this output side, a roughly twenty-foot drop to the water. We stood there staring at the angry rapids for several minutes before Cintron suggested that we take one last look at the platform.

Standing where Zaidoun had stood, I could understand why his body had not immediately floated to the surface. Zaidoun's water-logged body had probably been caught up in the undertow and trapped under the dam for some time before it surfaced downstream nearly two weeks later.

Gwinner's angry demand, "Where's the body? Where's the body?" kept playing in my head. If I were going to prosecute this case, I would need to prove beyond any doubt that Zaidoun was dead. The video showing Zaidoun's body was circumstantial evidence. The inherent distrust toward Iraqis would make it easy for the defense to cast doubt: just a few insistent voices claiming the soldiers saw the Iraqis standing on the side of the road as they pulled away. Never mind that their story was inherently incredible. I needed direct proof that the bloated body they recovered down river was Zaidoun.

Taking one last look at the narrow, steep grade of the shoreline that Marwan had struggled to pull himself up, Gwinner's persistent claim that the soldiers saw the two Iraqis on the side of the road again struck me as ludicrous. There was no way that anyone, having just been tossed fully clothed into the river, could have quickly swam to the shore, pulled themselves up and out, and rushed back to the road before the soldiers departed. And why would Marwan and Zaidoun risk being seen by the same soldiers who had just forced them into the river? Even a child would know better. Why tempt the bully to do it again by reappearing by the side of the road?

The fact that Gwinner had stood here, seen the drop, the water, the whirlpool, and the shore, and yet he still claimed that he had believed that nothing had happened, placed him in a new, unflattering light.

During the hour or more we spent at the bridge that day, Zaidoun's father had hung back near the pump house and in the clearing on the side of the road, uninterested in hearing or seeing the details of that night. He wore the same orange robe from our first meeting.

Looking up as we approached to leave, he nodded slightly to acknowledge us.

This time, when I asked him for permission to exhume and autopsy Zaidoun's body, he released a long, weary sigh.

"It will be important to obtaining justice for Zaidoun," I said to fill the space.

A long pause followed before he finally said, "We will consider it."

Hearing that, I resisted the urge to pressure him to say "yes" right there.

"Thank you for considering it," I said, assuring him that every step of the autopsy process would be carried out in a respectful manner.

"I understand that this is a difficult decision," I said, "and I appreciate your consideration because it is crucial to the . . ." Worried I might be talking too much, I looked up to find Zaidoun's father watching me, rather than the translator, very intently. There was no sign of anger or irritation in his face. He studied me with soft eyes and an almost sympathetic curiosity. His expression seemed to say, "I don't think you understand, captain. For a parent who outlives his child, there is no justice."

That evening, I learned that CID planned to interview Colonel Rudesheim the following day.

CHAPTER EIGHTEEN

Fish or Cut Bait

CARTER STOOD ON THE OPPOSITE side of our main table, a blend of dread, annoyance, and resignation on his face.

"Hold on a minute," I said, uncertain of what I'd just heard. "How come your packet isn't in yet? When's the deadline? I thought it had to be in by the first."

Raising his head, Carter exhaled. "Another problem with the computer system, ma'am. It got all messed up, and now they're saying they don't have my information." Anticipating my next question, he added, "Yes, I spoke to them. I tried everything."

"So when you log in at the site, it doesn't have any of your point information? That you completed your correspondence courses, none of that?"

"Nope, all gone," Carter said, bitterness finally evident in his voice. "And they acknowledged that it was their fault."

The army's promotion system was handled online, as were the correspondence courses Carter needed to complete in order to apply to be promoted. To even be considered, a candidate needed to accrue a certain number of points. As the candidate completed each course, the system would instantly update the points. It was a great system . . . when it worked.

"Wait, then what did they tell you to do?"

"There's really nothing I can do," he said. "Don't worry, ma'am. I'll just file it when we get back. It's not a big deal."

He might as well have told me that he'd changed his mind and now wanted to stay in Iraq. Carter's goal from the outset had been to return as a sergeant, and to leave the army as a sergeant. With just over a year of his four-year commitment remaining, Carter planned to cash in on his benefits and go to college. While Carter had been frequently tempted to stay, I encouraged him to get his degree and had been quietly relieved when the "re-up guy" offered a paltry bonus amount if Carter renewed his contract. Had the army known better, they would have tripled that amount and been ready to negotiate.

From the start, I'd considered Carter's promotion to sergeant to be a given. The hardest part was simply doing the leg work from Iraq. And, several times this year, even Carter had confronted the reality that it might not happen while we were here. I would have accepted his concession again had it not been for the quick darting of his eyes and a slight hesitation before he'd proclaimed it no big deal.

"Wait a minute, Carter, this is a big deal." I felt my blood pressure rising and Carter withdrawing simultaneously. Turning to Kolb, I asked, "Sergeant Kolb, were you aware of the computer problem?"

"Yes, ma'am. I looked into it and there wasn't much that we could do." Great.

Now leaning against the table, I made a concerted effort to appear relaxed. "Man, it's like one thing after the other with that stupid online system," I said, pretending to concede defeat. Carter didn't buy it.

"Ma'am, I tried everything."

"But, is there any way to somehow prove that you did finish the correspondence courses, that you have the points for promotion? Do you have printouts or something that we can submit?" Carter shot Kolb a look I couldn't discern. Anger. Fear. Panic?

"What? What is it?" I demanded, glad I wasn't just imagining things.

"Well, yeah. I could submit my paperwork showing that I took the courses, but . . ." Carter hesitated, his face contorted in misery. "I'm an idiot. I packed my file of paperwork in the trunk that we sent back with the Humvee."

"Oh, no! And the Humvee is on a ship in Kuwait now, right? Shit! Carter, why the heck did you send it back?"

"I don't know. I just got so mad and they wouldn't help me fix it. It doesn't matter now anyways," he said, looking away. "I'll just do it when we get home."

"So, you're just going to give up? After all that work, that's it?"

I might as well have slapped him across the face. Carter looked wounded. How dare I call him a quitter. It was a low blow. But under the circumstances, clearly necessary.

Meanwhile, Kolb watched from behind the laptop, content to be a spectator. In the distance, I could hear Sandra directing several soldiers to our workspace.

Turning, I spotted the soldiers and yelled, "Hey guys, the JAG section is closed at the moment. Come back in twenty minutes."

Seeing that, Carter went pale.

"Ma'am, I'm not quitting, I just can't do anything right now. I'll do it when we get back."

Ignoring him, I asked, "What papers are you missing exactly? What would they need to see? Is there any other record of this information? I mean, c'mon, the army doesn't just leave it up to you, do they?"

Yeah, Carter began, there was. If we were back at Fort Carson, he explained, he could go to the unit on post that handled all the personnel files and get it copied. It's in the Carson system, he explained, but he couldn't access it, for whatever reason, from Iraq. They'd already tried reaching the unit at Carson, he explained, and they demanded that he be there in-person

"When did all this happen? Why am I only learning about this now?" I asked. "Oh, for God's sakes! You've got to be kidding me!" Even as the words came out, I knew they belonged to my parents. To their credit, my parents are not coddlers. They are extremely supportive and loving parents, the sort of parents you can call at 0300 to talk about anything. In their world, however, there is no room for hand wringing.

As children, when a neighbor girl was bullying me and my sister, there was no "there, there." Instead, they sent us back to battle the bully armed with an impressive arsenal of verbal defenses: "Leave us alone, you bully!" "Be quiet, you're a bully!" "Go away!" At night, they had us rehearse these loudly. And just in case, my dad taught us how to punch: closed fist, thumb outside, with a locked wrist. While most parents would blanch at the thought of teaching their five- and six-year-old daughters how to punch, my parents' approach had its merits. Namely, it empowered us to stand up for ourselves. Carter needed a serious helping of that, right now.

"Ma'am, please," Carter lamented, "please, just leave it."

Kolb added, "Ma'am, we tried everything."

"There has to be a personnel unit here on Anaconda that can help us. I know there's a finance unit . . ."

"I think that unit already left, or is about to redeploy already," Kolb replied.

"Well, do you know where they're located?"

Kolb drew a map of the general location, and I grabbed my Kevlar. "Sergeant Kolb, what's the rule, does it have to be there by midnight on the first? We can do it online, right?" We had three days to recreate Carter's file. Grabbing Carter's forearm, I pulled him toward the door.

"I mean it, Carter. Get your gear on. We're leaving right now, to find the personnel unit. The worse they can say is no, right?"

Considering I had never laid a hand on him before, Carter was taken aback. Finally, he sighed, and mumbled, "Okay."

With that, I released him to get his vest and Kevlar on. Two minutes later, we left in search of the unit.

While frustrated and angry at the state of Carter's promotion file, it wasn't the only time-sensitive matter on my mind. By this point, Zaidoun had been buried for more than two weeks; he'd been dead for nearly a month. While I was no expert on autopsies or the manner in which the body decomposes, I knew enough to know that a cadaver immersed in water for two weeks wasn't in good shape. CID had also heard nothing from Zaidoun's family since we'd last met at the bridge.

There was, at least, some good news: CID had called that afternoon to confirm that Colonel Rudesheim was not involved in the cover-up. With the current state of affairs, this was reason enough to celebrate.

"And the exhumation?" I asked hopefully.

"Still checking," they said. "We'll call you back."

When Carter and I finally found the personnel unit late that afternoon, the soldiers were literally packing up the last of their computers. Several soldiers had just started dismantling parts of the tent. Unwilling to walk away empty-handed, I forced several NCOs and a captain to listen to our tale of woe.

They seemed genuinely sympathetic, but their answers were always the same: Fort Carson can help you.

And they would, I decided, as we departed. In no mood to have to shout down Carter's doubts, I kept this decision to myself as I considered whom I could enlist to help us back home.

We trudged back to headquarters in silence. When we were nearly halfway there, Carter asked, "So ma'am, what next?"

Suspicious, I stole a glance at his face, which appeared open and curious compared to the defeated look he'd worn all day. Encouraged, I forged on. "Okay, Carter, tell me who your closest friend is back at Carson. Who can we count on to go to that personnel office and get this done for you tomorrow? And that means they not only get the file but scan each page in that file and e-mail it back to us."

Carter was quiet.

Concerned that I'd gone too far, I added, "Okay, let's just assume that anyone you ask will say it's impossible. Who is the one person who might think it's impossible but would be willing to give it a try anyways?"

At least a minute passed before Carter said anything. By which point, I was already preparing my response to his "No one, ma'am. There's no one."

"Sergeant Farrand," Carter announced suddenly. "Do you know him, ma'am? He works at the courthouse now, but if there's anyone that can do it, it's definitely Sergeant Farrand."

Bingo. I slapped Carter on the back so hard that he stumbled forward. "Easy there, ma'am," he said, feigning distress as he fell back in next to me. "I need to be a sergeant before you can kill me."

At least we were making some progress. With sleep ever harder to come by lately, waiting in line at the computer lab that evening didn't bother me. It also assuaged my guilt over not paying more attention to Carter's plight. When my turn at the computer finally came up, I spent most of my thirty minutes writing a detailed e-mail to Sgt. Nick Farrand about Carter's situation. Admittedly, I was micromanaging at my worst, outlining what he could say to the clerks there to convince them. I also sent a plea to a good friend with connections at the Fort Carson personnel office.

When I finished, I decided to copy two additional people I hoped might help Farrand in his quest. They were fellow lawyers I used to work with. Or, I corrected myself, would soon work with again. A soldier hovering nearby cleared his throat. My time was up. I quickly scanned the e-mail one last time and hit send. It was 0200 when I left the computer lab and realized that I'd forgotten to e-mail home.

It was a torturous few days that followed, but ultimately, well worth it. Cintron called to inform me of the news: the family had agreed to exhume Zaidoun's body. Remarkably, even the stoic Cintron sounded happy.

"That's wonderful!" I screamed, thankful that the ALOC was deserted. "Did you see the form I e-mailed that they need to sign?"

Days spent worrying had led me to prepare a permission form in both languages, just in case. We couldn't spare any time, I'd figured, if they actually said yes. Cintron informed me that division had also been informed and that I should coordinate the exhumation with them.

After hanging up with Cintron, I left a phone message and e-mailed Colonel Barnes to let him know that we were eager to begin the exhumation right away.

The family's change of heart unleashed a whole host of questions about the current state of Zaidoun's body. Did Iraqis practice any sort of embalming? Do Muslims frown on it? As far as technology went, the country was twenty-five years behind; their embalming practices couldn't be much better. What state of decay rendered it impossible to determine a cause of death?

The idea of pulling a body out of the ground was tremendously disconcerting. I wondered what had prompted the family's change of heart. I wondered if, ultimately, it was the same matter-of-fact approach to death and exhumation that my mother had expressed over exhuming my grandmother's remains: it simply had to be done.

Several years ago, during a holiday dinner, my mother recounted a recent conversation she'd had with her siblings about relocating my grandparents' remains from Vietnam to the United States. Yes, this passes for holiday dinner conversation in my family. Local Vietnamese thugs in Saigon had taken to extorting the families of those buried in the cemetery. It was a "protection" payment to keep people from defacing the graves. After years of paying off these thugs, my mother, aunts, and uncles decided it was time to take action to ensure that our grandparents' final resting place was indeed restful. With no close family left in Vietnam, they felt it would be better for our grandparents' remains to be in the United States, where the majority of our family now lives.

I waited for my mother to lament how the younger generation doesn't understand the importance of respecting one's elders. Instead, my mother recalled the *first* time she had dug up her mother's grave, with her own hands.

I spilled my drink. "What? You?" I sputtered, horrified.

"Who else was there?" she snapped. "The family had to do it. There's no one to pay to do that."

During the Vietnam War, U.S. soldiers had set up camps next to the cemetery where my grandmother was buried.

"I was twenty-four when the family decided to move her body," my mother explained. "We were afraid that the soldiers would start storing equipment near the graves. They were so close, and they were already moving through the cemetery." Like many other families who had considered the sacred ground compromised, they moved her mother's remains to a more remote cemetery.

I understood the reasoning, sure, but I couldn't wrap my mind around the fact that it had to be done by my mother.

"There wasn't a shovel, Mom?" I asked, incredulous.

"The men shoveled, but you still have to push the dirt back."

Oh, of course. "So, what did you see? When you opened the coffin?"

She snorted, as if I was being hopelessly dim. "What do you think I saw?"

Gosh, Mom, the last time I dug up a body was, well . . . yeah . . . never.

"There's no body. It's just bones with some bits of clothes around them." Then, she added, "It's not hard to lift out," as if I'd been wondering how my five-feet-one-inch, one-hundred-pound mother had unearthed a cadaver all by herself.

As far as Zaidoun was concerned, the body needed to be intact. Then, a proper autopsy could be conducted to confirm the cause of death. That was secondary, however, to identifying the body. Was it really Zaidoun, the nineteen-year-old man I'd seen smiling in those photos? Gwinner still contended the whole allegation was a lie, and Zaidoun was still out there, laughing at us. We couldn't trust Iraqis, he'd said. "They lie all the time."

Although I'd met plenty of Iraqis who do, in fact, lie, Gwinner's hypo-critical statements were not only enraging, they were feeding a propaganda campaign at 1-8. Gwinner had the masses believing that Zaidoun was still out there, laughing, and scheming to make him and 1-8's Alpha Company look bad. Never mind that *Gwinner* had no evidence on his side.

Drowning In The Desert

My glory days as the JAG who sought justice against the two *traitorous* soldiers who had betrayed 1-8, were over. Now, I found myself in a position not unlike the one Tom had found himself in months earlier. Just as Sassaman's dislike for Tom had spread to 1-8's men, I discovered that Gwinner's anger towards me had infected 1-8's ranks. In the days following Sassaman's confession, 1-8's soldiers did not do what most soldiers would do and steer clear of the ongoing investigation. No, they steered right into it.

A good number of 1-8 soldiers, including several officers, stopped by my desk to challenge me on the merits of the case. "But how do we know that the guy really died?" each would inevitably ask.

I quickly learned that it was better not to engage. Whether these visits were encouraged or spontaneous, 1-8 was turning up the heat on me. So as I waited for guidance on when the exhumation would talk place, I made a concerted effort to keep a low profile with 1-8.

Exhuming the body was now more important than ever. We were losing critical evidence with each passing day. I was exhausted, weary from the investigation, and weary from the constant affronts. The thought of letting things slide, letting this investigation fall away, was more than tempting. Was all this aggravation worth it? Worth earning the contempt of the soldiers and commanders I had worked so hard for?

The next morning came and went without any word from division or CID. I began to worry that the delay would give Zaidoun's family time to change their minds.

CHAPTER NINETEEN

Standing Up

FEBRUARY BROUGHT A NEW TYPE of frenzy to the Administrative and Logistics Operations Center. Just a stone's throw from our workspace, a small crowd formed around a soldier who worked in the personnel section. Today, the quiet, dark-haired specialist appeared different. Chatting animatedly with the soldiers gathered around the personnel desk, he had the same look of thrilled disbelief you see on lottery winners.

Searching through his backpack on the table in front of him, he pulled out what looked like can of shaving cream. "Last chance. Speak up if you want any of this stuff," the specialist said, setting the can down next to two small bottles.

"Otherwise, I'm chucking it," he added with cheerful decisiveness. Even as he spoke, his generous mouth could not resist spilling into a smile.

It occurred to me that I had never seen the specialist's eyes before today, or even heard his voice all that clearly. The typically introverted specialist was polite every time I'd spoken to him, but he rarely made eye contact.

The same stab of envy I'd felt when I first heard that the specialist was redeploying early had clearly pricked the group standing around him. They watched with long, joyless faces, apparently drained by his good news. The specialist had just learned he would fill a last-minute open seat in the advance party that was the first group of soldiers scheduled to return home to Fort Carson.

"Yeah, they just told me. We're supposed to leave tomorrow, or the next day," the specialist explained to one of the sullen faces. Pressing a full bottle of aftershave into the palm of another soldier, the specialist chirped, "I have more stuff down at the trailer, so just stop by."

Must be nice. The rest of us had one to two months left to go in Iraq. Turning away from the jubilant specialist, I found Carter watching me with a cross look on his face.

"Ma'am, you still haven't gone through the claims?" Carter said, not hiding his frustration.

"Hey, I haven't had a . . ."

"Captain Semenko wanted you to look at this one, remember?" Carter said, plucking the first manila folder off the pile, he slid it toward me. "He's coming back today."

"Wait, what's it about?" I asked, as I logged in to the secure server to check for new messages.

"I don't know. He just said that he wanted you to look at it first. ASAP."

I shot Carter a knowing look and he rolled his eyes. These days everything was ASAP. Every unit wanted their legal loose ends tied off immediately.

"Okay, I'll look at it. Just leave it there," I said. The screen indicated one new e-mail. It was from the forensics guy in Baghdad I'd e-mailed several days earlier about a possible exhumation. According to his message, he just needed the information about the case and the orders from the commander. The team could probably arrive within twenty-four hours. He almost sounded excited.

Sure, I thought dejectedly, checking my watch for the umpteenth time that morning. Nearly two days had passed with still no word from division, or CID for that matter. My hope that they had simply moved forward without notifying me had been effectively dashed by the appearance of this new e-mail. The forensics guy knew even less than I did.

Carter cleared his throat, snapping me out of my haze. "Uh, ma'am, here he comes. Semenko," Carter warned.

Looking up, I saw Capt. Charles Semenko weaving through the crowd of soldiers gathered around Sandra's desk, admiring the collection of autographed photos from celebrities. Semenko bore a striking resemblance to the actor John Cusack. Tall, broad shouldered, and gangly, he had a blockish head with a wide forehead and dark hair.

Semenko was a bit eccentric; his goofy nature often made him the subject of jokes and ribbing among the captains at 3rd Brigade's field artillery battalion, but he was well-liked, regardless. An artillery officer, Semenko had assumed the job of 1-8's fire support officer sometime in the fall, and he now lived at Camp Paliwoda (formerly Eagle).

Shortly after his arrival at the battalion's headquarters, Semenko also had taken over the undesirable role of 1-8's claims officer. The recently promoted Captain Blake was more than happy to relinquish the position to Semenko in November.

Semenko hesitated when I didn't look up from the screen immediately. "Hey. Hey, just stopping by to see if you read that claims file yet. I dropped it off with . . ."

"I gave it to her, sir," Carter interjected, "and told her that you wanted her to read it ASAP."

I closed the e-mail and turned my attention to Semenko. "Sorry, Chuck, I haven't had a chance to read it yet."

"Oh, okay, well, I'll be here for another half-hour so I can come back," he said, assuming that I intended to pick it up right that second.

"Can you give me another day?" I asked, now understanding why Carter had been so abrupt. It was hard to tell if Semenko was acting clueless or he was just clueless sometimes. Although we were fast, he had just dropped off the claim file the night before. This wasn't a fast-food drive-through window.

Semenko hesitated. "Uh, well, can you just look at it now?" he asked softly. "I won't be back at Anaconda for a few days."

His earnest tone caused me to change mine, "Okay, okay." Sighing, I stood up and pulled the folder toward me as Carter slid the remaining stack of claims forward in its wake. "Hey, Sergeant Kolb, can you finish the reports for division? They need them within the hour."

"Great, I'll be back," Semenko replied, pounding the table a little too forcefully before bounding toward the door.

I read Semenko's cover memo first. It was a mandatory part of any claim: a form letter in which the claims officer describes the nature of the claim, what he believed actually happened, the sum total, and whether or not he recommended payment. In this instance, Semenko did not recommend payment. Reading quickly through the rest of the memo, it was easy to understand why.

The claimants, several family members, alleged that soldiers stormed their home in the middle of the night, sometime around 0200, rounded up everyone inside, and executed their father.

Two statements from lieutenants on the scene recounted the incident quite differently. The lieutenants described arriving at the target's home and, during a room-by-room search, encountering the target individual pointing a gun at them. One soldier fired his weapon, killing the target individual. On its face, they had shot the man lawfully, in self-defense, and in accordance with the ROE.

Several other aspects of the claim made me doubt its truthfulness. First, the claim had been filed recently, nearly a month after the incident occurred. Second, the claimants also alleged that the soldiers stole countless objects and gold jewelry worth 8 million Iraqi dinar. Although Iraqis routinely inflated the value of damage we inflicted, this claim alleged minimal property damage in proportion to the value of goods allegedly stolen. It was an outrageous amount, especially given that the claimants' themselves claimed a humble existence.

Another strike against the claimants was that their deceased family member, the person killed, appeared to have been an insurgent. The lieutenants' statements attested to the reasons why they had set out to capture him that evening. The Iraqi family likely felt they had no recourse at first but, in the weeks since, they probably saw they had nothing to lose in trying to obtain some compensation for the incident.

Lastly, it wasn't my claim to handle. The claim stemmed from an alleged incident that took place in Balad in early January. At the time, 1-8 was in Samarra leading Operation Ivy Blizzard. Therefore, the claim involved soldiers from the Stryker battalion that had temporarily replaced 1-8 in Balad. Closing the folder, I placed it back on the table.

As a technical matter, we could decide the claim, but I wanted Semenko's memo to clearly indicate that 1-8 wasn't the unit involved. I wrote a note indicating as much so that Semenko could include the point in his final memo, and stuck it to the outside of the folder. I agreed with Semenko's recommendation but I also wanted accurate information passed on to our replacement unit, just in case the claimants tried again.

Semenko returned an hour later, just as I was leaving for a meeting. Handing him the folder, I provided a short explanation of the note on top and finished with a "good job" regarding his diligence on the matter.

"But is there any way we can pay them the death money? The solatia?" he asked dubiously.

"No, solatia doesn't apply here. We killed the guy in self-defense," I replied, glancing at the time on my watch. It was 1430. Aside from being late for my meeting, I still hadn't heard a word regarding the exhumation.

"But can't we just pay the family anyway? Just give them something?"

Relatively new to the claims officer position, I suspected that Semenko had not encountered "these types of claims" yet. Recognizing some of my formerly naïve self in Semenko's anguished expression, I softened.

"Look, I understand how you feel. It wasn't their fault that they had a bad guy in the family, but I'm sorry, Chuck, we really can't."

Straightening up, he pushed the folder back toward me. "The whole thing just bothers me. Can you look at it again?"

I set down my Kevlar, annoyed. "What's going on here, Chuck?" I asked. I repeated the reasons why I concurred with his recommendation. He didn't interrupt, but when I finished, he took a deep breath and began to explain.

First, it was his fault that the claim was filed late. With a pained expression, he described how the family had approached him right after the incident and several more times after that. Their claim had sounded preposterous, so he kept turning them away. Each time they returned, he said, they were more adamant that he do something.

"If they're lying, they never return. I make it clear that I don't want to see them again," he said, affecting a stern, forceful expression. "So when the family kept coming back," he explained, "I began asking around, but the soldiers' answers weren't clear." Their oral responses also didn't match several written statements he'd found that were originally submitted for detention purposes that night.

He paused then, trying to recall the next point. "Oh, and 1-8 *was* in Balad that night," he added, as if that alone would clear the way for a solatia payment. "They went down to Balad to help the Stryker soldiers."

"Chuck, you're confusing me now. Is the allegation true?"

"Can we just pay them some solatia, or some money?" he implored.

Still uncertain where I'd failed to clarify things, but unwilling to make myself any later for the meeting, I said, "Look, I'll read it over again and call you at 1-8, okay? You're at headquarters, right?"

He nodded, thanked me profusely, and left.

Semenko's behavior was downright weird. I didn't know him well, but I'd heard he could be a bit unusual.

Prior to Brian Gebhardt taking his job at the brigade headquarters company, he had worked with Semenko at the field artillery battalion. When Gebhardt stopped by that battalion to visit some of his friends recently, he'd returned with some interesting tales. According to Gebhardt, one of the artillery captains was so frustrated by the dearth of intelligence that he had embarked on his own one-man intelligence gathering operation. Determined to go "undercover," the captain had donned an Iraqi tunic, appropriate native attire, and headed off into the local market alone. Aside from the fact that he didn't look like an Iraqi at all, Gebhardt said, already laughing, the captain also seemed to have forgotten that he didn't speak Arabic. He was lucky to make it back alive.

The story had sounded so outrageous, I speculated that the captain had probably done this as part of some bet he'd lost. It was ridiculous. Gebhardt had insisted that the captain in question had not lost any bet. The captain had ventured out to the market of his own volition. Gebhardt assured me that the guys in the unit knew better than to ever dare this guy to do anything. That captain was Charles Semenko.

What on earth had Semenko so worked up? Later that day, I sat down to review the file again. The only thing I came up with was that, perhaps, it was a questionable killing. Maybe Semenko thought the soldiers had responded with too much force. Still, even that wasn't clear. Nor would it have been the first time out here. Even when soldiers have rightfully defended themselves, afterwards they often start questioning their own actions, growing irrationally fearful that they might have done something wrong. When questioned, they sometimes clammed up, causing more undue suspicion.

When I reached Semenko on the TAC phone at 1-8 headquarters that evening to see whether this was what had upset him, he didn't elaborate.

"I'd really just like to pay the solatia and be done with it," Semenko said, repeating himself.

"Okay," I finally said, but added that I might be able to pay the solatia "if you gather a few more statements from the soldiers that had conducted the raid." Semenko agreed and I continued. "I just need routine information, nothing more, so I can substantiate the payment," I requested. "They probably made after-action statements so check with them first."

Between crackling zaps of the phone line, Semenko agreed, and I hung up satisfied the matter was resolved. It was just as well. I had no interest in doing any more digging around 1-8. As it was, 1-8 soldiers were still badgering me about the drowning investigation. And, according to my watch, it was already 1930. I was beginning to have a bad feeling about the exhumation.

By the time I spoke with Lieutenant Colonel Barnes that evening the excuses were fast and furious: exhuming the body would create a needless security risk; an autopsy would be of limited benefit to the case because of the advanced state of decomposition.

I felt broadsided. Having never even considered the possibility that division commanders would suddenly change their minds, it took me a moment to recover.

"Sir, that doesn't make any sense. Security? We attend meetings every day in town. And the Iraqis want this, they approved it."

"It's unfortunate, I know, but that's the assessment."

"Division said this?" I asked in disbelief.

His voice took a harder edge. "Yes, it's ultimately their call, there's nothing . . ."

"But sir, do they realize that without a body, we can't prove beyond a doubt that it was Zaidoun?" I knew I was pushing it, but disappointment and shock propelled me forward. "I don't understand. They already approved it. Don't they remember? I wouldn't have asked the family if they didn't!"

In the silence that followed, I realized that Barnes's reticence was not meant to offend me. He suffered the paralysis of a man trapped between duty and his own misgivings. He simply wasn't going to discuss this with me. It wouldn't be right, nor would it have made any difference.

What he said next surprised me. Barnes reiterated division's commitment to seeing the case through. In near-robotic fashion, he informed me that the

225

case was still active and that we would proceed with charges as soon as CID concluded the investigation. There also had been some discussion, it seemed, as to whether the soldiers involved would remain in Iraq pending trial, rather than return to Fort Carson.

What?

Until then, he said, I should preserve all the evidence I currently had and prepare to move forward with charges.

My subsequent attempts to point out the problems were quickly shot down. Barnes lost his patience with me; it was time to fall in line. Still, all I could manage was a wary, "Okay, sir," before hanging up.

That was it? An innocent man was dead, probably at the hands of U.S. soldiers. Didn't this warrant a full investigation?

I stayed at the JAG workspace for nearly an hour, paralyzed with disbelief. My conversation with Barnes looped through my mind as I forced myself to start closing down for the night. I had just finished securing my vest when I stopped, rigid with anger, over one of division's justifications.

Too dangerous. Too dangerous? Everything was dangerous. When had that ever stopped us from doing anything? Danger had never been an excuse not to pay claims each week, travel Highway One, or investigate the Cobb and Datray case. Danger had never prevented the constant trips into towns or visiting courthouses. It was a little late in the game to be worried about things being "too dangerous."

Too inconvenient, was more like it. I wondered whether division had hedged its bet. *It was easy to support an exhumation when it looked like it wasn't going to happen.*

The Hassoun family was wise to have been skeptical. It was my fault. I was the one who had pushed the exhumation, forcing it each time I saw them. I was the gullible one who believed we would do the right thing. Worse, I had convinced the family that we would. Recalling my assurances to the family, I cringed.

The next morning I was listless as Cintron informed me that CID was scaling back its investigation into the drowning. My silence prompted Cintron to explain that CID investigators were being called south to Baghdad to investigate detainee-abuse allegations at the Abu Ghraib detention facility. Hearing this, I could only shake my head.

Part of the reason I'd pushed so hard for a centralized detainment facility at the brigade, as well as a hearing process for detainees held on less serious changes, was to prevent what had happened in Abu Ghraib. Iraqis held indefinitely in overcrowded conditions, with no rights and no foreseeable legal process in place, created a situation ripe for abuse. Months ago, common sense had designated the entire detainment situation a legal landmine. Hanging up the phone with Cintron, I said nothing to Carter and Kolb, and headed outside in need of another walk.

Passing the trash dumpsters, I was surprised to see the jubilant specialist from the previous day scaling the side of one of them.

He didn't look nearly as happy today. It appeared his plans had changed. His seat on the advance trip home had been revoked. Welsch had apparently found someone else to fill the slot.

Now, the specialist was crawling through garbage, trying to retrieve some of his belongings as his friends stood by, ready to catch anything he might lob over. His friends were heckling him mercilessly.

"Come on man, get your nasty stuff. We don't have all day," one of the soldiers yelled.

"Dude, your stuff is going to reek. Just buy some new shit, " another said.

Seeing me, the soldiers took a break from heckling their friend to salute.

It seemed I wasn't the only one whose plans hadn't worked out.

CHAPTER TWENTY

A Bad Penny

SEMENKO WAS LIKE A DOG with a bone. He wouldn't let this claim go.

Weeks had passed since we'd last spoken. Now here he was back at my desk jabbering about wanting to "get this over with." Semenko had not, however, brought the one thing I required to approve the solatia payment.

"I need statements from the soldiers who were there that night," I repeated for what seemed like the hundredth time. "I need some record of what happened."

"The family gave me some photos of the house," he said, pushing a folder towards me.

It was as though he hadn't heard a word I'd said.

"They show the house, and the room where the guy was killed," he explained. "There's some other stuff from the family in there, too."

I offered him a stern stare and made no move to accept the folder.

"Sworn statements, Chuck, same as always," I repeated.

"There's some confusion with the statements. I'll get them as soon as I can. Just take a take a look at these right now," he said, opening the folder and pulling out a stack of Polaroid photos. He removed the rubber band that held them together and began shuffling through them.

"Chuck, hold on. I don't want to look at those pictures right now. I need you to get the statements first. I need a basic understanding of what happened, from the soldiers' perspectives. The lieutenants' statements are good, I just need more . . ."

"Oh, those statements are actually wrong," Semenko said casually. "I found out that the lieutenants just wrote that to process the detainees that were also arrested that night."

Hearing the conscientious Semenko's breezy explanation for the lieutenants' inaccurate statements made me want to tear my hair out. What he said reflected the harsh reality of how detainment and evidence collection were still handled down at the battalions: just another block to check during their nightly duties. Soldiers had to fill out statements to turn over detainees at the detention facilities, explaining the circumstances of their arrests. They were also supposed to fill out statements when civilians were killed during the course of a raid. And they did. Whether the statements were accurate or not was a different story.

This was the challenge I'd faced since our earliest days in Iraq. Getting soldiers and commanders to start using some basic police methods was one thing, but until division leadership enforced or emphasized the importance of doing so, the process would still be considered a necessary evil. At the brigade level, I'd found that a unit's adherence to these basic reporting requirements was largely determined by their leaders' attitudes. Some officers simply required more frequent reminders of the potential problems their unit could face if they let their soldiers slack. In the realm of legal landmines, unit and soldier accountability was a big one that I was always trying to steer the brigade away from.

For starters, requiring soldiers to provide basic statements explaining *why they detained this guy* discouraged some of the indiscriminate roundups of Iraqi men. There was nothing high-minded about it: we had neither the capacity nor desire to detain all the Iraqi males in the Sunni Triangle. Secondly, for the guys we did bring in, we needed to be able to distinguish the common criminals from the high-value insurgents. Without some way to process and sort the detainees, we would have no choice but to hold people indefinitely, as was done at Guantanamo Bay.

Just a basic explanation of who, what, where, when, and why. That was it. Nobody expected a treatise. I only asked that the information be accurate and that the battalion and company leadership stress this to soldiers down the chain.

"So, you mean they just wrote anything down just so they could hand over the detainees from Khalaf's house, right?" I asked so sharply it penetrated even Semenko's fog.

He looked up surprised, as though he'd just remembered that I was a lawyer.

"Uh, yeah. Pretty much," he said with a contrite smile. "But they said that they did take *real* statements from the soldiers about what happened. I saw some of them, but I gave them to the commander to read."

"Real statements, about what?" I asked, just to confirm.

"You know, about what happened at the house, shooting the guy," Semenko replied matter-of-factly.

I placed my hand over the Polaroids and pushed them down before Semenko could petition me to look at them.

"Chuck, I've read the file," I said. "Explain to me why this is so important?"

It was Semenko's turn to sigh, a small, thoughtful exhale that caused his chin and shoulders to drop. The appearance of polite frustration in the sometimes-spacey Semenko was disarming. Just as quickly, Semenko raised his chin and peered cautiously over his right shoulder, and then his left shoulder. Satisfied no one was within earshot, he leaned across the table purposefully. Semenko's cloak-and-dagger routine was trying my nerves.

"I told them 'no,' but the family just kept coming back," he said. I knew this already. Semenko explained that the family's persistence had prompted him to ask the soldiers about what happened.

"It wasn't like I expected anything," he added, "but the stories didn't match up." There were enough discrepancies, Semenko explained, that he felt he should probably interview a few more soldiers who were at the scene that night. When he approached them, he said, the soldiers were tight-lipped. Unsure how to proceed from there, Semenko turned over the statements he had to the company commander.

"He said he'd look into the matter," Semenko said conclusively.

I waited for him to continue. Several seconds passed before I realized Semenko was studying me intently, waiting for the import of his words to grip me.

"Oh, c'mon, Chuck," I groused, "I can't read your mind!" I had enough legitimate misconduct to deal with, and here I was speculating with Mr. Dense about possible wrongdoing. "Please, tell me what the problem is here. What's the issue?"

Semenko waited for my irritation to wane before beginning.

"There's an SOP for a cordon and search, right?" he said.

"Yeeaaah, okay. Please, keep going."

"Well, I asked a few soldiers to explain what happened in the house that night. All of them offered a different story that didn't match the original statements," Semenko said, "and none of their accounts were consistent with 1-8's standard operating procedures for a cordon and search."

Repeating the words to myself, I struggled to identify the nexus of his concern.

"Okay, let me just start over and explain the three different stories I got about that night," Semenko offered gamely.

The soldiers all claimed that they had good intel and arrived at the home of the target individual, Zadan Khalaf, around 0100 or 0200. They forcibly entered the home for a cordon and search. According to the soldiers, it was a big home with well over a dozen people staying there.

"Per standard operating procedures," Semenko said, "you go through the entire house first, clearing each room of all weapons and people, to make sure no one is hiding. Anyone found in the house is then brought to the main room." He paused after each sentence to make sure we were on the same page. "Once everyone is in the main room, the women and children are led outside. The men have already been searched and secured," Semenko said, bringing his wrists together behind his back to demonstrate. "So, we put them face down on the floor, in a row."

"Okay. And then you identify the target, right?"

"Right," he said. "You go down the line, lifting each man's head up and asking him in Arabic to say his name."

Nodding, I urged Semenko to continue.

"Well, that night, they went through the whole thing, lifting the heads and asking each man to say his name until they found Zadan Khalaf, the target. At least, that's how two of the soldiers remembered it," Semenko said.

But it was what the soldiers had claimed happened next that really concerned Semenko.

The first soldier told Semenko that Khalaf had resisted as the soldiers brought him from the main room into a separate room for questioning. Once they were in the side room, Khalaf lunged for a pistol he had been hiding. Seeing this, one of the soldiers shot Khalaf instantly.

Semenko took a deep breath before describing the second account of the evening.

The second soldier had told Semenko that Khalaf lunged for a handgun as the soldiers were handcuffing him.

The third, and most dramatically different, account had the soldiers encountering an armed Khalaf on the initial search of the house and shooting the man when he didn't drop his pistol.

I shrugged. "So, the first two stories are a little off, and the third guy, well . . . did you make sure he was actually in the room at the time? Not outside or something?"

Semenko ignored my question. "It doesn't make sense. The guy would have been zip-tied already," he said, clearly referring to the first two accounts of what had occurred. "And then this third guy tells me a completely different story?" Semenko threw up his hands in frustration.

"According to SOP, all males are zip-tied immediately. If he was zip-tied immediately, there is no way he could have lunged for a weapon." Even if he wasn't zip-tied, Semenko pointed out, there were other ways to take control of the situation before killing him.

I finally got it. According to standard operating procedures, soldiers would have zip-tied the men immediately, long before they began identifying the target individual. So, Semenko figured, how would the target individual have pulled a gun out if he were zip-tied? For Semenko, the soldiers' accounts were not only inconsistent, but a complete departure from the way they had been trained.

That wasn't the only thing: Zadan Khalaf was in his sixties. It strained credulity to believe that an old man had somehow broken free from not one, not two, but at least three soldiers' control.

"Either Perkins shot him when they moved him to another room, or he shot him right away," Semenko mused, oblivious to the fact that his words had hit me like a blow to the head.

"Wait. Back up. Did you say Perkins?" I asked. "Perkins was the shooter?"

Still lost in his thoughts, Semenko mumbled, "Yeah, but now I don't have that statement."

Perkins again? *Holy shit. I couldn't get away from this guy.* "Wait, if this is Alpha Company then . . . " I flipped the original claim file open and pulled out the two lieutenants' statements Semenko had just nullified. How had I missed this? The photocopies were faded, but the name block was legible. At the bottom of one of the statements, I saw the tidy signature of 1st Lt. Jack Saville.

Resting my elbows on the table, I stared down at the file as my mind raced, propelled by the tornado of concerns the mere mention of Perkins had whipped up. *Slow down, Viv. Slow down.* It doesn't mean anything. It's just speculation. The drowning investigation was still a little too fresh for me to trust that my judgment wasn't skewed. *Facts, Viv. Not emotions.* Plus, I reminded myself, there weren't enough facts to justify anything yet. I'd seen many statements where a more thorough interview would have cleared up some simple confusion. More likely than not, this was one of those situations that would have an easy explanation.

I did one last scan of the documents before closing the file again. Looking up, I met Semenko's expectant gaze.

"Okay, Chuck, I kind of see your concern, but just so we're clear: you think that the Iraqi, Zadan Khalaf, was killed unlawfully?"

Semenko tensed up instantly.

"No, it's not that, it's just . . . well," he stammered. "It was probably right . . . or okay . . . that Perkins shot the guy . . . I just . . . " Seeing my skeptical face, Semenko fell silent.

As grim as my expression was, my stomach was somersaulting at the thought of tangling with 1-8.

No wonder Semenko wanted to pay the family solatia and just be done with it. He wanted to mitigate some of the damage to the Khalaf family, but Semenko had no desire to stir up a hornet's nest at 1-8. While Semenko wanted to do right by the family, the last thing he wanted was to point an accusing finger at a guy like Perkins.

"So you said, before, that you gave the statements to the commander. Did you mean Cunningham?"

Semenko nodded and explained that Cunningham had seemed genuinely concerned. "I just haven't been able to track him down," Semenko said, explaining why he hadn't brought the statements today.

"When did you talk to him?"

"Uh, the first time I talked to him was about a week and a half ago. But I saw him briefly the other day—just real short—and reminded him I needed the statements back."

I stacked the pile of Polaroid photos that had cascaded like a hand of cards on the table. Securing them with the rubber band, I added them to the file.

"If you can bring me the statements you already collected, I may be able to pay the solatia," I offered flatly. "The statements are from the guys that were there that night, when the shooting happened, right?

Semenko's brows knotted with worry. "Well, I'm pretty sure that one of those earlier statements belonged to Perkins."

"Okay, well, just try and bring the statements you already had." It was hard to tell if he was anxious or confused. "Does that make sense?" I asked.

Semenko started to say something but just nodded instead.

As I watched Semenko leave that day, I worried over whether I'd just made a huge mistake. Usually, when Iraqis accuse soldiers of serious crimes, the unit's commander initiates an investigation, per Army Regulation 15-6. It wasn't a good sign, however, that over a week had passed with no action by Cunningham or Sassaman. Now, I was sending Semenko back to the den of wolves to retrieve statements that I feared others might not want found. Semenko needed to get the existing statements without arousing 1-8's suspicion. He'd have to do what my father had done once in an equally grim situation: he'd have to ignore the panic in his heart and "act natural." While Semenko would have the return trip to 1-8's headquarters to consider his approach, my father had had little more than a split second.

On that particular day in February 1979, my father found himself in the wrong place at the wrong time. Having just finished a meeting with an Iranian source at a safe house, he was headed back to his office at the U.S. Embassy. Turning the corner near the embassy, he discovered hundreds of people had gathered outside the gate, waving rifles and pistols. Furious about the U.S. government's support of the Shah, the mob yelled "U.S. go home!" as they brandished their weapons and fired shots into the air. Armed Iranian males filled every inch of his periphery. Worse still, he had already been spotted by several men at the edge of the crowd. With his sandy blond hair and blue eyes, they knew he must be an American.

Drowning In The Desert

He had a decision to make. If he turned and ran, the crowd would undoubt-edly pursue him and either beat or kill him. If he continued forward, he risked the crowd discovering the weapon he had hidden in the small of his back, a sure sign he was military or CIA, the most reviled sort of American. Seeing only slightly better odds ahead of him, he raised his arms to show he was unarmed, forced a smile onto his face, and waded into the crowd.

Act natural, he told himself, as the Iranians surrounded him, slapping at his arms and shoulders. All he needed was for one of them to slap him on the lower back and feel his pistol, and they'd tear him apart limb by limb.

"What do you do at the embassy?" they demanded.

"Contractor. Contractor," he repeated, affecting the goofiest, most civilian grin he could muster. *No trained killer here,* it said. Just a harmless working man caught in the crossfire. Their eyes narrowed at his athletic physique, but the open, innocent look on his face, longish hair, and beard threw them. Reluctantly, they moved to let him through.

The odds were not in Semenko's favor. His observation about discrepan-cies in the Khalaf statements may have already set off alarm bells at 1-8 and certainly within Alpha Company. Another misstep and things could get ugly, very fast.

A group of soldiers had formed to the right of the table and waited politely. Sitting down I ushered the first soldier over, and worked diligently through the line. When the last soldier stood to leave, I grabbed my Kevlar and headed to the TOC. I needed to see the intelligence summary from the night Khalaf was shot. It's a completely normal request, I told myself. I checked the INTSUM regularly, especially when I needed to verify claims.

The fresh-faced lieutenant on duty at the S2 intelligence section obliged and hopped up to fetch the reports as they came out of the printer.

"January 2nd through the 6th?" he asked.

"Yes," I confirmed, offering a smile that I hoped masked some of the turbulence inside.

"Here you go," he said genially, handing me the printouts.

I thanked him and turned away to examine them. I stood there for sev-eral minutes scouring the reports. Engrossed, I nearly jumped when he asked, "Looking for anything in particular, ma'am?"

"What?" I yelped, surprised to find the lieutenant still standing close by. "No, no," I assured him, embarrassed by my skittish behavior. "I'm just trying to verify some claims." I started back toward my workspace in the ALOC. *Get a grip, Viv.*

About halfway down one of the earlier pages, I locked in on 1-8's action report from the night of January 2 and morning of January 3. They reported conducting numerous cordon and searches at different locations in Balad to apprehend several target individuals suspected of conducting mortar attacks on Camp Eagle.

"During the cordon and search, eleven personnel were detained and two enemy personnel were KIA; 30 AK-47s were confiscated."

The report made no mention of the pistol Khalaf had reportedly lunged for, or held, whatever it was. Thirty AK-47s. Eleven people detained. Two people killed. No pistol.

That aside, the summary seemed to agree with the accounts detailed in the soldiers' statements provided to Semenko. Given soldiers' tendency toward sloppy reporting, part of me was happy to see that they had reported *something.* I knew from speaking with Semenko that the other killed-in-action was from an earlier raid that same evening, and that 1-8 had uncovered weapons at some locations. The absence of any mention of the pistol, however, bothered me. Did Perkins keep the pistol?

The family claimed that the soldiers took their father's body with them when they left. "They put him in a sack and dropped him into the armored vehicle." If they had gone to that effort, they certainly wouldn't have left a pistol lying around.

"Hey, have you eaten yet?"

I looked up to find Capt. Brian Gebhardt's cheerful face smiling down at me. Lots of time on the road, and in the sun, had given him a nice, deep tan and gold streaks in his light brown hair.

"Or, are you *too busy?*" he teased, echoing my frequent excuse for passing on meals.

Gebhardt's invitation felt like a ray of sunlight entering a dark and shadowy room.

"No, I'm hungry," I said decisively, tucking the report into the claims file. I was ready to momentarily escape the growing weight I felt looming over me. Buoyed by his unexpected and well-timed appearance, I added, "But do you need to grab your Kevlar? Because by the look of your hair, you don't wear it anymore."

Brian laughed and I hurried to get my gear on, suddenly eager to get away from the workspace. "Let's go," I said, feeling lighter and happier than I had in hours.

Over lunch at the chow hall, I listened happily as Brian recounted the details of his two-week leave to Colorado, several weeks earlier. A blanket of fresh snow had fallen just in time for Brian and his wife to do some late season snowboarding. It felt good to be reminded of Colorado's snowy peaks and crisp, cool air. Brian glowed with good health, even though his shoulder still contained shrapnel from a rocket attack on Anaconda last October. Fortunately, his wounds had not been life threatening, but he would have a problem with metal detectors the rest of his life. Two weeks of long showers and sleeping in the springy firmness of his own bed had reinvigorated him for the arduous task that awaited him back in Iraq.

Brian had spent the past few weeks leading multiple convoys of vehicles returning from Anaconda to Kuwait, where they were loaded onto a ship for redeployment. Sergeant Phil had driven our Humvee down as part of one those convoys, my appeal to hold onto the vehicle for one more week having been denied.

Sitting across from yet another friend who'd returned from leave reinvigorated, I regretted that I hadn't insisted on going home. Division had denied my post-holiday leave request on the ground that they needed me to oversee the drowning investigation. I fought back a surge of bitterness then as I recalled the abrupt manner with which division had aborted its plans to exhume Zaidoun's body. Determined not to let my frustration take my afternoon hostage, I changed the subject.

"So, you're keeping busy with the redeployment stuff, eh? What's the next step now that the ships have sailed?" I asked.

Brian laughed dryly. "Now Welsch has me in charge of getting all the remaining equipment together. My thanks for doing a good job."

I shook my head knowingly. Welsch could smell competence a mile away.

"So what's keeping you so busy? Isn't the drowning case done yet?" he asked. "Still can't believe it, really."

The shock of Sassaman's involvement in the cover-up still reverberated throughout the brigade. Still wary of the subject after my recent clashes with several 1-8 officers, I merely nodded in response and confirmed that the soldiers' futures were still uncertain. Eager to return to a safe topic, I shared how the JAG team had been inundated with war trophy applications from the various units. Even the support units, I told him, seemed to have at least one metal-plated AK-47 in their possession. Consequently, processing the applications took a lot of time, especially with Mendoza gone.

Brian had the opposite problem. He'd been given several more soldiers to help him run a makeshift car wash, one of the bonus redeployment duties Welsch had assigned to Brian.

"One of the guys is an E-7 [the pay grade for a sergeant first class]," he said with a laugh. "A funny guy, he was cracking us up with stories about driving his Bradley over hajji huts."

That comment stopped me cold. As the full weight of his words sunk in, I felt a strange numbness in my chest. "They gave you an E-7?" I asked, managing to keep my voice even.

"Yeah, crazy. An E-7 at a car wash."

"Brian, is the E-7 from 1-8?"

He paused, trying to recall. "Yeah, he is."

"What's his name?"

When Brian paused again, my frustration boiled over. "Is it Perkins, Brian? Sergeant First Class Perkins?"

He hesitated a second. "Yeah, it is. Perkins." Connecting the dots, his eyes widened with disbelief. "Wait. *That's* the guy facing charges . . . for the drowning? I mean, I knew he was in some sort of trouble, but . . ."

I confirmed that Perkins was related to the case, but I didn't elaborate. I was still focused on Brian's earlier comment. "So, Perkins told stories about driving over hajji huts?" I pressed, referring back to the shabby Iraqi stands that lined some of the roads.

"Well, yeah, he did. The guy was actually pretty funny."

"Perkins was laughing about it? Brian, it's really not funny," I said, my voice thick with disapproval. Hearing it, I tried to affect a more neutral tone. "So, what else did he say?"

Drowning In The Desert

It was too late. Brian was on the defensive. Aware that he had hit a nerve, he no longer wanted to discuss Perkins. From the set look on his face, I could tell this wasn't a matter for debate. I kicked myself for letting my emotions get the best of me, and my earlier rebuke hung in the air between us. I knew Brian well enough to know that he probably hadn't taken Perkins's story as anything more than a tall tale told by a particularly gregarious storyteller. Brian, the benefactor of my office chair and trailer-hooch, was as thoughtful as he was effective. As for Perkins, it didn't surprise me that he could be charming when he chose to be.

"Brian, I'll drop the Perkins stuff if you just tell me what he said about the hajji huts. That's all, nothing else," I said.

Brian agreed. He explained how he had only caught the tail end of Perkins's story that day, but that Perkins bragged about using his Bradley to pulverize a row of straw huts owned by Iraqi street vendors.

"Oh, okay. Thanks." As promised, I dropped the topic.

Outside the chow hall, the sun had shifted from broil to bake and we walked back leisurely. Brian and I chatted about the dangerous and monotonous drive to Kuwait, a good portion of which was off-road, straight through the southern desert. We laughed about Welsch's perturbing efficiency and Sergeant Hodson counting the days until he retired.

Although I didn't dare bring it up again with Brian, my mind kept drifting back to Perkins. A bad penny always turns up. How foolish I'd been to think I could escape him, even during a friendly lunch.

His actions in Samarra had already cost Sassaman and Cunningham their careers. Division's refusal to exhume the body would probably mean that Perkins wouldn't be convicted for the drowning. At worst, Perkins would get a slap on the wrist. As a senior noncommissioned officer, he would likely be retained by the army. If so, the chances were good he would come back to Iraq. His reign of terror would continue. Perkins had to be stopped.

Several slim, black plastic boxes were stacked neatly on the trunk at the back of the JAG workspace when I returned. Sergeant Phil sat with one of the boxes open on his lap. Using both hands, he carefully dislodged the shiny black 9mm pistol from its groove in the box's foam interior. Holding it up, he admired its lethal beauty before reading out the serial numbers etched into the gun's barrel.

Seated at the keyboard, Kolb typed in the numbers. Kolb and Philibert were putting together the temporary weapons cards that would allow the Iraqi judges' to carry pistols. The handguns I'd ordered, with Welsch's help, had finally arrived, and we wanted to ensure the judges encountered no problems carrying them. Seeing this reminded me that we were still at least one handgun short. In my initial order, I'd forgotten to include a lower-level judge at the Ad Dujayl courthouse. Because it was too late to order another one in time, I'd asked the guys to keep checking with the battalions for any confiscated pistols.

"Hey, ma'am," Philibert said, standing up. "Any chance we can keep one of these?" He held out the gleaming 9mm and proceeded to tuck the barrel of the pistol beneath his waistband in the small of his back. He let his uniform blouse fall over it. Turning back around, he affected a look of wide-eyed innocence. "Who would know?" he asked, doing a slow turn with his palms out.

"Sure, go on and keep it. Consider it a souvenir," I joked. "No one will ever know."

Even as the words came out, I thought of the mysterious pistol that the soldiers claimed Khalaf had lunged for. If that gun actually existed, it was technically seized property, and I could use it to arm the judge in Ad Dujayl. Reaching for the TAC phone, I dialed 1-8. The phone rang twice before a soldier answered.

"This is Captain Gembara at Brigade Headquarters. Is your S2 around, Captain Williams?"

"One second, ma'am."

I heard him querying others nearby about the S2's whereabouts.

My heart flew into my throat at my own impulsiveness. If Gwinner were there, he'd probably get on the line. He'd want to know why I was calling. I debated hanging up.

Still holding the receiver, I heard the soldier's voice crackle across the line.

"Sorry, ma'am," he said, "I can't find him right now. Did you want to leave a message?"

"Uh . . . no. No, I'll just try again later. Thanks."

Hanging up the phone, I waited for my insides to settle.

CHAPTER TWENTY-ONE

Ovem
lupo commitere

MORE THAN A WEEK PASSED before I saw Captain Semenko again. Collided into, actually, would be more accurate.

He was leaving the brigade ALOC just as I arrived.

"Hey, I just dropped some stuff off on your desk. I'll be back," he said, hurrying past me.

"Wait! When?" I asked, calling after him. "Today?"

Semenko's silence over the past week had given me some time to think about the claim. The revelation that Perkins was the shooter, and the uncanny timing of Gebhardt's story, had made everything seem horribly damning. With a little distance and perhaps a cooler head, however, I realized my initial suspicions were premature. I needed more evidence. I'd let whatever Semenko brought me today guide my next step.

Considering how sensitive 1-8 was these days, I also knew that my chances of ever learning the truth about Khalaf's death were slim. This close to the end of our tour, the odds of my convincing division to take the issue seriously were even slimmer. I needed only look to the aborted exhumation as evidence of

Ovem lupo commitere: To set a wolf to guard sheep (Latin).

their limited tolerance for any legal mess.

I was glad I'd had the sense not to storm into Rudesheim's office, or call Barnes, and demand that we investigate the Khalaf claim immediately. I would have come off as the overeager prosecutor stirring up trouble. And besides, any last-minute messiness would leave a bad taste in everyone's mouth. It would cancel out all of the good work I'd done this year.

As pissed off as I was about the decision not to exhume Zaidoun, I took some comfort in the fact that Rudesheim, Barnes, and my countless other bosses were pleased with my work and were confident in my abilities. Both trials had been a success. The MEK disarmament had gone well. Although I had to strong-arm the brigade into moving on the detainee standard operating procedures, we could even point to that issue as one we were ahead of the curve on. With just a few weeks remaining in theater, I just needed to ride our success home to Fort Carson.

"Morning, guys," I said, reaching for the stack of papers on the desk. "Did I miss anything? What's the latest?"

A flurry of furtive glances passed between Kolb, Phil, and Carter. No one said anything. Kolb twisted the cap off a water bottle and pulled his Gatorade container from beneath the table.

"What? What is it?" I asked, feeling strangely playful. "What?"

Their blank expressions felt suspect. It was an act or something, I was sure of it. "Okay, then, let me guess: We detained an entire town? Or wait, division wants Sergeant Phil now to help them pack up?"

Carter's lip quivered the slightest bit, just enough to encourage me.

"No? Okay, I know: First Sergeant Hodson has us back on shit-burning detail. That's it, isn't it? We have to report out there with large sticks to stir the pots." I was amusing only myself now.

"Nope, ma'am, but I wouldn't put it past him," Kolb drawled, as he carefully tipped scoops of orange powder into his water bottle.

Carter and Kolb offered polite smiles. Sensing their restraint, I sobered instantly. Something really was wrong. Philibert turned to help a soldier.

"They posted the points list today," Carter said, his face inscrutable as he straightened the stack of folders in front of him.

Kolb secured the cap on his water bottle and began to shake it vigorously.

"Well, what's that mean?" I asked. I was all business now. Was that bad or good?

Phil began sorting through temporary weapons cards in search of those from the soldier's unit. The soldier, a corporal, waited patiently, enthralled by the drama he sensed was about to unfold at the JAG desk.

Neither Kolb nor Carter elaborated. They were clearly waiting for the soldier to leave. My heart sank. If this were good news, it wouldn't matter whether the soldier stood there. Taking their cue, I picked up an investigation report and pretended to scan it. Meanwhile, Philibert had apparently forgotten the alphabet, because an eternity passed before the corporal left.

I glanced warily towards the door, willing it to remain clear. "Okay, what happened? The point list, what's that mean? Just tell me, Carter. It's not the end of the world."

Kolb spoke first. "Well, ma'am. The cut-off number to make sergeant this month was high," he said somberly. "A lot higher than I expected, actually. You know it fluctuates each month depending on how many people put their packet in and how many sergeants they need in a certain specialty."

"But can't he just resubmit next month? Or is it better to get more points and then resubmit?"

Carter no longer hid his disappointment. He set the folders aside. "Ma'am, I don't want to do it," he huffed. "It's just not worth it. If I resubmit, they'll just say no."

"What?" I felt a headache coming on. "Carter, please don't start this again. Giving up isn't . . ."

"They'll just say no, ma'am, because I already made it. I made the list! I got promoted!" Carter punched the air like a prize-fighter and Kolb grinned.

"What?" I asked, studying each of their faces, unsure whether I could trust this positive news.

Phil shook his head approvingly. "Yeah, that was definitely worth it. Definitely," Phil said and turned to high-five Carter and Kolb.

"That whole thing was an act? You made it?" I asked, still not trusting this positive development. "Oh, Carter, I'm so happy. You deserve it!"

"Thanks, ma'am," Carter beamed.

In the midst of this good cheer, Phil remembered the folder Semenko had left and passed it to me.

Grabbing a legal pad off the desk, I headed to the library to discern the folder's contents in private. Settling into one of the abandoned office chairs that now lived in the library, I debated whether I should get a cup of coffee first. Tom, if he were here, would probably have accused me of procrastinating. Could you blame me? How much more did I really want to know about what Perkins had been up to?

As well-intentioned as Semenko was, he was about as stealthy as a rampaging elephant. Within hours of Semenko's last visit, I'd found myself on the phone with Gwinner. He had called to clarify exactly what I needed from 1-8. It was our first conversation since I'd learned that he was involved with the cover-up.

"Sir, because of the Iraqi family's claim, I was just trying to get the statements that the unit made after the shooting. Captain Semenko said the soldiers that were in the room that night made them," I said in as neutral a tone as possible.

"Oh, okay, "he said, "I know there was some confusion about the statements they had at the detention facility," Gwinner started to explain.

I murmured something to indicate I had heard him, but didn't offer much beyond that. Then he surprised me. Gwinner attempted to explain Khalaf's death. The man was shot because he had lunged for a pistol that he had hidden between some blankets that were stacked on a bureau.

Again, I just murmured noncommittally.

"He went straight for it," Gwinner added.

"Sir, I understand. I just wanted Semenko to get the statements that were made after the shooting, to verify it and include in our denial of the claim." Gwinner promised to get me the statements.

That conversation gave me a heads-up not to expect any smoking gun in the soldiers' statements. Flipping the file open, I finally got down to work. Inside were three statements and the medical records provided by Khalaf's family. I made a note to ask Sergeant Phil to get the medical records translated.

As for the statements, they were brief, nearly identical in language and content, and suspiciously "legal" in tone. For starters, all three soldiers identified Khalaf as "head of a local terrorist cell responsible for attacks against U.S. forces." Doesn't quite roll off the tongue, does it? Soldiers typically didn't offer justifications for why the person was a target. They usually leave that to their commanders. At most, a soldier might say something like, "There was an HVT [High Value Target] in the building so we surrounded the perimeter." They're less concerned with the intelligence that led them there and more focused on the action, what they had to do.

Flipping to the third statement, I saw that the soldier didn't even identify Khalaf as an Iraqi, but only as a "hostile threat." It was a phrase I drilled repeatedly during ROE briefings. Hostile threats are those that present an imminent danger to your life and, once identified, soldiers can use deadly force to stop them.

I set it down, amazed by the degree to which someone had gone to ensure these statements spoke directly to me. They were just a little too good.

Several hours later, Semenko was back at our workspace.

"Hey, Vivian, we're about to leave. I just wanted to make sure you got the stuff," he said, tapping his pen on the table.

"Oh, okay." I hurried to retrieve the folder. "Yeah, I looked at it, and read the statements. But it's still not clear if these soldiers were in the room when . . ." Looking up, I found Semenko staring at the door. "Chuck?"

He jumped in response, almost as if he'd forgotten I was there. "I'll be really quick, I promise," I added, hoping to allay his fears that his ride might leave without him.

When the nervous pen tapping resumed, I continued. "Okay, I read the statements, but these soldiers, they didn't actually see Khalaf get shot. One of them even says that. And I don't think the other two guys were there either. I needed the statements from soldiers that were actually there. If not Perkins, then maybe Staff Sergeant [Carl] Ironeyes made a statement. Wasn't he there, too?"

Semenko looked like a deer caught in headlights. "Chuck? Are you tracking?" Halfway through his nod, his eyes darted back to the door.

"Hey, uh, I should have called you earlier but, you know, I talked to Cunningham and the soldiers and, you know, I actually, uh, think I was wrong about it all," he said.

"What?" I leaned across the table, not sure if I'd heard him correctly.

Clearing his throat, Semenko started over. "I mean, uh, I don't think there's any need to investigate the claim anymore. I think I just misunderstood . . ."

"Hold on," I said, raising my hand. "Look, I just need one statement from someone who was in the room."

"I think I got it all wrong, though," he said, his eyes still on the door.

He was no longer tapping his pen but clutching it in his hand, clearly ready to bolt. He had all of the calm of a child waiting for a safety lecture to finish so he could hop in the pool. Even the sound of Jay Arthurs rearranging folding chairs in the civil affairs section seemed to unnerve Semenko.

And then it hit me: Semenko wasn't worried about missing his ride, he was afraid to be seen with me.

"Chuck, please, look at me," I said evenly. "What's going on here? Did someone at 1-8 pressure you to stop investigating this claim? Be honest."

He blinked before rolling his eyes unconvincingly. "No, no. Nobody's pressuring me." The pen tapping resumed, this time in a staccato rhythm. I stared, not quite believing that he was acting this way.

Glancing toward the doorway, he said, "Uh, look, I'll explain over e-mail, okay?" The pen disappeared into his cargo pocket.

"Uh, yeah, okay. E-mail works."

Whoever he spotted in the hallway then must have signaled that they were leaving. Grabbing his Kevlar, he made it as far as Sandra's table before rushing back towards the JAG workspace.

"Hey, Vivian, do you have a regular e-mail address I can send it to?"

Confused, I said, "You mean my Carson e-mail?" He shook his head as he fumbled to retrieve his pen. It took me about that long to understand what he was asking. "Oh! Yeah. Yes, I do." Before he could respond, I grabbed his pen and scribbled my Hotmail address on a scrap of paper and shoved the pen and paper back at him.

He stuffed them both in his pocket and hurried toward the door.

"I'll be sure to check it tonight," I yelled after him.

When I returned from the BUB that evening, Philibert had succeeded in locating a translator on short notice.

"He's waiting in the library, ma'am. He says he can't stay long because his ride is leaving soon."

That seemed to be theme of the day.

A middle-aged Iraqi man dressed in a suit stood up as I struggled to push open the library's warped plywood door.

After a brief introduction, we got down to business. I handed him the papers that the Khalaf family had provided concerning their father's medical history. The copies resembled standard pages pulled from any medical file, except that everything was in Arabic. The only thing I could discern was that most of the entries were dated in 2001 and 2002, though the final few appeared to be from September 2003.

To justify the raid on Khalaf's house, 1-8 claimed that Balad's police chief had told them that he had seen Khalaf running away from the scene of a recent IED attack. The family had provided these pages as proof that their father suffered from a debilitating back condition that made it difficult for him to walk, much less run.

I waited patiently as the translator examined each page. After several minutes, he looked up and said, "This is an old man. You are looking for a young man?"

"No, no. I want to know about this old man." I asked him to explain the medical entries and tell me what the old man was being treated for.

He made quick work of it. "The man is old. He sees doctor because he doesn't feel well. His hands, his back, they hurt." He pointed out the series of entries over the years, documenting how the man had returned repeatedly complaining of pain in his joints. Initially, the doctors recommended bed rest and warm compresses but eventually, they prescribed medication.

"The medicine helped him for a little bit," the interpreter said, pointing at a longer entry, "but his back still hurt. In the morning, it hurt more."

Flipping to the last page, he scrutinized the final entries.

"Does it say what it is that is causing the pain?" I asked, still unclear what exactly the man had suffered from. Having a stiff back didn't mean he couldn't run.

The translator looked confused. Returning his attention to the papers, he said, "The doctor said it will get worse, but nothing more."

I tried again. "What will get worse? Does the doctor give the problem a name?"

The translator paused and examined one of the later entries more closely. A second later his face lit up with recognition. "Ah!" he cried, "this man, he suffers because he is old!"

It took another ten minutes of back-and-forth before the translator understood that I wanted the exact translation of the words.

Zadan Khalaf suffered from spinal osteoarthritis, a degenerative disorder that could cause loss of normal spinal function. He also suffered from peripheral neuropathy, a condition where the brain has problems communicating with the spinal cord. Neither condition, however, canceled out the possibility that he was still mobile. Both disorders, while potentially debilitating, could be managed. In other words, as the translator aptly put it, he was old.

The Khalaf family had been smart to provide the medical records proving their father's debilitated condition. Had we been in the United States, it would be significant evidence that weighed heavily in their favor. Unfortunately, even if the records indicated that Khalaf was a quadriplegic, Perkins would probably claim that the man had given him a nasty look. Or, rather, that Khalaf used his eyes to signal *another* Iraqi to lunge for a gun.

Recalling Gwinner's version of events, I tried to imagine for a moment how a sixty-something-year-old man with osteoarthritis had broken free from several soldiers and managed to reach a gun he'd hidden among some stacked bedding. Even Semenko found the idea that Khalaf would be moved without first being zip-tied ludicrous. Khalaf was, after all, the target of the raid. If there's one man you want to handcuff, it's him.

The idea that Khalaf would be able to reach for anything with his hands behind his back, much less a gun, before Perkins noticed, wasn't just hard to believe, it was crazy. Perkins and the others were in the prime of their lives. This was a senior citizen with an inch-thick medical file.

I started to sigh but found myself laughing instead. It was all so preposterous. Khalaf may, in fact, have been a leader of the local insurgency, but I doubted that he posed any threat to Perkins and company in the house that night, as the soldiers contended.

As we stood to leave, the translator grasped my right hand with both of his hands.

"My wife, she wanted me to ask if there was cream for women's skin," he asked, before releasing my hand and lowering his eyes.

"Do you mean lotion?"

He rubbed his palms together and daintily patted his face and neck, mimicking a woman smoothing on moisturizer.

"What they have here is no good. Iraq no good," he repeated, affecting a sour expression. "She wants from outside Iraq, made in Europe, America.

She can't find so she tell me to ask." Shaking his head, he added bashfully, "I forget."

Holding his palms out toward me, he said, "You are lady, so I ask."

"Stay here," I said, "I'll be right back." Ten minutes later I returned with several different bottles of lotion culled from the bin of free supplies donated by charitable organizations back home.

He accepted the bottles with both hands and turned to put them in his bag. I waited for him to finish before handing him a folded piece of paper.

"What is it?" he asked, straining to read it. I stopped him before he reached for his glasses.

"Just keep it. At the gate, they may ask why you have so much lotion," I explained, pointing at the bag.

It took a second. "Yes. Yes," he finally said, tucking the note inside his jacket. His mission accomplished, he smiled. "Thank you, captain."

Semenko's e-mail did little to allay my concerns. The e-mail began, "I didn't realize it until tonight . . ." and went downhill from there. I closed my eyes momentarily. Beads of sweat formed on my brow. Semenko was in full retraction mode.

Semenko insisted that it was all his fault; he'd made a mistake. "It all appears to be valid and I jumped to conclusions, reading the statements and then hearing the stories. I am alone and under no duress. It seems like a clean shoot and that is why there is no 15-6."

I stared at the computer screen for a long time that evening. The statement "I am alone and under no duress" succeeded only in conjuring up an image of Semenko sweating in front of a keyboard surrounded by 1-8 soldiers in full battle rattle. "Now everyone is answering my questions because you are involved," he wrote.

Semenko apologized for causing such a "stink" and went on to say that he didn't want to investigate the claim any further. "I now understand the soldiers didn't do anything wrong."

He even claimed that he was confused, and that there was never an earlier statement by Sergeant First Class Perkins. "I didn't pay close enough attention." Again, it was entirely his fault.

Drowning In The Desert

Just when I thought Semenko's e-mail could not become any more disturbing, I read his closing paragraph:

If you can/if you believe it and it's possible, please tell Major G that, now that you "now understand that it was Chuck's mistake for submitting the wrong documents that led to the confusion, and now you realize it was a good shoot."

Had he lost his mind? *Semenko sounded like the one with a gun to his head.* No duress? He'd even scripted what I should say to get Major Gwinner to back off.

I wasn't even sure how to begin to respond. *Dear Chuck, Help is on the way. There will be a Humvee waiting outside Camp Paliwoda's southern perimeter at 0330. Bring everything. Good luck, Vivian.* I sat in front of the computer for at least another half-hour before I pounded out a quick thanks to Semenko for his e-mail. "I understand your decision," I wrote, and asked that he bring me any other information he had regarding the claim. More than anything, I wanted to talk to him in person.

I crawled into my sleeping bag that night with all of the recent discoveries swirling around in my brain. Khalaf's spine condition. The Stepford statements from Alpha Company. Perkins's lost statement. Semenko's "no duress" e-mail.

All of the new information made sense, even Semenko's bizarre e-mail. And yet I still felt unsettled, like I needed to catch all of these loose bits of information before they floated away.

I reached for my headlamp and the claims file so I could examine all the paperwork one more time. The file was just as I'd remembered, but I couldn't shake the feeling I was missing something. No answer presented itself.

Frustrated, and no closer to sleep, I decided to start over and read everything one last time, beginning with Semenko's initial memo regarding the Khalaf claim. I read it closely this time, all the while scribbling down the known facts, with a side note explaining his delay in presenting the claim. As obvious as the facts were, I suspected the fog in my brain was denser.

I forced myself to slow down and make sure to note even the most minor details. My list of who, what, when, and where grew longer. It was only then, as I reviewed my notes and noticed a minor discrepancy in the recorded dates, that the missing link finally presented itself. Shit!

Hunting through the papers I'd scattered across the top of my sleeping bag, I pulled out the three recent statements. My face felt hot. I had been close to it for days. Why hadn't I noticed this earlier? I tossed open another file to confirm it before pulling the lamp away from my forehead so I could blot the sweat with a tissue. The files were now spread out in front of me, the tops of the important pages visible. It had been right there all along.

The execution. The drowning. Everything happened on the same day.

CHAPTER TWENTY-TWO

Bloodstains

IT ALL WENT BACK TO Captain Paliwoda. Eric's death at Camp Eagle late in the afternoon of January 2 was the spark for the violence that would erupt after sunset. A night that began with a vengeful mission in Balad would ultimately end with the same soldiers returning to Samarra for an ill-fated patrol. By sunrise the next day, two Iraqi men were dead, and the lives of everyone involved hopelessly fractured. What happened in the twenty-four hours after Eric's death would consume us for years to come.

As the senior ranking soldier inside Khalaf's house that night, did Perkins know he'd get away with it? Was that the real reason that Perkins moved Khalaf to a different room?

By the time the soldiers of 1st Platoon, Alpha Company, 1-8 Infantry, turned their Bradleys onto Highway One for the trek back to Samarra, they already had blood on their hands. Emboldened by the deadly mission they conducted in Balad, Perkins and company took greater risks during their evening patrol in Samarra. It was the first time they'd thrown *two* people into the river, and the first time they'd done it at night.

I was halfway back to my trailer to retrieve a file I'd left there when a figure leapt from the shadows of a trailer and yelled, "Boo."

Drowning In The Desert

Stifling a scream, I jumped back, certain that the surprise had been intended for someone else. It took several seconds of squinting into the sun before I realized that I was wrong, and that the laughing soldier before me was Tom Roughneen.

"Tom!" I screamed. "What the hell are you doing here?" I'd gone from startled to annoyed to relieved in a heartbeat. Before he could respond, I threw my arms around him and gave him the warmest hug possible between two people in armored vests. It was my turn to laugh when I saw the discomfort on his face.

"Sorry, I just can't tell you how wonderful it is to see you. I still can't believe you're here. I really need to talk to you. I need your opinion on something. I have no one to talk to. I swear, I'm starting to lose it."

"Well, kiddo, it's good to see you, too!" Tom said, grinning. "Your e-mails have been short though, so you'll have to fill me in."

"I will. I will. Why are you here?"

"Well, turns out that we're flying home through Anaconda. Our flight is supposed to leave sometime in the next twenty-four hours. You know, wheels up. Bye, bye, Iraq."

His timing was brilliant. My counsel, my advisor, my friend had arrived in my hour of need. As Tom explained his unit's wait status, another small wave of relief washed over me. We had a few hours to talk.

Safe in the knowledge that he wasn't leaving immediately, I took a deep breath and started over. "So, how was Kirkuk? Been to any good restaurants?" I teased.

Tom filled me in on Kirkuk: his final projects with the city council, the latest power struggle in his unit, his sad farewells to his Kurdish friends and his beloved interpreter, and, of course, how he handled the local family that kept trying to persuade him to marry their daughter.

We stood there on the walkway between the rows of trailers for half an hour, just laughing.

Warmed by the sun on my back and the comforting presence of my closest friend in Iraq, I felt muscles in my neck and back unclench for the first time in weeks. Seeing Tom, I realized how lonely I'd been, and how much I missed laughing and thinking about things other than work, or the mounting tension with 1-8. So many of my friends had already gone home or onto different assignments. Welsch had Brian Gephardt so busy I hardly saw him.

"Okay," Tom said, with an air of finality. He studied the ground for a few seconds before continuing. "Well, I gotta say, I'm sorry to hear about the drowning debacle," he said. Lifting his head, he looked at me, his blue eyes now darkened with concern. "I didn't realize it was so bad until I read the *Slate.com* article. Don't you ever get a break?"

"Oh, Tom, Tom, Tom," I said, shaking my head, "I think it's just the tip of the iceberg."

Over dinner at the chow hall that evening, I filled him in on everything that had transpired. When I was done, I pushed away from the table, exhausted even in the retelling of it.

"Well, what do you think? Be honest," I said, settling back in my chair. "Am I completely off base? Everyone keeps acting like I'm stirring up trouble, but Perkins, this guy is out of control." I stopped myself. I could see that Tom was digesting my question.

"Viv, look at where you are. Who do you work for? These guys don't want to hear it because it's also their careers, don't you see? They want to go home and forget this place and what happened. Off-base? They're murdering people! They went from soldier to executioner and no one blinked. When does it stop?"

The ferocity of his response surprised me. A prosecutor, I'd expected him to whip me with questions, confirm distinctions, and search for qualifications. Tom rolled his eyes and exhaled before beginning again.

"Do you really think this was the first time for any of this? Of course not. Someone looked the other way the first few times, and 1-8 took that as a sign to do as they pleased. It was out of control months ago. This didn't happen overnight."

"Tom, I know," I sighed dejectedly. "I have no doubt that twenty years from now, Gwinner will be swearing that Zaidoun is still out there somewhere, laughing about how he really got one over on those Americans! The worst part about it is that he'll say this stuff, and yet Odierno nixed the exhumation, so . . ." I stopped then, unwilling to waste any more energy on stuff I couldn't change. "So, at most, Perkins gets a slap on the wrist and he's back here in another year."

Tom shook his head in disbelief.

"Don't you see? That's why this Khalaf claim is actually pretty important. Besides the fact that the whole unit has been strange about it, what's going to stop Perkins from ordering other soldiers to kill people?"

Drowning In The Desert

Tom stared at me wide-eyed. "Wait. Do you think Sassaman ordered him to kill that guy?"

I shook my head dismissively. "No. He's not that stupid. Perkins just did what he wanted, and no one is going to ask too many questions because they're happy. It's like they have a wild animal they can unleash and look the other way. They had their revenge."

"Yeah, but they cover for him, so technically that makes them complicit."

"You're right, but that's way too legally nuanced for the chain of command. They would probably need to see a video of Perkins shooting the guy in the head before anything happened," I said bitterly. "I'm supposed to go forward with the drowning case, but they cancel the exhumation? Think about it."

"Yeah, but they sought justice!" Tom said, pretending to bang a gavel against the table. "It's pretty clever, really." He smiled and took a bite of his food

"Another investigation is the last thing they want to hear. We're leaving in less than two weeks. Division leaves in a week." My mood had soured. "Plus, there's no way I could ever prove it. Gwinner's the gatekeeper over there. He's monitoring who talks to me, what they're saying. It's crazy." I pushed my tray away in frustration. "And then, there's poor Chuck."

"I just can't believe they're all still in their positions," Tom said. "Why didn't Odierno remove them? Aren't they getting letters of reprimand?"

"That's the word, at least," I said.

"Have you seen what Sassaman says to the reporters? It's like he's some one-man terminator," Tom said, referring to a *New York Times* story in which Sassaman was reported to have said, "With a heavy dose of fear and violence, and a lot of money for projects, I think we can convince these people that we are here to help them."

Tom clucked with dismay, "Why doesn't anyone at division or corps do anything about it? I mean it's in the papers; it's not a secret."

"Tom, you may not remember this but division *approved* those tactics," I said. Expelling a frustrated sigh, I reminded him about the town of Abu Hishma, how the tactics were condoned by division. The town had made headlines right before Tom returned to Kirkuk. The Rules of Engagement had basically been set aside as Sassaman had his men blow up many homes, all for the same reason: insurgent stronghold, terrorists lived there. There was no immediacy factor. He just returned days later and blew the places up or peppered them with bullets.

"You have to teach 'em a lesson" was another answer I got from some 1-8 officers.

Stateside, my father had also been disturbed by the Abu Hishma situation and had sent me the newspaper article. He'd even highlighted Sassaman's "fear and violence" quote. In the margins, he had scribbled, "Be careful–you're more likely to teach them how to really hate you. Soon, they won't even want your money."

My father had called it the "cowboy approach": running around flashing guns and intimidating people into submission by brute force. Special forces guys pride themselves on their ability to keep their cool in a chaotic situation and strategically using violence as a tool. After being shot at on three different continents, my father was convinced that a hot-headed approach was a huge liability, especially in low-intensity conflicts like Iraq.

My father was not squeamish about violence or use of force. This was a man who taught my siblings and me to fire pistols as children. He also had intimate knowledge of how lethal an insurgency could be. In Vietnam, during the Tet Offensive, my father's patrol had come under attack in an alley in Phan Thiet. A Viet Cong grenade exploded right next to him, blinding him in his right eye and causing deafness in his right ear. Rocked by the blast, he took a bullet in his right shoulder seconds later. His philosophy: go after the enemy, just be smart about it. To him, violence, like any tool, had to be used strategically to be effective. Sassaman's response in Abu Hisma struck my father as reactionary and appallingly short-sighted.

A heavy silence fell between Tom and me. I watched blankly as the chow hall workers began wiping down the tables. Tom finished the last of his food.

I was unprepared for what he said next.

"Viv, I think you should talk to Lieutenants Larson and Hudson. Remember them? I worked with them at Paliwoda's company. I actually told you about this once, a long time ago."

Tom described a situation I remembered well enough. It concerned a tactic several 4th Engineer officers had told Tom about. They claimed that 1-8 soldiers would conduct "recons by fire." Days after they had been attacked, 1-8 soldiers had returned to the area they believed the attack had been launched from, an overgrown section of a well-traveled road, and sprayed the entire area with bullets to "send a message" to the community. This "recon by fire" had reportedly killed a woman hanging laundry in her backyard. The woman's family feared retaliation if they came forward, but the neighbors had been outraged and mentioned it to several 4th Engineer soldiers who were also working in the area.

This was fourth-hand knowledge, but Tom had wanted me to look into it. At the time, I'd told him to have the soldiers report it, or to find someone with more credible knowledge. It had been a sticky point between us.

"I don't know if the lieutenants were the ones that talked to the family, but maybe they'll tell you who did." He paused, then added, "And if not, at least you know you tried. I just know they were the ones who told me about the recon by fire and the dead lady." Crossing his arms, he sat back. "It's a pattern of recklessness."

When I agreed, Tom offered to call the lieutenants to see if they'd be willing to come up to headquarters to speak with me, "just so they won't feel weird."

Later that night, Tom stopped by the ALOC one last time to say goodbye to me and the guys. His civil affairs team was headed into the "waiting pen," where they would remain until their flight arrived. As he left, Tom told me that he had talked to Lieutenants Larson and Hudson and they had agreed to stop by the following day.

Tom's unmitigated outrage offered me the clarity and perspective I needed to move forward. The past few weeks had brought to the surface every molecule of self-doubt I had. I'd been thrown by my commander's discomfort, 1-8's intimidation, and the coolness from my peers. As bad as all that was, I'd allowed myself to internalize the bullshit about what made a "real soldier." I'd let myself be cowed by my gender, my branch, and my own desire to make nice. I'd also forgotten the one thing I knew about courage: it had nothing to do with convenience.

Tom was right. He'd been right about everything. About 1-8. About my trials. About the fact that I'd been working my guys too hard. "There's a serious problem at 1-8. Don't let it blow up in your face," he'd said. Recalling how quick I'd been to doubt Tom, rather than 1-8, I felt flush with shame. I had relished my insider status even though I knew how fleeting and fickle it was. And even then, I longed to be back in "good standing" with Sassaman, Gwinner, and the others.

Today, there had been no "I told you so" from Tom. His advice, as always, was level-headed and pragmatic.

"Circumstantial evidence is still evidence," he'd said. "Give up the idea that you'll find a smoking gun. It doesn't exist. What you do have is a pattern of recklessness."

It didn't surprise me that the lieutenants, when they arrived the following morning, weren't interested in divulging much of anything. Hudson and Larson were friendly, respectful, but tight-lipped. While they acknowledged 1-8's aggressive tactics, they were careful not to remember anyone in particular. As for the recon-by-fire incident, they had only heard about it from others, always several nameless people removed.

I wished them a safe redeployment and bid them farewell, satisfied, as Tom had predicted, that I'd at least pursued the matter, however late.

For all of 1-8's recklessness, I knew I couldn't be anything less than thorough if I was going to recommend a formal criminal investigation into the Khalaf shooting. The first order of business was to confirm the standard operating procedures for raids. That would be key to establishing that 1-8 had gone off course.

Everywhere I went the next day, I canvassed soldiers about raid SOPs. I chatted with soldiers while they took smoke breaks, at the chow hall, and in the JAG workspace. Each soldier I spoke with echoed the protocol: When entering the home of a target individual, all males are zip-tied immediately, as well as any uncooperative females. Men are taken to the main room of the house, and women and children are taken outside. Then, with help from interpreters, the individuals are identified, and the suspects are separated for questioning.

The official accounts offered by Khalaf's family reflected the soldiers' standard operating procedures to the letter. Baha Muhamed Khalif, a male guest at the home that night, described being woken up by the sound of soldiers attempting to kick in the door.

"I opened the door and was quickly placed on the ground and restrained. Zaidon (the deceased) was brought out also restrained and placed on the ground. A U.S. soldier holding a pistol began asking everyone for their name. When Zaidon was identified, U.S. soldiers lifted him up and took him into a separate room."

Drowning In The Desert

According to Khalaf's daughter, soldiers even handcuffed a young boy before sending him outside to wait with the women.

Feeling daring, I even struck up a conversation with 1-8's liaison officer, a captain stationed at brigade headquarters. After broaching the issue as a protocol question, his answers were the same. Then, something clicked, and he seemed to remember who it was that was asking. *You know, the enemy.* Instantly, his tone changed. Straightening up in his chair, he crossed his arms, and appeared to be contemplating the matter deeply.

Narrowing his eyes at me, he asked, "What exactly are you looking for?"

"Nothing really, just curious," I said doing my best to sound breezy.

"Of course, there are situations where things might go differently," he said.

"Like?"

He was quiet for a moment. "If the number of people in the house were greater than you expected and you didn't have enough zip ties, you might not be able to handcuff everyone," he offered.

"You would try and cuff as many of the men as you could wouldn't you?"

"In most cases, but not all."

"When wouldn't you cuff one of the men?"

"If you didn't have enough zip ties, you might not be able to."

"If you did have enough zip ties, at what point would you restrain the men?"

"Right away . . ." Catching himself, he added, "Well, it depends."

"On?"

"What the circumstances are."

"Under what circumstances would you not cuff them right away?" I asked.

"In most cases you probably would," he said. "But not always."

Convinced I'd heard enough, I thanked him and mumbled something about needing to get back to the workspace.

I was a few feet away from his desk when behind me I heard, "Our SOPs can be different depending on the circumstances."

It certainly seems that way.

He wasn't the only 1-8 officer covering his bases. The next day, Gwinner dispatched Semenko to deliver two fresh and unsolicited accounts of the Khalaf shooting, from Perkins and Ironeyes. Gwinner also made sure Semenko apologized for "misplacing" Perkins's and Ironeyes's original statements. Semenko was as skittish as ever, and it looked as though he hadn't slept in days. Dark crescents hugged the bottom of his eyes.

"That Captain Semenko sure is a character," Kolb said in his signature drawl as we watched Semenko leave. "But you can't deny that he's brave." Kolb had just finished constructing a paper model of a Mini Cooper, part of a sales packet his wife had sent him. He was contemplating buying one when we returned. Turning the car in his hands, he checked to see if he'd secured the paper flaps. "Especially 'cause he's out there all alone with those guys. Nope, I can't say I would have done it."

As bad as the tension with 1-8 was, I realized later that it would have been a lot worse had it not been for Kolb. Kolb took it upon himself to become the unofficial point person for the dozens of legal and administrative matters we needed to address with 1-8 as part of redeployment. He fielded most of 1-8's phone calls and handled the majority of follow-up calls. When soldiers from 1-8 would confront me, he'd find ways to interrupt and disperse the crowd. There was no fanfare or loud declaration; Kolb's support was quiet, thoughtful, and consistent.

An hour later, the phone rang. Covering the mouthpiece, Kolb whispered, "Hey, Captain G, it's Major Gwinner. You look at that claim yet?" He was referring to the file Semenko had brought.

I shook my head. Having spent the entire hour trying to finish reports for division, I'd barely glanced at the file.

Kolb didn't miss a beat; he hung up seconds later.

"Just a hunch, ma'am, but I think he'll call back, even though I told him I'd have you call him."

Kolb volunteered to finish the reports so I could read the file.

Perkins's statement was one of two in the folder Semenko had left. They were recently prepared statements, not the originals I had asked for. Semenko also included an amended-claims memo that attempted to explain the mysterious whereabouts of the earlier statements made by Perkins and Ironeyes.

Perkins and Ironeyes had done a commendable job of syncing their statements. Ironeyes offered a general account while Perkins provided the details. Both statements were written two days earlier, on March 3.

According to the time on the form, Ironeyes had been awakened between midnight and 0100 to provide his new statement. He wasn't happy. "It is now the middle of the night and I was woken up to write another statement about something that happened about two months ago."

His memory proved clear, however, despite his allusion to it being a distant event. He stated that their mission was to "capture a suspected planner of attacks against coalition forces." In parentheses, he wrote "Zadan Kalef [Khalaf]." Ironeyes described entering the house, clearing the rooms, and searching and detaining everyone inside. They separated the women and children and began searching the males, he said. As they searched, Ironeyes recalled that Khalaf "was putting up a struggle so I told my guys to move him to another room thinking he might calm down a little." His platoon sergeant, Perkins, stepped in to assist. As Khalaf was moved, Ironeyes stated that he saw Khalaf grab something, at which point Ironeyes shouted a warning and Perkins shot Khalaf. In parentheses, Ironeyes added that what Khalaf had grabbed turned out to be a gun.

Perkins should have offered a more general account. It would have been easier to believe. Instead, he concocted a story of self-defense that wasn't plausible. In it, he recalled that "the target individual Zadan Kalef was struggling with members of first squad so he was moved to another room." Perkins went into the room "to help calm the individual down." When he felt the man "had settled down enough to detain," he turned to ask someone for some plastic cuffs. While Perkins was turned, "SSG Ironeyes shouted something to the effect that the man was grabbing something." Perkins turned back around and "saw a pistol in the man's hand and fired a controlled pair. The arm was still coming up and I fired a third shot in his head."

Each time I read this I felt a new surge of anger and disgust that the shooting had happened, and that Perkins, Ironeyes, even Gwinner were trying to feed me some bullshit story all over again. Perkins must have felt pretty confident. All he needed to say was that he responded to the threat by firing a "controlled pair." That would have been sufficient. Not one for modesty, however, Perkins made a point of mentioning that he'd shot Khalaf a third time and offered that pithy explanation about Khalef's hand "still coming up." This third shot to the head was gratuitous. Perkins knew he could get away with it, though.

Ironically, the statements provided by Khalaf's family members more accurately reflected the soldiers' standard operating procedures for a cordon and search than the tale Perkins and Ironeyes had proffered. Baha Muhamed Khalif, a male guest at the home that night, gave the following statement: "U.S. forces came to the home and woke up the family while trying to kick in the door. I opened the door and was quickly placed on the ground and restrained. Zaidon (the deceased) was brought out also restrained and placed on the ground. A U.S. soldier holding a pistol began asking everyone for their name. When Zaidon was identified, U.S. soldiers lifted him up and took him into a separate room. I was taken outside with the females. The U.S. forces came out of the house with a body bag."

The account by Khalaf's daughter was more consistent with standard operating procedures, too. She stated that "soldiers stormed into the house taking women outside the house and arresting our young guest, tightening his hands together and placed him in the outdoor. They kept our father inside and pulled him to the west room where they shot him dead."

The idea that Perkins, or any other soldier for that matter, couldn't have used physical force to subdue the old man was absurd. Perkins was the same guy that ordered his soldiers to throw an Iraqi man off a bridge after the man allegedly made an obscene gesture at him. Perkins was the same man that his own soldiers feared would physically harm them. Bowman's statement came to mind: "Sergeant First Class Perkins would not have any problems putting his hands on me."

Perhaps most damning to the soldiers' version of events were the pictures of the room where Khalaf died. It was small, no bigger than eight by ten feet, and cluttered with stuff: an old loveseat, two dressers, a trunk, boxes, and a small desk. Except for a small portion of the loveseat that was uncovered, clothes, blankets, and more boxes were piled on top of the furniture that bordered the room. As you entered the room, the loveseat was directly to your left, against the wall. Only a narrow strip of carpet, about three-and-a-half-feet wide, was visible, directly in front of the loveseat. Several photos zoomed in on the massive blood stain on the carpet in front of the loveseat. The dark stain, where blood had pooled, disappeared beneath the loveseat. The two dressers, piled with clothing and bedding, were on the far wall of the room.

Even if I overlooked the wild inconsistencies between the statements, the soldiers' departure from basic procedures, and their recent history of lying, the space was too small to support the soldiers' version of events. If both Khalaf and

Drowning In The Desert

Perkins were in the room at the same time, as Perkins claimed, Perkins could only have been an arm's length away from Khalaf at any given time. If Khalaf had made a move for a gun, Perkins needed only to step and kick or punch the back of the debilitated man to stop him.

Because Ironeyes claimed he could see Khalaf grab for something, Ironeyes must have been standing at or near the door, with Perkins between Ironeyes and Khalaf. Otherwise, Ironeyes could have skipped the warning shout and shot Khalaf himself.

And there were other questions that the soldiers' statements did not answer. For example, if the soldiers planned to question Khalaf, why wasn't there an interpreter present? And, where was the pistol they alleged Khalaf was holding?

When the phone rang again, I signaled to Kolb that I'd take it.

CHAPTER TWENTY-THREE

The Leap

AT THE U.S. ARMY AIRBORNE School in Fort Benning, Georgia, teams of instructors known as "black hats" or "Sergeant Airborne" spend weeks training soldiers how to jump out of an airplane and survive. After three weeks and five jumps, we'd lose our status as "legs," earthbound, fear-consumed, nonairborne folk. First, however, we needed to master what is known as the "parachute landing fall," a landing technique that is supposed to distribute the shock evenly throughout your body. We spent the first few days practicing our falls in a sawdust pit. As our skills improved, so did the height of the apparatus we were required to leap from. En route to the plane, we still had a thirty-four-foot-high tower and a 250-foot-high tower to conquer.

Surprisingly, it was the day we had to tackle the thirty-four-foot tower that proved to be the longest and most challenging day of airborne school. The height wasn't the problem, it was the extended wait we had to endure before reaching the platform. Waiting with fellow soldiers on the tower's support platform was excruciating. Any confidence or ease you had going in was undone after fifteen minutes of exposure to your fellow soldiers' fears and mounting anxiety. Tuning out the trepidation around me, I tried to focus on the soldiers ahead of me. Every time one of them would freeze on the platform,

Drowning In The Desert

Sergeant Airborne would yell, "You dirty, nasty leg! You forget what you came here for?"

It was so beautifully army. Of course they expected us to be afraid, they just expected our sense of purpose to override that fear. I didn't hesitate when I got to the platform, but only because I'd benefited vicariously from Sergeant Airborne's screams to the soldiers ahead of me. All of this was in preparation for the day you found yourself in the doorway of an actual C-130 with Sergeant Airborne screaming "Go!"

Sergeant Airborne's taunt was on my mind a lot these days. What was I here for? My suspicion about the Khalaf shooting was upsetting my bosses. The soldiers whose approval I'd once gloried in now considered me a bad guy. I felt queasy a good amount of the time.

My stomach wasn't helped in any way by Kolb holding his hand over the receiver and mouthing "Gwinner." Taking the phone, I made every effort to keep my tone as cool and as neutral as possible.

Thankfully, Gwinner got right to the point. He wanted to know if I'd received the additional statements that I had requested to complete the claim.

"Yes, sir, Semenko dropped the folder by this afternoon. Thanks for taking care of that so quickly."

"So you have everything you need?" he asked, testing the waters.

For the sake of keeping things cordial, I could have said "yes," but that would only make it more difficult if I called back requesting something else. I left myself an out.

"Yeah, well, I think so, sir," I said as brightly and agreeably as I could.

A worthy opponent, Gwinner tried again. "You have the statements from the guys in the room that night. Isn't that what you wanted?"

Well, technically I wanted their first statements. I just kept it general to see what showed up.

"Yes, sir, but I haven't really had a chance to read through all of them yet. I don't know if that's all I'll need until I read them, sir. I need to read them first."

"I know there was the confusion with the statements," Gwinner continued. "And I have Captain Semenko right here." His voice faded as he moved his mouth away from the receiver, presumably to say something to Semenko. I imagined Gwinner yanking Semenko by the front of his uniform toward the phone.

"If this is about those statements, he can explain to you right now what happened," Gwinner offered.

I cringed. "No, sir," I hurriedly assured him, "Chuck explained about the statements. I understand about the statements."

Carter and Kolb had stopped what they were doing and were now watching me. Carter mouthed, "What's wrong?" while Kolb held out the folder of statements, his face quizzical. I mouthed "Nothing," and gestured for them to go back to what they were doing.

"What is the problem here, Captain Gembara?" Gwinner demanded. "We've given you what you need. What more is there to this claim?"

You tell me, sir. Why can't I just read the statements first?

"Sir, thank you again for getting them to me so quickly," I said, "I just haven't had a chance to read them. I'll read them tonight," I repeated as cordially as I could.

Gwinner correctly interpreted this as a bad sign for his unit and launched into a defense of Perkins's decision to shoot Khalaf. "Khalaf was reaching for a gun when Perkins shot him," Gwinner insisted angrily. "It was a legal kill."

"Sir, like I said, I will go through the statements this evening," I repeated, unwilling to engage Gwinner in a dialogue about the substance of the soldiers' statements. My measured tone only stoked Gwinner's anger.

"There is no truth to this claim. This man was behind several attacks," he roared before reiterating that Balad's police chief had seen Khalaf "running" from the site of the attacks.

Recovering from his outburst, Gwinner hissed, "These people are lying opportunists."

Lying opportunists? I closed my eyes, unable to believe that we had come full circle. The image of the other family he had called "lying opportunists" instantly sprang to mind: Zaidoun's family, with their red-rimmed eyes, their refusal to accept solace money, and their haunting pleas for justice. Lying opportunists?

It was then that I recognized it, that same feeling I had in the door of the C-130: unbridled fear. It had all been preparation for this very moment. I could almost hear the Sergeant Airborne screaming, "Go!" I did not come to Iraq to be bullied. I came here to uphold the laws of war. If I didn't do that, no one would. No more waiting, it was time to jump.

"Sir, I'm confused," I began, careful to keep the sarcasm out of my voice. "Why didn't the soldiers follow their standard operating procedures? Why wasn't Khalaf zip-tied?"

There was a second of silence on the other end, and my heart clenched. Gwinner, it seemed, had also been waiting for this moment. No longer restraining himself, his anger boiled over in a scathing tirade.

"Captain Gembara, do you even know what our standing operating procedures are? Do you? You're not out there, are you?"

It was a question intended to silence me. I didn't take the bait. I felt a strange calm come over me as his anger grew.

"But, sir, I just want to know— please, can you explain to me then— why would soldiers zip-tie all the men except for the target?"

Gwinner's voice exploded across the line. "Captain Gembara, have you ever even been on a patrol? With people trying to kill you?" I pulled the receiver away from my ear. "With people shooting at you?"

I swallowed, only partially aware of Kolb, Carter, and now Philibert and Jay Arthurs watching me, their faces frozen in wonder.

"Have you?" Gwinner hissed, his hatred so apparent it took my breath away.

With persistence, he had hit his mark, and the fury he triggered seemed poised to consume me. My heart was beating wildly in my chest, that primal instinct to render an equally scathing personal attack was on the tip of my tongue. *Careful, Viv. Don't do it. He still outranks you. He's a major. Don't do it.*

His fury continued unabated. "You should come out sometime. On a patrol. See how it is to have people shooting at you."

His comments were so unacceptable, so beyond reasonable that they had the effect of restoring my equilibrium. I felt my calm returning almost as swiftly as it had disappeared. Gwinner had shown his hand, completely and irrevocably. The man was out of control. *Disengage, Viv.*

"Sir, I don't . . ."

He cut me off. Gwinner returned to insisting that I tell him who else was needed to close out the claim. "The company commander? Perkins? Other soldiers? Who?" he demanded.

"Sir!" I yelled. "At this time, I do not need anything else from you or the unit regarding this claim. I have nothing else to say on the matter." With that, I hung up.

Standing there, my hand still on the receiver, a current of angry electricity coursed its way through my body. The audience of silent, stunned faces around me confirmed that I had, in fact, shouted down and hung up on a senior officer. "Captain G, what happened?" Philibert finally asked.

"Geez, guys," I said. Letting out a deep breath, I leaned against the table and crossed my arms, still shaken. "Gwinner just lost it, you know, completely. Did you hear me trying to get off the phone?" I offered them an abbreviated version of the call, but even hours later Gwinner's cutting words still lingered in my mind.

It would be difficult to prove that the Khalaf shooting was an execution-style murder, but there was plenty of evidence suggesting a troublesome command climate at 1-8. It wasn't an infantry thing, as they liked to suggest, it was most definitely a 1-8 thing.

My next step was clear. I had to go forward. Doing so, however, would antagonize my superiors, complicate my life, and likely fail in the end. Picking up the phone, I called division to notify them that I would be sending an urgent e-mail about the Khalaf claim.

Fully aware of the ramifications of my request, I wrote to division, strongly recommending that they escalate the Khalaf claim into a full-blown criminal investigation. To make the case as easy to understand as possible, I typed up a concise summary of the entire file. I included a timeline of events and high-lighted significant details including the fact that 1-8 never reported confiscating a pistol that night, a point that would raise the eyebrows of any investigator.

As I typed my summary that evening, the action report from the January 3 raids caught my attention for another reason. I'd forgotten that 1-8 had reported killing *two* men that night. Fingers suspended over the keyboard, I did a mental inventory to see whether I'd seen any information regarding the second killing. Nothing. Then, I forced it from my mind, distrusting my sudden interest in the second killed-in-action as an excuse to delay my report on the Khalaf matter. *Focus, Viv.*

With less than two weeks remaining in theater, I knew the likelihood of a full investigation was slim. It was equally clear that my silence would buy me nothing. Not peace of mind. Certainly, not justice. And, most importantly, not self-respect. I wasn't searching for my unit's approval and acceptance any longer. I had found my voice and it was resonant. The boldness of Perkins's savagery demanded an equally bold pursuit of justice.

CHAPTER TWENTY-FOUR

Failure to Repair

The truth will make you free,
but first it will make you miserable.
— James A. Garfield, 20th President of the United States

HOT CHOW AT FORWARD OPERATING Base Animal was like any other hot meal served in the field. There was the same muddy looking "meat thing," the same preservatives-laden vegetables, and the same choice of cheerless carbs, wet, amorphous snowballs of rice or battle-tested Wonder bread.

I'd hitched a ride with a supply convoy out of Anaconda that day and found myself hostage to the circuitous route the convoy was making among several bases. With some time to kill before the convoy left Camp Animal, I chit-chatted with soldiers lining up for lunch.

"C'mon, ma'am, why don't you stay?" the first sergeant insisted, after joining the group.

"Thanks, First Sergeant, but I'm about to leave."

"Aw, c'mon," he said, ushering me to check out the grub. The hot chow looked like the food at Anaconda, with one exception: the scowling soldier who ladled it out. He looked vaguely familiar. I scanned his nametag and then, to confirm my eyes weren't deceiving me, I checked his rank. *No way.* Still not quite sure I had read the nametag correctly, I asked the first sergeant what the soldier's name was. Yes, that one, the one slopping the food down in angry splashes.

Oh, no, they didn't. Stepping forward, I checked the nametag again, confirming in fact, *Oh, yes, they did.* The lunch attendant that day was none other than Pfc. Paul Lightfoot, known far and wide in 3rd Brigade as the doofus who had shot himself in the foot to get out of Iraq. Yes, his plan had worked out well.

Lightfoot probably did not realize that his return to Iraq was as much a surprise to me as it was to him. Last I'd heard, he'd been transported in June 2003 from a combat hospital near Baghdad to Fort Carson via Ramstein Air Base in Germany, where the brain trust must have decided that, instead of sending me the camera battery I needed (or anything but old, scribbled-on file folders), they would send back a misbehaving soldier. I'd been in such short supply.

Up to my ears with the investigations and trials, my colleagues back home had grudgingly agreed to handle the Lightfoot case after we learned that doctors had sent him home to heal. I'd confirmed that the case file, with corresponding witness statements, had reached the Fort Carson JAG office soon afterwards.

Somewhere, somehow, between the Fort Carson JAG office, the medical unit treating Lightfoot, and his own unit, Lightfoot was never tried for stealing from Iraqis or for shooting himself in the foot. No, they just sent him back here. At some point, you would think, somebody at Fort Carson might have mentioned this to me. A simple heads-up would have been nice. You know, so we didn't put the guy in daily contact with the unit's water and food supply. Apparently, it had never occurred to anybody that a soldier foolish enough to injure himself might be a threat to other soldiers as well.

F. Scott Fitzgerald's declaration that there are no second acts in American lives clearly did not apply to the army. Every day at noon, and again at dinner, the soldiers of 1-68 Armor Battalion bore witness to that phenomenon.

Although Lightfoot's surprising Act II came as a result of Fort Carson's incompetence, word about an extended first act in another matter had made its way around Anaconda. Even before I had heard that it was official, soldiers were talking about the fact that Lieutenant Colonel Sassaman, Major Gwinner, and Captain Cunningham were expected to receive letters of reprimand from General Odierno for their parts in the cover-up of the drowning incident.

While the punishment was expected, the fact that Odierno allowed all three officers to remain in their positions surprised many soldiers.

Back at the JAG workspace, Brian Gebhardt seemed keen on continuing our lunch conversation from the other day. I, however, was happy to forget he'd ever mentioned Perkins's name, or the drowning. While I still wasn't accustomed to the enmity from 1-8 soldiers, I'd accepted it. With a good friend like Brian, the discord was upsetting, particularly because we'd never had any, and because I considered Brian a level-headed guy. His casual tolerance of Perkins had thrown me for a loop. Granted, Brian only knew him as the funny guy at the car wash, not the guy who chewed soldiers out for throwing people in the river the wrong way. Either way, I was willing to shelve any discussion of Perkins or the drowning in favor of a return to our friendship.

Unfortunately, with the guys still at lunch, I was on my own that day. Brian tossed out a few softballs before getting to the real reason for his visit.

"Is it true?" he asked. "Did Odierno give Sassaman, Gwinner, and Cunningham letters of reprimand?"

Where was this interest coming from, I wondered. The other day, he'd seemed to think Perkins was one funny guy. Had Perkins said something more?

"Yeah, it looks like it," I said, hoping that would satisfy him and we could navigate our way back to less choppy waters.

"Yeah, but what about Perkins," he asked, "and the lieutenant?"

"Well, it's still not clear. They may be charged back home." A second later I added, "You do realize that as an officer, if you receive a letter of reprimand, it ends your career progression, though, right?" I'd thrown it out there as neutrally as I could, hoping to spur a reaction. I turned back to my computer to check my inbox. Nothing new.

Taking a seat on our trunk, Brian placed his hands on his knees. He seemed lost in thought.

"So that's it, huh?" he finally said, more to himself.

While he sounded frustrated, I approached cautiously. "Well, it's the division commander's decision. He's the approval authority." And because Sassaman, Gwinner, and Cunningham had not been removed from their jobs in the battalion, it was safe to assume that would, in fact, be it for them.

"Really?" Brian remained inscrutable.

"Well, yeah," I replied. Impatient to know where he was headed, I continued, "Plus, they were just the cover-up; they didn't push the guys in the river that night."

"Yeah, I know, I know," Brian mumbled.

"It happened after Paliwoda died," I offered, echoing some of the leadership's explanations for their actions. "1-8 was devastated and angry, so when these Iraqis accused their guys of drowning some guy, I think the knee-jerk reaction must have been to protect their soldiers, right? It was probably a hard call," I said before shifting my attention back to the computer screen.

Brian digested my words for several seconds before saying anything. When he finally responded, the conviction in his voice surprised me.

"Viv, but *they* are the officers," he said, staring hard at me. "*We* are trained to make those tough calls. All the hard decisions. That's why we're the leaders." He cleared his throat. Continuing, he admitted, "I thought about this for a long time the other day, and then I got it, why it bothered me so much." Leaning forward, he rested his elbows on his knees and paused as though he were organizing his thoughts. "What's the point in having officers if we can't expect them to make these tough calls? That's what we took an oath to do. Soldiers depend on officers to tell them what's right and wrong. Even with your JAG bosses, they outrank you, so you do as they say, right?"

"Well, yeah, of course," I said, shrugging my shoulders.

Brian stood. "Even Perkins, he may be an E7, but *they* outranked him, and no one told him 'no' or tried to stop him. Instead, they covered for him! So what's he supposed to think then?"

Not to mention Logan, Martinez, and Bowman. I nodded silently in agreement

"Think about it. If the officers don't stop it, who will? Isn't that why we're held to a higher standard?"

As bad as Perkins was, yes, any officer who didn't stop him was worse.

Gebhardt had hit the nail on the head, capturing perfectly the ambiguous, gloomy disappointment I'd felt about Sassaman's involvement. I'd struggled to articulate it to Tom, who having never gotten along with the lieutenant colonel, didn't really understand why I felt so let down. Regardless of Sassaman's intentions, by instructing his soldiers to lie, Sassaman had condoned their actions and compounded the matter. His order hadn't protected Logan or Martinez or Bowman, who seemed desperate to tell someone about the oppressive command climate they lived in. Sassaman's order certainly hadn't protected Gwinner or Cunningham, who would now lose their careers over it.

Whether he realized it or not, Sassaman had basically sent a message saying that Perkins could continue doing as he pleased and the commanders would protect him. Even if Sassaman didn't know just how bad Perkins was, the message was still the same.

While Brian's comments had crystallized the reasons for my disappointment, the relief was fleeting. I felt no better knowing what it was that upset me so much about Sassaman's involvement in the ordeal.

Brian paced back and forth, now consumed by his fervor on the role of officers. I wondered whether he was reflecting on his training at West Point. I was tempted to say I agreed with him, but I didn't want to disrupt his train of thought. I could tell he was dancing close to the whole "officer and a gentleman" idea.

While Richard Gere may have brought the idea into the mainstream with his movie *An Officer and a Gentleman*, the idea is at the heart of military doctrine. As a commissioned officer, it is simply not enough to be a good infantryman or engineer, you're supposed to be the embodiment of discipline and integrity. Officers aren't just held to a higher standard in theory. The concept is actually codified in military law: Article 133—Conduct unbecoming of an officer and a gentleman. The thinking is that if the nation is going to trust you to lead its soldiers, you better be someone worth saluting.

Congress, the body responsible for military law, recognized that a soldier's trust in his or her leader is inextricably linked to that leader's moral integrity. Anything about your life that raises even a pinch of doubt about your character becomes an issue. There's no separation of the professional and personal, the public and private. You should be a role model in *both* your professional and personal life. You cannot pick and choose what rules and laws you abide by.

That's why things like having an affair with a subordinate, or chronically bouncing personal checks, are taken very seriously. You're supposed to embody the army's values. Anything that could cause one of your soldiers, or your peers, not to trust you is a dangerous trait, raising serious questions about whether you are fit to lead. By telling his soldiers to lie, Sassaman eschewed the laws he had sworn to uphold in favor of his own judgment.

Later that day, I learned that Odierno would appoint an informal investigation into Khalaf's death. While encouraged by the news, I wondered why CID wasn't involved. If professional investigators found 1-8 challenging to investigate, what were the chances that a regular officer could ferret out the truth? It was out of my hands, however, so I packed up the file's contents, including the photographs and Khalaf's medical records, for delivery to division headquarters.

I spent the remainder of the afternoon helping the guys handle the heavy foot traffic through the JAG workspace. Adding to the chaos was the arrival of my two JAG replacement officers. Bright-eyed and earnest, they wore more body armor than I'd ever seen, and they couldn't wait to hear everything about my job. Keeping with the army's fondness for PowerPoint presentations, I showed them one I'd prepared called "Lessons Learned." Next to them, I felt a hundred years old. Even twenty-one-year-old Carter looked weathered and worn as he maneuvered around the new JAGs who said they just wanted to hang around and "take it all in."

My replacements were from the 1st Infantry Division, which was replacing our 4th Division in Iraq. They would be responsible for covering 3rd Brigade's area of operations after we left. The good news was that 1st Division had assigned two JAG officers to the area. The bad news was that the two JAGs would not be located in Balad at Camp Anaconda. Instead, one lawyer would be based out of 1st Division headquarters in Tikrit, while the other would be located at an air base north of Balad, in Ad Duluyiah.

This new arrangement did not go over well with the judges in Balad. At our final meeting, they insisted I change this and tell the new unit to put *both* lawyers at Anaconda. Laughing, I asked them how their boss, the chief judge in Baghdad, would react if they demanded to work in the towns where they lived, or demanded a pay raise? They saw my point and eventually dropped the matter, but they remained concern about this new setup.

Most of their anxiety stemmed from the growing tension they felt with Balad's police force. Post-Saddam, the roles of the judiciary and the police were still evolving, and the adjustment period had been difficult. The judges worried that the police had become too empowered by their work alongside U.S. infantry units and now regularly dismissed any questions or objections the judges raised over their conduct. It helped to have an army lawyer nearby to consult with when these tensions arose. The judges also felt that an army lawyer's involvement provided weight to their inquiries with the local police commanders. To the Iraqi judges, moving the army lawyers to Tikrit was too far, the move too bureaucratic, and signaled the drawback of Coalition forces that they feared was imminent.

"Don't be discouraged by the distance," I said repeatedly. "I think it is a good sign that they've assigned two lawyers to this area. It shows the army realizes how important supporting the legal system is to keeping peace."

Several of the judges nodded politely.

Philibert had wisely suggested I wait until the end of the meeting to issue the judges their guns. Seeing how heavy with worry the judge's faces were, I was thankful I would finish on a positive note.

Philibert's reasoning, on the other hand, was bizarre. He feared that by arming the judges early, they might be tempted to take me hostage.

"And just think, ma'am," he'd said a little too excitedly, "1-8 would hear that it was you they'd taken hostage and then they'd never show up."

Naturally, Kolb, Carter, and I had ignored Phil. We attributed Philibert's increasingly morbid sense of humor to short-timer's syndrome, just oddly manifested in the eccentric Phil.

Locating the weapons cards in my backpack, I moved on to the good news with the judges.

"You will each receive a weapon today, along with a weapons card that permits you to carry it for personal protection. I know it has been stressful for you, and I hope this helps."

As the interpreter explained, I watched the judges' angst-ridden faces relax into cautious excitement. Some smiled, and several pulled their seats closer as I began stacking the black gun cases on a rickety coffee table.

After matching the weapons cards with each corresponding box, I issued both to their new owners. The judges were genuinely surprised that I'd delivered on my promise to arm them. Their delight only increased when they saw the brand new 9mm pistols nestled inside their cases.

"Please, safeguard your guns and never carry them without the weapons card." Smiling, I added, "Remember, we have the serial numbers of each gun on record. You don't want your gun turning up in the wrong place."

This was a warning intended to ensure their vigilance in safeguarding the weapon, but not because I was concerned they would commit crimes. Although we had prepared a database of all the weapons cards we'd issued in 3rd Brigade's region, along with the corresponding weapons' serial numbers, I was skeptical that 1st Division would continue the program after we left. So, without informing the judges of my concern, I hoped that by issuing each of them a weapons card that contained their photo, position, and weapon's serial number, along with 3rd Brigade's insignia, it might deter follow-on soldiers from confiscating the weapons outright, as had happened before. Iraqi judges theater-wide had been authorized to carry a personal weapon, but lower-ranking U.S. soldiers who ran our checkpoints were (rightfully) sometimes hesitant to simply take a man on his word when he claimed to be a judge.

One of the judges snapped the box closed and stood up. He placed his hands neatly over his heart and thanked me, his eyes moist.

"We have enjoyed working with you, captain. Thank you for not forgetting us," the chief judge said as we walked out. When we reached the gate, he turned and offered his hand. "God willing, we will meet again in a peaceful Iraq. Ma Salama."

Shaking his hand, I replied, "I hope so. Ma Salama." A peaceful Iraq. It took a moment to register. "I hope so," I repeated more to myself.

With so few feel-good moments in my job of late, my mind lingered over the meeting as Philibert and I sped back to Anaconda. I was glad I'd heeded Tom's advice: concentrate on what I could accomplish, and not allow myself to be overwhelmed by the larger frustrations. Small, concrete steps, Tom had insisted, were still improvements. He was right. I felt proud knowing that I'd laid down at least a few of those steps and that they were headed in the right direction. I departed with no regrets.

With the controversy swirling around 1-8, it came as no surprise that the follow-up meeting with the Christian Peacemakers and the citizens of Balad attended by Lieutenant Colonel Sassaman and myself—Cunningham did not attend— did not go quite as well as had my meeting with the judges. Before the meeting began, however, an Iraqi reporter approached me and handed me a photo from our previous meeting with the townspeople and the Christian Peacemakers. He boasted that it had run in a prominent Iraqi newspaper, along with a story.

Smiling, I thanked him for the photo, all the while cringing at what I imagined must have been written about the meeting. The reporter explained that he wanted me to have the photo to show my family. Continuing, he said he wanted me to have the photo "as a memory," he said, before correcting himself, "*to remember*"— he waved his finger around the room—that "we all worked together."

While I had considered the earlier meeting a barely averted disaster, the Iraqi reporter had been encouraged by the fact that there was an attempt at dialogue. Like the Balad judge's comment about a peaceful Iraq, I was struck by their hopefulness. If they were able to envision a peaceful and prosperous Iraq, was it that remote a possibility? I debated the point in my head for a while. By the end, I wasn't much more optimistic, but I longed for it all the same.

"Captain G, you realize this may be the last time we're on this road?" Philibert asked as we headed back to Anaconda. He sounded almost wistful.

Shifting in my seat, I turned and looked out the window, really paying attention to the landscape for the first time in weeks. I tried to record the images in my mind, finding it hard to believe that this now-familiar surrounding would soon be only a memory: the dusty roads, straggly vegetation, and the random scattering of low-slung, cinder-block homes between the larger gated homes. Would Iraq, in ten, twenty, or even thirty years, ever be like Vietnam, now a top travel destination in Asia? Would I ever return and drive these roads in a civilian vehicle?

No chance. The idea was laughable. Yet I could practically hear my father chiding, "Never say never, Viv."

Navigating the crater-filled roads that evening, I couldn't help but think about what was ahead for Iraq and for the soldiers who replaced us. Would the road get smoother? Would the risk ever lessen?

We will meet again in a peaceful Iraq, the judge had said.

Back at the ALOC, I learned that Captain Semenko had dropped something off at the JAG workspace, apparently at Gwinner's instruction. It was another statement regarding the Khalaf claim.

"I didn't read it, ma'am, but it's from Captain Cunningham," Carter said, handing me the document.

"You're kidding, right?" I responded. Cunningham volunteering an unsolicited statement to explain what happened? Again?

"I know, I know," Carter muttered.

Unsure whether I had the stomach for Cunningham's version of the truth, I set the file on the table and made a beeline for the computer, eager to see if I'd received an update on the Khalaf investigation. I was particularly interested to learn who had been tapped to be the investigating officer. Plenty of e-mails. None of them from division. While I was tempted to call, I knew my nagging wouldn't help.

Whoever ended up investigating the incident would have to hit the ground running. Last night's blow-up with Gwinner had underscored that fact. When it came to 1-8, there was no middle ground. You were either with them or against them. They'd supported the Cobb and Datray investigation because 1-8 considered them traitors. Perkins, on the other hand, was one of them, still a member of the team.

This begged the question: *Why?* Why would Gwinner and Cunningham remain so stubbornly loyal to a man whose actions had already damaged their careers? Perkins's arrogance, his sneering disregard for the Code of Conduct, made him an incredible liability. His twenty-four hours of terror had resulted in casualties in Balad and Samarra. Perkins was a menace, a danger to the U.S. mission, and a frightening figure for the men who had to execute his orders. Why would Gwinner and Cunningham continue to stick their necks out to protect this man? Did Perkins have something on them? If so, what?

Later that evening, I would have my answer. Amazingly, it would come from Cunningham himself.

Having exhausted every conceivable excuse to put off reading his statement, I finally forced myself to sit down with it late that night. In his sworn statement, Cunningham continued to insist that Khalaf had been responsible for the mortar attacks in Balad, just as the other 1-8 soldiers had parroted. And, as previously stated, the day after Khalaf was killed, Cunningham had asked Lieutenants Saville and Schneider to write statements about the incident. Cunningham also acknowledged that he did not ask Sergeants Perkins and Ironeyes to write statements about what happened until Semenko had asked

Cunningham about the incident. Cunningham blamed Semenko for losing the sergeants' original statements.

It wasn't until the very end of his statement that Cunningham unwittingly resolved the Perkins mystery. He explained that at the time of the raid he was standing outside Khalaf's house, speaking with the women through an interpreter, when he'd heard the gunshots inside. Shortly afterward, Perkins and Ironeyes briefed Cunningham on what had happened. To answer the unposed question of why he didn't ask Perkins and Ironeyes to write contemporaneous statements describing what had happened, Cunningham offered this: "Based on my proximity to the action and the Battalion Commander outside in the courtyard, I did not have the individuals write full statements. . . . I was confident all actions were within ROE."

The battalion commander was there?

There it was. Sassaman had been standing outside of Khalaf's house the night Khalaf was killed by Perkins. Because units are supposed to police themselves, especially when there have been KIAs, Cunningham's statement suggested that by having both himself and the battalion commander on site during the raid, the need for diligent reporting was less pressing. In other words, because the big guy was there, it was all kosher: written statements weren't necessary because the commanders were confident that there was nothing to explain, or at least nothing that they wanted to explain.

This said a lot, not only about that night, but also about the drowning and 1-8's senior leadership. I had the answer to my question, and it was a miserable one.

My rotten-apple theory about Perkins didn't hold. Perkins may have pulled the trigger, but there were officers above him who implicitly condoned Perkins's illegal tactics, or even worse, may have given Perkins an order to kill Khalaf. Without question, Perkins was a bad guy, but a bad guy who flourished in a command culture that valued his cruelty.

Did Sassaman order the hit? One way or another, this was a question the army would have to answer. The timing was suspicious. The shooting occurred within twelve hours after Paliwoda's death. Having been assigned to patrol Samarra and participate in Operation Ivy Blizzard, Alpha Company seemingly would have had no reason to be in Balad on the night of January 2 and the early morning of January 3, that is, not unless they had been called to Balad for a special mission.

We learn from our leaders. Sassaman had said it himself at the Cobb trial: he believed most military justice issues boiled down to either a failure to lead or a failure to repair. In this case, it was clearly the former. We would never know whether a guy like Perkins could repair himself, because 1-8 had never asked him to. They had other plans for him. First Battalion, 8th Infantry Regiment was a world unto itself, one where unlawful, even brutal, acts were, at best, condoned and, at worst, explicitly ordered.

Every man is vulnerable in a climate that embraces bad behavior and secrecy. It suddenly made sense how even a mild inquiry regarding a civilian claim could provoke a heated response from Gwinner. It wasn't *loyalty* that compelled Gwinner or the other officers to cover up the drowning, it was fear. Fear that outside scrutiny would collapse this alternate universe on top of itself.

CHAPTER TWENTY-FIVE

The File

FROM THE AIR, THE TRAILER village probably looked like three seemingly endless rows of white rooftops separated by an equally endless line of drab wooden walkways. Brightening this bland linear spread were large splotches of black and tan and specks of green, the various gear and supplies soldiers had dragged out from their trailers as they began packing up to go home. The trailer village hummed with activity. Soldiers were everywhere. They lingered in doorways that were now propped open all the time. You could see them smiling as they hauled bags of garbage to the dumpster or inventoried their belongings in the middle of the walkway. For most of them, it had been a good year, no injuries, no bad behavior. Nothing left to do but pack up and go home.

My own belongings, with the exception of two rugs I'd purchased in Kirkuk, fit easily into a large green duffel, a rucksack, and my backpack. Setting them near the door, I couldn't help but laugh recalling my mother's proud purchase of a new roll-away suitcase for me to take to Iraq. Wheeling it toward me, she'd announced, "It'll be better for your back." At the time I'd wondered where exactly she thought I was going. A *roll-away bag*. I could already hear the guffaws from the guys. My large, green duffel, no more than a cylindrical, canvas trash can with its short loops for handles, was no friend to anybody's back. At the time, I'd attributed my mother's bizarre purchase to her pre-deployment jitters and maybe a bit of denial about where I was headed.

I'd spent the previous days tethered to the JAG workspace, waiting for an update on the Khalaf investigation. Nearly a week had passed since Odierno appointed the investigating officer, a senior Military Police officer from division, and the investigation began. I'd considered the officer's police background good news but I felt less optimistic today. He had never contacted me to discuss Khalaf.

With all of the bustling in the trailer village, the brigade headquarters building was deserted. Most of the equipment and supplies had been sent home earlier in the week, with only the most basic supplies remaining. Operations outside the wire were officially over, and most of the battalions had relocated to Anaconda to wait for their flights home.

On the floor of the workspace, we sorted the files by urgency. Pending files went in one stack. Everything else was packed into trunks that would arrive a month after us. I placed the bulky drowning file in the pending stack.

The clock on the computer said 1600. Division was set to pull the plug on all of their communications in just over an hour, and I still had no answer regarding the Khalaf investigation. I imagined my phone messages accumulating in a dusty heap on the corner of a desk, just waiting for someone to sweep them into a garbage bin before division headquarters closed for good.

By this point, Carter and Kolb had realized that a lot of my job was an excruciating wait for answers from my bosses. They did what they could to ease the wait, gamely tackling lingering administrative issues. When those were done, they stayed close by in the rec area, playing ping-pong with a newfound fervor.

As fine a soldier as Carter had become in Iraq, he was also a ping-pong prodigy. He'd returned from his two-week leave not only rejuvenated, but determined to wipe the confident smile from Kolb's face at their next game. By mid-January, the student had become the master. Kolb accepted his defeat graciously and cheered as Carter advanced in the brigade headquarters tournament, ultimately fighting for the title against none other than the brigade commander, Colonel Rudesheim.

With still no word from division nearly an hour later, I began punching the numbers for Tikrit. I expected the phone to ring and ring as it had the last few times, so I was caught off guard when I heard a voice on the other end.

In spite of myself, I felt a spoonful of hope that almost immediately spilled to the floor. After interviewing several soldiers from 1-8, the investigating officer had deemed the Khalaf matter "inconclusive," and no further action would be taken. Division shut down operations twenty minutes later.

The days that followed were quiet, quieter than they'd been all year. I spent most of them packing and sleeping.

Eager to unload myself of a small package and two letters I'd never mailed home, I headed to Anaconda's makeshift post office where a line of soldiers snaked its way around the building. I took a spot at the end of the line and resigned myself to the idea of at least a thirty-minute wait.

Waiting. Always waiting. It had certainly been the theme for that past month. The excruciating days I'd waited for division to move forward on the exhumation had been a warm-up for the past week. I felt foolish for not having realized it sooner. The conclusion of the Khalaf investigation had left me shell-shocked.

The line moved slowly, but I didn't mind. I soaked up the redeployment giddiness around me in the hope that it would distract me from my contemplative mood. Directly ahead of me, a group of soldiers discussed the vital issue of what their first meal back home would be. A few said steak. Another soldier insisted on fried chicken, until one of his buddies mentioned pizza and caused everyone else to rethink the issue. I quietly voted for pizza before allowing myself to be consumed by the conversation behind me.

The soldier behind me was in a tough spot. He suspected his girlfriend had cheated on him while we were away, despite her repeated denials. His most compelling evidence: the time one of her male friends answered her cell phone well after midnight. The jury, consisting of his two friends, supportively declared her a "bitch," but counseled him to "get some" before he launched any accusations at her.

The other major topic of discussion was the big purchases soldiers planned to make when we returned. So far, I'd heard numerous mentions of motorcycles, cars, and stereos. Philibert was splurging on the cruise with his daughter, and Kolb would likely get that Mini Cooper. Carter and I were still undecided. For me, it was still difficult to get past the idea of a long shower and my own bed. When I'd mentioned the possibility of buying an elliptical trainer, the guys shook their heads disappointedly at the lack of horsepower.

My part of the line inched forward inside the small main room. The rectangular space was covered with warnings about shipping home weapons and other contraband. Seeing these, I was reminded of my hopefulness earlier in the week when I had received a call from CID. Surprised, I assumed it was about the Khalaf investigation. Perhaps the informal investigation had been escalated to a criminal investigation and they were now scrambling to get as much done as they could before we redeployed.

"No, ma'am," the agent said, "it seems a bunch of contraband came up in the X-rays of boxes soldiers were sending home."

A sarcastic "Awesome" was all I could muster. I'd gone out of my way to warn soldiers not to ship confiscated weapons and other contraband home. "Do not ruin a year of great service by doing something so stupid," I'd implored them.

"Yeah, it looks like some of them took the weapons apart thinking it wouldn't look as suspicious," the agent said with a chuckle. "One guy had a pistol grip wrapped inside a T-shirt and a bolt assembly for an AK-47 stuffed inside a shoe." Legal problems, it seemed, were already en route to Colorado.

As for the soldiers of the brigade headquarters company, we left Iraq in waves. Carter and I were scheduled to leave a few days before Kolb and Philibert. I figured this must have been First Sergeant Hodson's parting shot: to split up my team on the way home. While this bothered me, I simply couldn't muster the will to tangle with Hodson over the trivial slight.

On our assigned departure date, Carter and I were transported, along with about sixty other HHC soldiers, to the designated holding area for those due to leave imminently. Located near the airfield, the holding area was a plot of dirt about the size of two basketball courts. The perimeter was enclosed by a tall, chain-link fence and the ground was covered in a thick layer of rocks to deter dust and mud. A patchwork of large tarps overhead offered some shade.

To reach the holding area we had to pass through two tents. The first one drew a silent gasp from those of us who'd just arrived. The tent's interior bore a striking resemblance to an airport customs inspection station. Behind evenly spaced rows of white cafeteria tables stood soldiers, hands sheathed in latex, ready to inspect our baggage for contraband. One of the inspectors even wore a face mask. A tremor of fear reverberated through our group. *What are they looking for? Do they check every bag?* Even I began a mental inventory of what I'd packed. *What wasn't allowed again?* When my turn finally came, I hurried forward, heaved my bags onto the table, and stood by nervously, ready to argue the rightfulness of their contents. The gloved soldier opposite me, however, seemed less concerned with uncovering contraband than with catching some fatal disease. After carefully removing two items from one of my bags, using just her index finger and thumb, she peered cautiously inside. Stepping back just seconds later, she exhaled deeply, her face a mask of relief.

"Pack it up, ma'am," she said gruffly, already stripping the top layer of latex from her hands. I felt strangely insulted.

The next stop was the smaller amnesty tent where we had "one last chance to dump the goods," a sergeant yelled. Hearing this, Carter shot me a look. He'd had a similar experience at the contraband search. The line continued to plod forward toward a screen that partially concealed a barrel near the tent's exit. I stepped behind it, glanced quickly in the amnesty barrel and stepped back out. No surprise. Just gum wrappers and cigarette butts.

By the time Carter and I entered the holding area, it was already crowded with soldiers who were not part of the brigade headquarters company. They barely looked up as we maneuvered around them. Several leaned against each other, and many were splayed across bags or curled up napping on the rocks. All of them looked terrible. How long had they been here? Carter and I decided to split up to search for a place to squat, assuring ourselves that the disheveled soldiers must be leaving very soon.

I spent the next six hours cowering in the only space left: in the sun. Soldiers continued to stream in, but none appeared to be leaving.

We would spend the next two days there. We spent a lot of this time arguing over whose turn it was to ask for a status report on our flight and devising schemes to break out to get a soda, go to the PX (Post Exchange), or just stretch our legs.

Three porta-potties were lined up against one of the chain-link fences, but the nearly eighty of us penned there were allowed to use only two of the three. The third toilet was reserved for the half-dozen soldiers who worked at this makeshift detention facility. *Brilliant, guys.*

Turning to add some T-shirts to the makeshift bed I was assembling on the gravel, I couldn't help but laugh at the irony. I'd spent the entire year trying to keep the detainee issue from detonating only to spend my last days broiling in the Iraqi sun on a bed of rocks not too far from an overused porta-potty that seemed poise to regurgitate human waste into the confinement area. The list of detainee standard operating procedures that my JAG team had prepared now mocked me. *Detainees should have access to facilities and a place to wash their hands. Detainees should have a place to lie down. They should also be protected from the elements.*

As wild as our drive into Iraq had been—think bumper cars with Humvees—I should have known that our departure would be just as memorable.

Finally, just when I thought I might become mentally unhinged if we were forced to stay there any longer, we were informed that our plane had arrived to take us home.

Recent attacks on aircraft in Iraq made a traditional takeoff too dangerous, so we launched skyward in what felt like a near-vertical ascent. This terrifying takeoff behind us, I slept all the way to Turkey. Still in the Middle East, two days after we were supposed to have flown home.

We spent two more days in a Turkish military hangar, lounging on the concrete and watching countless movies on a massive projection screen that dominated our area. The booming volume made it nearly impossible to sleep or do anything but watch whatever movie was playing. Stretched out on the floor, I was simply grateful for the smooth surface and to be out of Iraq.

When someone announced that we would enjoy a commercial flight home, I joined the rest of the group in a crazed dash for the United Airlines 747. Eager to stake out good seats, soldiers littered the tarmac with discarded bags that they planned to retrieve after they secured their seats.

When we finally left Turkey, we made it as far as central Europe before making another stop. Deplaning in Prague, I followed a sea of soldiers into the relatively modern airport. Off one corridor, a small group had formed in front of a store window: the airport's duty-free shop. Several had their faces pressed against the glass, eyeing the merchandise.

"What time are they supposed to open?" I asked.

"We're trying to find out, ma'am," a lieutenant said. "You know all the liquor is duty-free, right?"

It was then that I noticed the major standing next to him, staring at the liquor display with open longing. "I just hope they've got more in the back," he said.

The group hooted their agreement.

Nodding, I turned to see where everyone else had disappeared to. I took a few steps before stopping and asking, "So, what unit are you guys with?"

The lieutenant proudly relayed their unit name but all I heard was "combat stress team."

Combat Stress. Of course. After a year of handling soldiers on the brink, the combat stress counselors had certainly earned the right to booze a little.

I slept all the way from Prague to Colorado Springs, waking only when a stewardess bumped into my knee as she made her way down the aisle. Opening my eyes, I found the cabin bathed in a tawny light, and rows of soldiers sleeping soundly around me.

I was tempted to pull out Semenko's last e-mail to me. I'd printed it so I could examine it later. The e-mail was a belated response, but interesting nonetheless. Semenko reiterated his earlier statements, that Cunningham was at fault for the missing statements, not he.

In response to Gwinner's call, "No grief," he wrote. "Major Gwinner is all spun up. 'She doesn't know our SOP, we don't zip-tie males unless they are fighting us or the target suspects.'"

Target suspects, eh? I finally pulled the folded paper from my cargo pocket, and reexamined the line again. Even now, after reading it a dozen times, I found it disconcerting. Amazingly, after spending what must have been a harrowing last few days with 1-8, he felt compelled to offer *me* encouragement. "Keep your chin up, Vivian, and God bless."

Midmorning on March 19, 2004, we finally landed at Peterson Air Force Base in Colorado Springs and boarded a waiting bus. None other than Lieutenant Colonel Welsch was there to welcome us home. He'd arrived a few days earlier and looked more relaxed than I had ever seen him. Still groggy from the flight, and filthy after five days without a shower, my eyes crackled as I opened them.

"Welcome home, guys! Glad to see you made it," Welsch announced gregariously as his warm slaps on the back unleashed minute puffs of dust from our uniforms.

He was all smiles, which, even in my haze, I found jarring. If Welsch looked this good, there was hope for all of us. As aggravating as I sometimes found Welsch's logistical decisions to be, the man was a class act. The embodiment of the army's ethos of quiet professionalism and selfless service. Among the brigade leadership, it was Welsch who seemed to understand my position best, who understood that our job was to serve the army's best interests.

Stepping off the bus at Fort Carson, Colorado's crisp spring air enveloped us. The vibrant scenery struck me: patches of wild color at the foot of the mountains, the pristine Pike's Peak with small pockets of snow, the green of actual trees and grass. Iraq's monochromatic landscape seemed blighted in comparison to the lush display here. As cliché as it sounds, the urge to kiss the ground didn't feel all that silly. It felt good to be on American soil and even better to be in Colorado.

After a brief stop to turn in our weapons, we formed up outside of the gymnasium where our family and friends had gathered inside. The building vibrated with anticipation. It seemed almost too good to believe that on other side of that door were Mike and my family.

"Leave your gear, people! Just your Kevlar," a sergeant yelled as we sorted through the chaos of bags. Even when Carter found our bags, I still couldn't adjust to the loss of my weapon, holster, and vest, and had to repeatedly remind myself that I'd turned them in. Their weight, I realized, had lent me a sense of security I suddenly craved as Carter and I hurried to join the loose formation of nearly 200 soldiers.

"Now, don't over-think it, people!" the sergeant instructed. "Just march in, follow the commands, and when you hear dismiss, you're free to go." He finally smiled.

Cheers and applause greeted us as we marched into the field house. The bleachers overflowed with smiling, screaming faces of families and friends. Ahead of me in the formation, Carter turned and winked.

The formation pivoted and we turned to face our friends and family. Hundreds of pairs of eyes scanned the formation searching for the soldier they'd been waiting for. Seeing the faces, I couldn't help but think of Eric Paliwoda's fiancé and the families of the other soldiers who never made it home. Tears welled in my eyes at the thought of their tragic reunions. My fingers shook and I willed my palm to hold my salute for the rest of the national anthem. *Come on, Viv. Now is not the time.* The sea of faces grew soft and blurry. Eric's words,

"I couldn't go home fat," taunted me. He had never looked more alive and commanding than he had that day with Sassaman. I clung to that image and tried to still my heaving chest.

Slowly, the large dots of color in front of me began to come into focus, and the tan, handsome face of my fiancé stood out against them. He'd already spotted me and waved furiously with his free hand while holding flowers in his other. Over the PA system, someone read off the names of the units present.

I shifted my gaze from Mike to Deb and finally to my parents, whose tear-streaked faces glowed with happiness. Their only wish had been granted. I'd made it home. So many times I'd feared it would not happen, that we would never have this moment. I was grateful that I'd been so lucky.

My mind collapsed under the pressure of all the emotions that vied for my attention. Everything surged forward: the heartbreaking losses, my immense gratitude, the loss of innocence, the painful lessons learned, and the joy I felt in being home. Tears fell for the soldiers we were and the soldiers we'd become. We had come home, but we would never be the same.

"Dismissed!" boomed a voice in the distance. The order sent families surging from the bleachers to infiltrate our loose formation. Mike found me quickly and we clung to each other amid the onslaught of people. My parents soon appeared, rushing forward, seemingly oblivious to those around them. Both hugged me tightly, almost desperately. When they finally released me, they remained close, their bodies sagging with relief. They knew better than anyone the horror of war. Turning to hug my sister, I found myself face to face with Majors John Rawcliffe and Kerry Cuneo, my former boss from the criminal law section.

"Hi, um, hi, ma'am, hi," I said, surprised that they'd made the effort to come welcome me home. Except for a few brief, work-related e-mails from Rawcliffe and a handwritten note from Cuneo in the package of used folders we had received, I had not spoken to either of them in over a year.

"Welcome back," Rawcliffe and Cuneo seemed to say in unison.

Still riding the wave of euphoria, I hugged Cuneo and gave a handshake and half-hug to Rawcliffe, truly touched that they'd come out but still wanting to hug my sister. Cuneo and Rawcliffe smiled uneasily, their arms hanging at their sides, long and awkward.

Several feet behind Rawcliffe, Deb watched at us with a quizzical look on her face. Because of their rank, she assumed this was official business and hadn't objected when Rawcliffe pushed past her to get to me.

"Good to see you, Vivian," Cuneo said

"Good to see you, too," I said reflexively, causing their already tight smiles to tighten further. They looked as though they were each waiting for the other to say something.

"It's great to be back," I said, still feeling giddy. Cuneo glanced furtively at my parents and Mike. Rawcliffe shifted his weight from one leg to the other before adjusting his glasses.

"Um, sorry to interrupt," Rawcliffe started. "Did you happen to bring the file?"

The file? What file?

"We were told about a case file you were supposed to hand-carry back. The drowning," he said.

Still dazed by the emotions of the past fifteen minutes, I struggled to assign meaning to his words.

They just wanted to take it off my hands, he said, so they could move forward with it while I get some much-deserved down time.

Meanwhile, Carter had extracted himself from my parents and appeared at my side. Soldiers and their families weaved through our loose group.

"The drowning file?" I asked for confirmation.

"Yes," he said.

I stared at him and Cuneo in confused disbelief. The cold, hard reality of the drowning case, with all its disappointments, hadn't just followed me home, it was there to greet me. Closing my eyes, I willed myself to process everything in order. *The file was so important to them that they interrupted the happiest moment of my life.*

Deb, now impatient with this protracted exchange, slid in to hug me.

"Yes, I have it," I finally said, "but it's back in my duffel bag somewhere. You want it now?" I asked. They nodded. "Okay, if you'll just give me a second to find it."

"Viv, is everything okay?" Mike asked, stepping forward.

"I'll be right back. Just stay here," I said as I ran outside to search the hundreds of identical bags for the one with my name on the tag. When I finally located mine, I dumped half of its contents onto the gravel to reach the pending files I'd wrapped in plastic and packed at the bottom.

Grabbing the file, I ran back into the gymnasium where only a few stragglers remained. Spotting Sergeant Farrand next to Carter, I momentarily forgot the file and embraced him, still grateful for all of his assistance with Carter's promotion packet. Turning, I found Rawcliffe and Cuneo again. The protective half circle of Mike, Carter, and my family studied the two interlopers politely. I handed the file to Rawcliffe, who thanked me. Cuneo mumbled a final "welcome home" and they headed for the exit.

Even before I could say a proper hello to my family, I had my answer: there would be no justice for the drowning in the desert.

Epilogue

THE MINUTE I REALIZED TWO senior officers had been dispatched to my homecoming to collect the drowning file, I knew I would have no role in prosecuting the case. I handed it over with mixed feelings. Part of me was relieved and happy to begin my post-Iraq life. Another part of me was reluctant to hand over to someone else something that I'd worked so hard on. I felt I was the best person to prosecute the case. When the army decided to appoint JAGs from Fort Hood with limited trial experience, I wasn't entirely surprised. All too aware of the challenges they would face in bringing charges, I made sure they knew I was available to help in any way.

In July 2004, I was asked to testify at Perkins's Article 32 hearing, similar to a civilian grand jury proceeding. I testified about the events surrounding the exhumation request. At the same hearing, Gwinner and Cunningham testified under immunity and claimed that the JAG section attempted to prevent Perkins and other 1-8 soldiers from speaking to a lawyer. Sadly, it seemed, some things never changed. This was my final involvement with the case following our return.

I completed my active-duty commitment to the army in October 2004. After the year apart, Mike and I tried to spend as much time together as possible. We went fly-fishing and watched movies, but were just as happy running errands. My soul mate and best friend, he cheerfully reacquainted me with some of my favorite carbs: pizza, bagels, and French toast. We also made the rounds, catching up with friends and families at countless parties and barbeques. Invariably someone would ask me, "What exactly does the army need lawyers for?"

It is a fair question and one I've become used to. I set aside my usual smart aleck remark in favor of something more relevant. Army lawyers have responsibilities similar to those commonly associated with civilian lawyers, prosecuting and defending soldiers in criminal matters, representing the army in civil litigation, and providing a broad range of legal services to soldiers. In times of war, however, army lawyers fulfill their most important role, to advise commanders on how to lawfully conduct military operations, in accordance with the laws of war. It is critical to the legitimacy and credibility of our nation's military operations and foreign policy that we follow the laws of war and demonstrate our national allegiance to the rule of law. That was especially important after we invaded Iraq. If we hope to inspire Iraqis to strive for democratic ideals, our military must embody all that is good and fair in our system of government and justice. If our presence in a place like Iraq represents only oppression and offers no glimpse at the democracy we promised, war no longer becomes a method or means, it becomes the ultimate destination.

It was the next question that always tripped me up. "What was the scariest part of being in Iraq?" I knew the answer they were looking for. They wanted to hear about the gunfire in Samarra, or the mortars that shook the ground and made me wonder if today would be "The Day," or the Blackhawk falling from the sky. They wanted to hear about the close calls, the near misses, and the moments that made me believe in God. If only it were that easy.

How do you explain to someone who has never been to war that the scariest moments are just after sunrise and that the only good morning in a war zone is the morning you leave? Until then, the dawn of a new day is nothing but a fresh challenge to everything you think you stand for. Will I have the strength to be the person I was when I came here? Will I find the courage to cry foul when the only answer they want is silence? Will I risk going forward even if I have to do it alone? The challenges are endless. IEDs, mortars, and enemy fire are frightening, but for me, the scariest thing was the fear that I might let the ease of false camaraderie steal my voice and silence my outrage.

I was awarded a Bronze Star for my service in Iraq. It was presented to me by the Staff Judge Advocate at a small ceremony at Fort Carson. I thanked everyone, shook hands, and smiled for photos. While the recognition from the army was nice, nothing compared to the satisfaction of pinning on Carter's new rank at his promotion ceremony. I pinned the chevrons on one lapel and Sergeant Farrand got the other. The thrill of seeing Carter wear the rank of sergeant stayed with me for days.

I thought often about my father's words: "You may not win all or any of the battles you fight. You *can* guarantee that you return with honor." The worldwide outrage over Abu Ghraib sent a clear message to the army. Seeing how much anger there was over the humiliation of Iraqi detainees, some senior military leaders were even more worried about the possible fallout from the day Zaidoun drowned, a day that had ended with three unarmed Iraqis dead in U.S. custody.

Drowning In The Desert

With the entire world watching, the army knew it could not avoid a trial in the drowning case. By cancelling the exhumation, creating numerous delays, and assigning the prosecution to inexperienced trial counsel, the army ensured, however, that there would be no justice for Zaidoun's family.

I will always be disappointed by my chain-of-command's cowardly handling of the murders of Zadan Khalaf and Zaidoun Hassoun. Their deaths did nothing to advance our mission in Iraq. Samarra and Balad were no safer in the months and years that followed. The victims of the night of January 2-3, 2004, were both American and Iraqi. The soldiers who carried out some of the orders that night were placed in a terrible position by their leaders. They, like all soldiers, deserve to train and operate in an environment that fosters their skills and embraces their best instincts.

I would be lying if I said the losses didn't overshadow the victories. They do. They always will. They were devastating, even haunting. They were, however, a consequence of going to battle and refusing to shrink into a quieter, more convenient version of myself, and resisting the temptation to do the bare minimum rather than fulfilling my duty.

My year in Iraq was miserable and challenging, but the chance to serve my country was one I would never trade. Almost everyone who puts on the uniform aspires to serve nobly. While some are not fit for the challenge, there are thousands more who are. JAG lawyers will always be necessary to ensure that the army aspires to its highest calling, that it never loses sight of its values, even in the heat of battle. When we ignore intimidation, condone cruelty, or simply remain silent, we not only impede our mission, we rob our soldiers of their greatest desire: to serve nobly and return with honor.

The army I know and the army I love is made up of soldiers like Tom Roughneen, Charles Semenko, Eric Paliwoda, Ralph Logan, and my team: Benjamin Blake Carter, Michael Kolb, John Philibert, and Kissthopher Mendoza. Soldiers of conscience and commitment. For soldiers like these, and the generations that follow, I pray that they have leaders worthy of them.

In January 2005, Sgt. 1st Class Tracy Perkins was convicted of aggravated assault in connection with the attack on Marwan Fadel Hassoun and for ordering another Iraqi man thrown into the Tigris River in December 2003. Perkins was acquitted of involuntary manslaughter in the alleged drowning of Zaidoun Fadel Hassoun and acquitted of making a false statement.

The six-man jury considered a sentencing range that included no punishment, a dishonorable discharge, rank reduction, and eleven-and-a-half years in prison. The government trial counsel recommended five years in prison and a dishonorable or bad conduct discharge. The military jury reduced Perkins's rank by one grade to staff sergeant, sentenced him to six months in military prison, and elected to retain him in the army.

At Perkins's court-martial, his attorneys argued that the absence of a body made it impossible to prove Zaidoun was dead. Agent Cintron testified to the army's decision to reverse its plans to exhume the body:

> We did have a date planned out that we were going to go get the body exhumed and it came down to the 4th ID general saying that he didn't need the body to be exhumed to take prosecution against the soldiers involved. Therefore, it came to if it's not going to be of any value then why get the body because we were risking ourselves for something the general said he didn't need. Of course, it would have been of value today if I could bring in a pathologist to say that they tested the body, but I can't do that.

Cintron also stated that, "In my experience, I have not had any alleged homicide cases where there was no body. I suppose I haven't even heard of such a thing before."

When Perkins was asked about his leadership philosophy as a platoon sergeant during the sentencing portion of his trial, Perkins responded, "especially in Iraq . . . if you're going to do something, do it aggressively, lead by example." Indeed.

First Lieutenant Jack Saville was convicted of a lesser assault charge for doing nothing to stop an Iraqi man from being forced into the river in Balad in December 2003. He plead guilty to assault and other crimes for forcing Marwan into the river in January 2004. Saville was sentenced to forty-five days in a military prison for his role in forcing three Iraqi civilians into the Tigris River and fined $2,000 of his military salary each month for six months before he was discharged from the army.

Drowning In The Desert

The army dismissed the criminal charges against Sergeant Martinez and Specialist Bowman in September 2004.

Both Lieutenant Colonel Sassaman and Major Gwinner received an Article 15, a form of nonjudicial punishment, for obstruction of justice. Their punishment under the Article 15 was a letter of reprimand. Sassaman and Gwinner have both since retired from the army. Captain Cunningham received a letter of reprimand for his involvement in the drowning cover-up and has left the army.

The drowning trial was not the only legal issue that dogged 1-8 following its return from Iraq. There were new allegations that soldiers killed an unarmed Iraqi man the same evening that Khalaf was killed. As previously stated, an informal investigation into Khalaf's death had deemed the evidence inconclusive.

In the fall of 2004, several months before Perkins's trial, a 3rd Brigade soldier, Pfc. Nathan Stewart, confessed to his wife and a psychologist about the possible illegal killing of an Iraqi, Naser Ismail, that still troubled him from his tour in Iraq. The Iraqi was killed by Stewart's squad leader, Staff Sgt. Shane Werst, during a raid in Balad during the early morning hours of January 3, 2004, in which his squad of engineers was attached to none other than 1st Platoon, Alpha Company, 1-8 Infantry Battalion. Stewart would later testify that he felt like he had been part of an execution.

Stewart's concerns prompted a CID investigation into the death of Ismail, the second Iraqi who was killed the night of 1-8's raids in Balad. The investigation revealed that in the wake of Captain Paliwoda's death, a series of new raids in and around the area was planned by 1-8 for later that evening. Their mission was to capture or kill insurgents responsible for the mortar attack that killed Paliwoda. Lieutenant Colonel Sassaman was in overall command of the mission, with Captain Cunningham responsible for leading Alpha Company.

According to Saville, prior to the operation, Cunningham gave a mission briefing that was attended by all of Alpha Company's squad leaders, platoon sergeants, and platoon leaders. At the briefing, Cunningham distributed a list of eighteen suspected insurgents and stated that five of the target individuals had been identified as the most dangerous and "were not to come back alive." These target individuals were identified by asterisks next to their names.

Saville approached Cunningham about the order. He was concerned that Cunningham had just authorized the illegal killing of Iraqis and asked him to clarify the order. According to Saville, Cunningham repeated his earlier statement that the specified individuals were "not to come back alive." Saville said the message was implicit: his platoon and the others involved were expected to do whatever was necessary to "make it happen if you can."

Saville repeated the order to his men, including Staff Sergeant Werst, but claimed he also told them that they should not do anything they were uncomfortable with, and to notify him immediately if they captured one of the targets. For repeating an illegal order and ultimately failing to stop an unlawful killing, Saville was charged with dereliction of duty

Saville later stated, "I think the platoon knew what was being asked of them after hearing Captain Cunningham's briefing. That is, to ensure the high value targets did not 'come back alive' and for us to 'make it happen' if we could. Sergeant First Class Perkins reiterated that if any of the targets were captured that he or I must be notified."

Toward the end of the raids the morning of January 3, Saville received a call over the radio that Werst had identified a detainee who was marked on the target list distributed by Cunningham. As Saville started moving towards Werst's location, Werst said over the radio, "There is about to be contact." Saville then heard several shots fired. Stewart was in the room when Werst fired those shots, killing Ismail.

Saville later stated, "I think that the stage was somewhat set for Sergeant Werst. Werst perceived it as an opportunity to kill those responsible for Captain Paliwoda's death and the command would support it. I don't think that Sergeant Werst would have pulled the trigger if not for Cunningham's order." Saville denied having any knowledge of Sassaman's involvement in the mission planning or any specific orders given by Cunningham.

In August 2005, Werst was court-martialed for the premeditated murder of Naser Ismail and acquitted by a military jury.

While charges were brought against Werst and Saville stemming from Cunningham's order, none were ever brought against Cunningham. No charges were brought against Perkins for the alleged execution of Zadan Khalaf, the other Iraqi killed by 1-8 that evening.

* * *

Drowning In The Desert

Benjamin Blake Carter served his final year in the army at Fort Carson. His lifelong passion for running led him to Oregon, where he began life as a college student.

Michael Kolb did get that navy blue, striped Mini Cooper when he returned from Iraq. He went on to serve the army as a recruiter in South Dakota. Kolb's marriage suffered under the strain of our extended deployment and the demands of military life. Within months of our return, Kolb and his wife decided to divorce.

Jonathon Philibert took that cruise with his daughter before returning to Iraq for a second tour with the 3rd Armored Calvary Regiment, which also is based at Fort Carson. And, yes, I received dozens of cheerful postcards from him during his second tour. In September 2007, Philibert returned to Iraq for his third tour with the 2nd Stryker Cavalry Regiment.

Since returning from Iraq, Tom Roughneen has been promoted to major and has switched his branch designation from civil affairs to the Judge Advocate General Corps. He served as an army defense counsel at the Office of Military Commissions in Washington, D.C., and Guantanamo Bay, Cuba, and continues to serve as a JAG officer in the Army Reserves. Shortly after obtaining his master's degree from the Johns Hopkins University School of Advanced International Studies in 2007, he married Dr. Alice Tzeng. They reside in New Jersey where Tom is in private practice.

Brian Gebhardt finished his active duty commitment to the army shortly after we returned and went on to receive his master's in business administration from Harvard Business School. Upon graduation, Brian and his wife, Cathy, relocated to Texas and started a family. His shoulder still sets off metal detectors.

Charles Semenko continues to serve in the army. He assumed command of Bravo Battery, 1-6 Field Artillery (Towed) in April 2007 and deployed to Afghanistan in support of Operation Enduring Freedom in late June 2008.

Index

1st Infantry Division, 278, 280

2nd Infantry Division, 3rd Brigade, Stryker Battalion (1-23), 117–118, 126–127, 129, 222–223

4th Infantry Division, 2, 17, 84, 103–104, 117, 150, 278, 299

   1st Brigade, 66th Armored Regiment, 113–114, 118, 121, 129, 150, 158

   3rd Brigade Combat Team, 2, 4, 15, 37, 51, 55, 84, 104, 121, 128, 181, 192, 221, 274, 278, 280, 300, 302

    1st Battalion, 8th Infantry Regiment (1-8), 4, 10, 13–15, 17–19, 21–22, 28, 31, 33–34, 36–37, 43, 47, 51, 54–56, 58, 66, 69–74, 76, 84, 86, 92–94, 99, 109–110, 113, 115, 117, 121–122, 126–127, 129, 138, 140–142, 154–155, 181, 184–186, 188, 190, 196, 199, 201, 217–218, 221–225, 232, 234–237, 239, 241, 243, 246, 248–249, 251, 255–257, 259–263, 271, 275–276, 278–280, 282–284, 287, 291, 296, 300–301

    Alpha Company, 180, 186, 194, 196, 217, 234, 236, 252, 255, 283, 300

    4th Engineer Battalion, 71, 74, 127, 136, 259–260

    Bravo Company, 71–72, 74, 127

    68th Armored Regiment (1-68), 3–4, 10–11, 15–17, 19, 21, 29, 77, 94, 274

    Alpha Company, 16, 29–30

101st Airborne Division, 105–106
173rd Airborne Brigade, 55

A
Abu Ghraib detention facility, 226–227, 297
Abu Hishma, Iraq, 109–110, 258–259
Ad Dujayl, Iraq, 15, 241
Ad Duluyiah, Iraq, 15, 37, 113, 118, 278
Adams, Staff Sgt. Bryant, 29–30
AK-47, 3, 5, 237, 239, 288
ALOC (Administrative and Logistics Operations Center), 47, 50, 52, 63, 100,
    122, 144, 154, 192, 216, 237, 243, 260, 281
Anaconda, Camp, 2, 16–17, 33, 49, 57–58, 61, 63, 66–68, 75–76, 80, 86, 98, 100,
    102, 104, 106, 108, 110, 113, 115–116, 121, 123–126, 128, 137–139, 152, 174,
    178, 192–193, 214, 221, 238, 256, 273–274, 278, 280–281, 286–287
Animal, Camp, 16–17, 19, 61, 273
Arthurs, Sgt. Jay, 100, 107–109, 121, 172, 248, 270
Article 6, 101–102, 104
Azawi, Thanna "Donna," 39, 76, 202–203, 206
Azawi, Tina, 39, 42, 122

B
Baghdad, Iraq, 17, 19, 30, 56, 62, 102–103, 113, 137, 157, 160, 169, 194, 201, 205,
    220, 226, 274, 278
Balad, Iraq, 4, 15, 17, 19, 30, 42–43, 51, 54–56, 76, 84, 86, 92, 99, 109, 113,
    115, 117–118, 125, 129–130, 138, 155, 160, 172, 180–181, 183, 188, 194, 199,
    201, 203–204, 222–223, 237, 249, 255, 269, 278, 280–283, 298–300
Barnes, Lt. Col. Tracey, 51, 66, 82, 94, 101–103, 147, 194, 197, 216,
    225–226, 244
Battle Update Briefing (BUB), 23, 26, 37, 50–51, 53, 139–140, 150, 192, 248
Blackhawk helicopter, 56, 103–105, 148–149, 297
Blake, Capt. Francis, 33–36, 38, 45–46, 48, 92, 221, 298, 302
Bowman, Spc. Terry, 152–154, 179–181, 183–185, 265, 276–277, 300
Bradley Fighting Vehicle, 31, 33, 71, 109, 113, 143, 161–163, 179–180, 184, 186,
    239–240, 255

Brassfield-Mora, Camp, 114, 116, 118, 121, 138, 158, 179
Brown, Capt. Robert, 91–92

C

C-130, 56, 268–269
Caine, Capt. Hartleigh, 130, 155, 189
Campion, Capt. Clinton, 82–83, 90–92, 124
Carter, Spc. Benjamin, 2, 11–17, 19–20, 27, 33, 37–38, 50–52, 60, 79, 81, 86,
    93–95, 99, 105–106, 111, 120–121, 127, 130, 133–137, 142, 169–170, 172,
    174–176, 190–192, 211–215, 220–221, 227, 244–245, 269–270, 278–279, 282,
    286–289, 292, 294–295, 297–298, 302
Chavez, Capt. Sandra, 114–115, 144, 213, 220, 248
Christian Peacemakers Team, 138, 194, 201–202, 204, 280–281
Cintron, Special Agent Irene, 142, 150, 152–155, 157–164, 166–167, 187–188,
    207, 216, 226–227, 299
CMOC (Civilian Military Operations Command), 169, 171
Coalition Provisional Authority, 30, 56–57, 90, 110, 113, 157, 194, 205,
    164, 279
Cobb, Pvt. Thomas, 10–12, 15–19, 21, 24, 26–34, 38–39, 42, 45, 47–49, 51, 53,
    66, 68–69, 75–77, 80–82, 84–85, 88, 91–95, 97, 102, 115, 121, 124, 139,
    140–141, 152, 173, 185, 226, 282, 284
Criminal Investigations Division (CID), 12, 18, 138, 140, 142–143, 152–155, 158,
    184, 188–189, 195, 199, 209, 214, 218, 220, 226, 278, 288, 300
Croswell, Capt. David, 115, 116, 122, 142
Cuneo, Maj. Kerry, 293–295
Cunningham, Capt. Matthew, 153, 183–186, 188, 190, 196, 200–203, 205–206,
    234–235, 240, 247, 274–275, 277, 280, 282–283, 291, 296, 300–301
Cunningham, First Sergeant, 66–67

D

Daquq, Iraq, 113, 171
Darpino, Lt. Col. Flora, 147–149
Datray, Pvt. Jason, 10–12, 15–19, 21, 24, 26–34, 38–39, 42, 45, 47–49, 51, 53, 66,
    69, 7577, 88–93, 97, 115, 122, 124, 126, 138–142, 152, 185, 226, 282
Dawood, Donald, 50, 91

E

Eagle, Camp, 16–17, 19, 30, 33, 35, 38, 41, 43, 67–69, 72, 89, 126–128, 141, 221, 237, 255

F

Fadel, Murtdadah, 39–43, 45–51, 53, 76–77, 88–89, 91–92, 94, 122, 140–141
Farrand, Sgt. Nick, 215, 295, 297
Fedayeen, 46–47, 51
Fort Carson, 6, 14, 21, 24–26, 63, 80, 104, 119, 121, 134–135, 138, 158, 173, 181, 213, 215, 220, 226, 244, 248, 274, 292, 297, 302
Fort Hood, 104, 121, 296
Fort Leavenworth, 94
Fujimoto, Capt. Dave, 171–172

G

Gebhardt, Capt. Brian, 75–76, 121, 201, 224, 237, 243, 275–276, 302
Gembara, Capt. Vivian, 4, 13, 17, 21, 23, 26, 71, 81, 90, 107, 142, 147, 241, 263, 269–271, 281
Geneva Convention, 55, 70, 119
Gil, Mike, 101
Gilmore, Sgt. Maj. Cornell, 104–106
Gonsalves, Lt. Col. Ryan, 113, 120, 150, 155, 199
Gray, Spc. Roy, 44
Gwinner, Maj. Robert, 26–27, 32–33, 54, 56, 58, 70, 140, 153–155, 158, 184–185, 189–190, 193–196, 199–200, 208, 217–218, 241, 246, 250, 252, 257–258, 260, 262–264, 268–271, 274–275, 277, 281, 282, 284, 291, 296, 300

H

Hassoun family, 138, 150, 182, 195, 226
Hassoun, Marwan Fadel, 139, 143, 151–153, 159–167, 179, 183, 207–208, 298–299
Hassoun, Zaidoun Fadel, 139, 152–153, 155, 157–166, 168, 179, 183, 185, 207–208, 214, 216–218, 225, 238, 244, 257, 269, 297–299
Henley, Judge Stephen, 79, 82–83, 93, 141
Highway One, 3, 15–16, 19, 27, 29, 93, 102, 122, 125, 226, 255

Hodson, First Sgt. Jerry, 60–62, 75, 240, 244, 288
Hudson, Lt. Tim, 129, 259–261
Hughes, Capt. Brian, 55
Humvee, 16–17, 29, 33, 35, 45, 49–50, 59–60, 71, 73, 75, 100–103, 112–113, 116,
    122, 124–125, 148, 172, 201, 206, 212, 238, 252, 290
Hussan, Amar, 30–35, 39–42, 53, 76–77, 88–92, 122, 141
Hussein, Saddam, 18, 46, 56, 103, 113, 118, 148, 278

I
improvised explosive device (IED), 9, 27, 29, 84, 86, 102–103, 122, 178,
    249, 297
Iran, 4, 50, 113, 145–147, 149, 235–236
Iraq, 1–6, 9–10, 12, 14, 16–19, 21, 25, 28–30, 34–39, 41–42, 45–46, 48, 50, 53–57,
    64, 66, 69, 74, 76–77, 80, 84, 87, 89–90, 92–93, 95, 97, 99, 101–102, 104, 109,
    112–113, 115–117, 119–120, 122, 125–126, 130, 134, 137–139, 141, 143,
    145–146, 148–150, 152–157, 162, 166, 171–174, 178–181, 184–185, 187,
    190–195, 198–199, 201–206, 208, 212–213, 216–217, 220, 222, 224–227, 230,
    234–235, 238–241, 246–248, 250, 255–256, 259, 265, 269, 274, 276, 278–281,
    285–286, 288, 290, 292, 296–302
Ironeyes, Staff Sgt. Carl, 247, 262–266, 282–283
Ismail, Naser, 300–301

J
JAG (Judge Advocate Gen.), 2–6, 11, 15, 18, 22–25, 31, 37, 39, 47, 50–51, 55, 58,
    61–62, 66, 75–76, 79–80, 86–88, 93–94, 98, 100–107, 110, 114–115, 118–119,
    121–122, 124, 127, 135–136, 138–139, 141, 144, 147–150, 169, 172–173, 176, 193,
    213, 218, 226, 239–240, 245, 248, 261, 274–276, 278, 281, 286, 290, 296, 298, 302

K
Kevlar, 17, 31, 32, 58, 60, 81, 83–85, 99, 106–107, 123, 155, 158, 178, 192, 214,
    223, 236, 238, 248, 292
Khalaf, Zadan, 231–234, 236–237, 241, 243–244, 246–247, 249–250, 252, 255,
    257, 261–262, 264–266, 268–271, 278, 281–283, 286–288, 298, 300–301
Kirkuk, Iraq, 51, 54–55, 76, 87, 99, 113, 116, 171, 256, 258, 285
Kolb, Staff Sgt. Michael, 2, 12–14, 18–21, 27, 36–38, 43–45, 49–50, 53, 60, 75,

79–82, 86–88, 93, 95, 99–100, 102–107, 109, 120–121, 130, 135–138, 142, 148, 169–170, 172, 174–176, 190–191, 212–214, 221, 227, 241, 244–245, 263, 266, 268–270, 279, 286–288, 298, 302
Kuwait, 11, 51, 60, 93, 124, 201, 212, 238, 240

L
Larson, Lt. Ryan, 129, 259–261
Lightfoot, Pvt. First Class Paul, 137–138, 274
Logan, Spc. Ralph, 143, 152–154, 158, 179–181, 183, 185, 276–277, 298
Love, Maj. Robert, 6–7

M
M16, 9–10, 30, 39–40, 100, 151, 172
Martinez, Sgt. Reggie, 153–154, 179–185, 187, 276–277, 300
Marwan. See Hassoun, Marwan Fadel
Mendoza, Spc. Kissthopher, 86, 94–95, 121–122, 130, 134, 170, 174–176, 190, 201, 239, 298
Mike, 20, 38, 99, 122, 124, 173, 292–296
mortar, 3, 16, 34, 43–46, 51, 62, 64, 66–67, 84, 92, 94, 118, 123–125, 127, 129, 171, 178, 203, 237, 282, 297, 300
Mosul, Iraq, 56, 117
Mujahedin-el-Khalq (MEK), 146–150, 244

O
Odierno, Maj. Gen. Raymond, 110, 147–149, 200, 257–258, 274–275, 278, 286
Operation Ivy Blizzard, 113, 115, 117–119, 121–122, 127, 171, 190, 222, 283

P
Pace, Capt. Noel, 61–65, 73
Paliwoda, Camp, 141, 221, 252
Paliwoda, Capt. Eric, 71–73, 126–129, 134, 183, 199, 255, 259, 276, 283, 292, 298, 300–301
Panchot, Staff Sgt. Dale, 109
Perkins, Sgt. 1st Class Tracy, 153, 180–185, 188, 195, 233–235, 237, 239, 240, 243, 246–247, 250–252, 255, 257–258, 262–266, 269–271, 275–277, 282–284,

296, 298–301
Philibert, Sgt. John, 12–14, 19–21, 23, 24, 27, 38, 50, 52, 59, 61, 76, 81, 86, 93,
    95, 105–107, 120–122, 130, 144, 170, 172, 174–176, 190, 201, 241, 244–245,
    248, 270–271, 279–281, 287–288, 298, 302
Pohl, Col. James, 141
Provost, Capt. Matt, 21, 114
Prystulska, Capt. Magda, 79, 82, 102–103, 139

Q
Qatar, 99, 106–109, 174

R
Rawcliffe, Maj. John, 293–295
rocket-propelled grenade (RPG), 16, 29, 84, 86, 109, 169, 171, 178
Romig, Maj. Gen. Thomas J., 101–102, 105–106
Roughneen, Capt. Tom, 51–58, 76, 80, 86, 92, 97–100, 107–108, 171, 218, 246,
    256–261, 276, 280, 298, 302
Rudesheim, Col. Frederick, 9, 14, 18, 50, 55, 61–62, 94, 113–114, 119, 126,
    147–148, 192–193, 197–200, 209, 214, 244, 286
Rules of Engagement (ROE), 1, 5–7, 9, 37, 54, 115, 222, 247, 258, 283
Rumsfeld, Donald, 111
Ryan, Capt. Kevin, 66–67

S
Samarra, Iraq, 4, 19, 36–37, 111–122, 127, 129, 138–139, 155, 160–161, 169,
    170–173, 176, 179, 182, 187, 194, 199, 207, 222, 240, 255, 282–283, 297–298
Sassaman, Lt. Col. Nathan, 22–23, 26–27, 29, 31, 39, 54, 69–76, 85–86, 93, 99,
    109–110, 113, 127–130, 141, 183, 193–196, 198–206, 218, 235, 239–240,
    258–260, 274–278, 280, 283–284, 293, 300–301
Saville, First Lt. Jack, 153, 179, 182–184, 187–188, 195–196, 199–200, 234, 282,
    299–301
Semenko, Capt. Charles, 220–225, 229–237, 243, 245–248, 250–252, 262–263,
    268, 281–283, 291, 298, 302
Springman, Lt. Col. Jeffrey, 37, 55
Stewart, Pfc. Nathan, 300–301

Sunni Triangle, 4, 15, 18, 110, 230
Swartsworth, Chief Warrant Officer Sharon T., 105–106

T
Tactical Operations Center (TOC), 4, 35, 47, 50, 127, 146, 147, 192, 236
Taylor, Capt. John, 139–140, 144
Tikrit, Iraq, 17, 19, 23, 51, 66, 70, 79, 82, 101–105, 115, 124–125, 140, 144, 147, 154, 181, 201, 278–279, 286
TJAG, 101–103
Toops, Capt. Emma, 114, 128
Tuz, Iraq, 112–113, 171

U
U.S. Army, 1, 3–4, 6, 8, 11, 15, 20, 22, 24–25, 30, 36, 41, 64, 72, 74, 83, 87, 92–94, 100–102, 111, 117, 127–128, 137, 141, 145, 149, 151, 166–168, 174, 190–191, 195, 197–198, 200, 203–204, 206, 211–213, 235, 240, 267, 268, 274, 277–279, 283, 292, 296–300, 302

V
Victory, Camp, 87, 104
Vietnam, 8, 101, 216–217, 259, 281
Vriesinga, Stewart, 202–203, 205

W
Weatherspoon, Spc. Willie, 79–81, 139, 144
Welsch, Lt. Col. Paul, 1, 3, 9–11, 13–15, 26, 47, 53, 61–63, 76–77, 81, 94, 98–99, 111–112, 116, 126, 139, 191–193, 200, 206, 227, 238–241, 256, 291–292
Werst, Staff Sgt. Shane, 300–301
West Point, 22, 72–73, 91, 127–128, 130, 182–183, 198, 200, 277
Westin, Capt. Tom, 59–61, 75

Z
Zaidoun. See Hassoun, Zaidoun Fadel